Plastic Money Terminology

Ewald Judt
Jeffrey Waldock

Plastic Money Terminology

An English-German Glossary

3., überarbeitete und erweiterte Auflage

Fritz Knapp Verlag
Frankfurt am Main

Bitte besuchen Sie uns auch im Internet unter
www.knapp-verlag.de

ISBN 3-8314-0762-2

© 2004 by Verlag Fritz Knapp GmbH, Frankfurt am Main
Gestaltung: Service & Agentur H. Nöbel, Hofheim
Satz: Multimedia & Preprint Rosemarie Sitte, Tautenhain
Druck und buchbinderische Verarbeitung: A. Hellendoorn KG, Bad Bentheim

Printed in Germany

Vorwort zur 3. Auflage

Seit Anfang der achtziger Jahre des vorigen Jahrhunderts sind Plastikkarten aller Art auch in Europa im Vormarsch begriffen. Dabei gibt es Debit- und Kreditkarten, Karten mit Zahlungs- und / oder Bargeldfunktion, Karten mit / ohne Elektronische Geldbörse, Karten mit globalen / nationalen / regionalen Einsatzmöglichkeiten und Karten für face-to-face und / oder virtuelle Transaktionen. Und dabei gibt es unterschiedliche Annahmemöglichkeiten: von der Verwendung von Imprintern über Terminals bis zur Akzeptanz im E- und M-Commerce.

Über all diese Karten, ihre Funktionen und ihre Akzeptanzabwicklung gibt es eine Vielzahl von Publikationen, sei es über die Kartenstrategie, das Kartenmarketing, das Kartenservice, das Kartenprocessing, das Kartenrisiko oder sei es über das Händlermarketing, das Händlerservice, das Händlerprocessing, das Händlerrisiko.

Für diejenigen, die sich nicht ausschließlich auf deutschsprachige Bücher und Zeitschriftenartikel verlassen wollen, gibt es eine Fülle von englischsprachigen Beiträgen, die allerdings eine ganz spezielle Terminologie verwenden. Diese Plastikgeld-Terminologie ist für jemanden, der nicht direkt in dieses Geschäft involviert ist, oft unverständlich. Darüber hinaus sind diese Termini oft schwer ins Deutsche zu übersetzen, das es für eine große Anzahl von Plastikgeld-Ausdrücken keine entsprechenden deutschen Worte gibt. Aus diesem Grund haben die englischen Ausdrücke zum Teil Eingang in die Fachterminologie gefunden und kommen daher auch in deutschsprachigen Publikationen vor.

Um die englischsprachigen Termini der Plastikkarten und ihrer Akzeptanz zu erläutern, wurde 1993 die 1. Auflage der „Plastic Money Terminology" veröffentlicht. Eine 2. überarbeitete und erweiterte Auflage erschien 1998. Nunmehr liegt die 3. Auflage vor. Gegenüber der zweiten Auflage wurde sie in einigen Bereichen überarbeitet (z. B. durch das Auslaufen des eurocheques) und ergänzt (z. B. im Zusammenhang mit dem E-Commerce).

In diese Übersicht der wichtigsten Plastikkarten-Ausdrücke wurden die am häufigsten vorkommenden Termini aufgenommen, wobei aufgrund des Umfangs der Materie und der Begrenztheit der zur Verfügung stehenden Seiten eine subjektive Auswahl getroffen werden musste.

Das Glossar ist alphabetisch nach den englischsprachigen Ausdrücken geordnet. Die Erläuterung des Begriffes erfolgt in Englisch. Bei Mehrfachbedeutungen wurde nur auf die Bedeutung im Plastikgeld-Bereich Bezug genommen. Ergänzt wird die Begriffserläuterung in englischer Sprache durch Querverweise, die in drei Formen vorkommen: *cf.* bedeutet die Gleichheit des Begriffes, *opp.* bedeutet das Gegenteil des Begriffes, *see also* benennt verwandte Begriffe.

Wien, Mai 2004

Ewald Judt
Jeffrey Waldock

Preface to the 3rd Edition

Since the beginning of the 80's of the last century, plastic cards of all varieties have also been making rapid headway in Europe. There are debit and credit cards, cards with payment and/or cash advance functions, cards with / without electronic purses, cards with global / national /regional possibilities of use, and cards for face-to-face and/or virtual transactions. There is also a large range of possible ways of acceptance: imprinters, terminals, e-commerce, m-commerce, etc.

There have been numerous publications concerning all of these cards and their functions, be they on card strategy, card marketing, card service, card processing or card risk, or even merchant marketing, merchant service, merchant processing and merchant risk.

Readers who do not wish to rely exclusively on German books and articles can choose from a wide range of English publications which use highly specific terminology. This kind of plastic money terminology is often difficult to understand for persons who are not directly involved in this business. Moreover, the terms are often difficult to translate into German, as frequently there are no corresponding German words for many plastic money terms. For this reason, English terms have in many cases been adopted and incorporated into the special terminology, and are therefore used in German publications.

In order to explain the English terms and their acceptance, the first edition of "Plastic Money Terminology" was published in 1993. A second revised and extended edition was published in 1998. The third edition has now been released. With respect to the second edition, the third edition has been revised (e.g. in connection the expiry of the eurocheque) and amended (e.g. in connection with e-commerce) in a number of areas.

The most frequently used plastic card terms were included in the glossary, whereby a subjective selection had to be made owing to the vastness of the available material and the limitations imposed on the available number of pages.

The glossary is sorted alphabetically according to the English terms. The English term is listed first. It is followed by an explanation in English. Only the meaning in the plastic money field is included in the case of multiple meanings. Cross references are then provided which are given in three forms: *cf.* synonyms of the term, *opp.* antonyms of the term and *see also* reference to related terms.

Vienna, May 2004

Ewald Judt
Jeffrey Waldock

An English-German Glossary

.

above floor limit fraud – fraud arising despite an authorization granted by the issuer because information as to the unauthorized use of the card was not known at that time
opp.: below floor limit fraud, under floor limit fraud

Betrugsfall über der Genehmigungsgrenze

above floor limit transaction – a transaction that requires the merchant to call his authorization centre for authorization because the transaction amount is over the merchant floor limit
opp.: below floor limit transaction

Transaktion über der Genehmigungsgrenze

accept a card, to – to honour a presented card
cf.: honour a card, to

eine Karte akzeptieren, eine Karte annehmen

accept a cheque, to – to honour a presented cheque
cf.: honour a cheque, to

einen Scheck akzeptieren, einen Scheck annehmen

acceptance – the process of honouring a presented card by a merchant / an inserted card by an ATM
see also: ATM acceptance, merchant acceptance

Akzeptanz

acceptance brand – the logo of a card organization indicating the acceptance of their cards at that location
cf.: acceptance mark
opp.: issuance brand, issuance mark, issuing brand, issuing mark
see also: decal

Akzeptanzmarke

acceptance business – all card business activities concerning the collection of transactions from merchants and the payment of the respective amounts to the merchants on the basis of a merchant agreement
cf.: aquiring, aquiring business, merchant aquiring business, merchant business
opp.: card issuance, card issuing business, issuance business, issuing, issuing business

Geschäft im Zusammenhang mit der Vertragsunternehmensabrechnung, Vertragsunternehmensgeschäft

acceptance gap – a region or a market sector where a specific card is not sufficiently accepted

Akzeptanzlücke

Akzeptanzdichte	**acceptance level** – the density of a merchant / ATM network depending on the number of available merchants / ATMs cf.: coverage see also: ATM acceptance level, ATM coverage, merchant acceptance level, merchant coverage
Akzeptanzmarke	**acceptance mark** – the logo of a card organization indicating the acceptance of their cards at that location cf.: acceptance brand opp.: issuance brand, issuance mark, issuing brand, issuing mark
Vertragsunter-nehmensbestand, Vertragsunter-nehmensnetzwerk	**acceptance network** – the entirety of all merchants honouring a specific card cf.: merchant base, merchant network
Niederlassung eines Vertragsun-ternehmens	**acceptance point** – a location where goods or services can be paid for with a card cf.: acceptance location, merchant outlet, outlet
Abnahmeverfahren	**acceptance procedure** – the steps for testing the operational capabilities of a device and/or a system see also: acceptance test
Akzeptanzqualität	**acceptance quality** – the level of service that is defined by merchant network density and convenience, as well as speed and as well as security of the transactions
Abnahmetest	**acceptance test** – a method to test the operational capabilities of a device and/or a system see also: acceptance procedure
nahezu 100 %-ige Kartenakzeptanz	**acceptance ubiquity** – an acceptance level with coverage more or less everywhere
Kartenakzeptant, Vertrags-unternehmen	**acceptor** – a legal entity with which there is an agreement to accept cards as a means of payment for goods or services when properly presented

cf.: card acceptor, ME (member establishment, merchant establishment), member establishment (ME), merchant, merchant establishment (ME), SE (service establishment), service establishment (SE)

access card – a card granting access to facilities other-   *Zutrittskarte*
wise barred to unauthorized persons
see also: access code, access control, access function

access code – a code granting access to facilities other-   *Zutrittscode*
wise barred to unauthorized persons
see also: access card, access control, access function

access control – a method to ensure that only authorized   *Zutrittskontrolle*
persons are granted access
see also: access card, access code, access function

access function – a feature on a card granting access to   *Zutrittsfunktion*
facilities otherwise barred to unauthorized persons
see also: access card, access code, access control

access point – an entry point into a network   *Zugangspunkt*

access products – payment instruments that allow bank   *Zahlungsmöglich-*
customers with a current account to dispose their available   *keiten, die es erlau-*
funds   *ben, über ein Giro-*
       konto zu verfügen

account detail file – a file with individual parameters of   *Datei mit individu-*
specific cardholders which are checked during authorization   *ellen Karten(inha-*
processing   *ber)limits*
opp.: account range file
see also: account limits, account parameters

account detail parameters – the individual limits (e.g.   *individuelle Kar-*
maximum amount and/or number of transactions that can be   *ten(inhaber)limits*
authorized within a defined period) set by the issuer for spe-
cific cardholders which can be found in the account detail
file and are checked during authorization processing

opp.: account range parameters

see also: account limits, account parameters, activity limits, acitivity parameters

Hauptkarten-inhaber

account holder – the person holding a card account which is charged with card transactions of his card and/or additional cards

Karten(inhaber)-Limits

account limits – the parameters (e.g. maximum amount and/or number of transactions that can be authorized within a defined period) set by the issuer either for individual accounts in the account detail file or for a range of accounts in the account range file which are checked during authorization processing

cf.: account parameters, activity limits, activity parameters, authorization limits, authorization parameters, card limits

see also: account detail parameters, account range parameters

Kontobewegung

account movement – any addition to or deduction from an account

Kartennummer

account number – a unique series of digits on the card created by the issuer to identify the issuer and the cardholder

cf.: card account number, card number, PAN (primary account number), primary account number (PAN)

see also: non-standard account number, non-standard card account number, non-standard card number, standard account number, standard card account number, standard card number

Karten(inhaber)-Limits

account parameters – the limits (e.g. maximum amount and/or number of transactions that can be authorized within a defined period) set by the issuer either for individual accounts in the account detail file or for a number of accounts in the account range file which are checked during authorization processing

cf.: account limits, activity limits, activity parameters, authorization limits, authorization parameters, card limits

see also: account detail parameters, account range parameters

account range – a defined segment of an account number series

cf.: card account range, card range

definierter Teil einer Kontonummernserie

account range file – a file with parameters which are common to all card numbers situated within a defined range and which are checked during authorization processing

opp.: account detail file

see also: account limits, account parameters, activity limits, activity parameters

Datei mit Kartenserienlimits

account range parameters – the limits (e.g. maximum amount and/or number of transactions that can be authorized within a defined period) set by the issuer, which are common to all card numbers that fall within a defined range and are checked during authorization processing

opp.: account detail parameters

see also: account limits, account parameters, activity limits, activity parameters

Kartenserienlimits

account statement – a paper-based or electronic record showing all effected transactions on an account within a defined period

Kontoauszug

accountability – the ability of an issuer to draw up shadow balances of electronic purses after receiving the respective transactions from the acquirer

see also: shadow accounting, shadow balance

Abstimmbarkeit

accounted (electronic) purse – an electronic purse where loading, payment and unloading transactions are centrally stored

opp.: unaccounted (electronic) purse

elektronische Geldbörse mit zentral geführten Schattenkonten

account-linked card – a card whose debits are deducted from a predetermined account

Karte, die über ein Girokonto abgerechnet wird

Clearingzentrale

ACH (automated clearing house) – a centre for the automated clearing of payment transactions
cf.: automated clearing house (ACH)

Vertragsunter-
nehmen abrechnen

acquire, to – to collect from merchants the transactions which are submitted to the interchange system and to pay the respective amounts to the merchants on the basis of a merchant agreement
cf.: collect, to
opp.: issue, to
see also: contract merchants, to

vertragsunter-
nehmens-
abrechnende Bank

acquirer – a bank which collects from merchants the transactions that are submitted to the interchange system and which pays the respective amounts to the merchants on the basis of a merchant agreement
cf.: acquirer bank, acquiring bank, acquiring institution, acquiring member, collecting bank
opp.: card issuer, card issuing bank, cardholder bank, issuer, issuer bank, issuing bank, issuing institution, issuing member

Genehmigungszen-
trale der vertrags-
unternehmensab-
rechnenden Bank

acquirer authorization centre – the site where the merchants call for authorization codes and which routes the authorization requests to the issuer
opp.: issuer authorization centre
see also: authorization centre

Transaktion, die z. B.
wg. eines Netzwerk-
ausfalls zwischen der
vertragsunternehmens-
abrechnenden und
der kartenausgebenden
Bank von der ver-
tragsunternehmens-
abrechnenden Bank
autorisiert wird

acquirer authorized transaction – a transaction which is authorized by the acquirer, e.g. as a result of network failure between acquirer and issuer
see also: merchant authorized transaction, store-and-forward transaction

acquirer back-office – the processing of all merchant functions not related to processing authorization

opp.: issuer back-office processing

see also: acquirer batch processing

Verarbeitung von vertragsunternehmens-bezogenen Daten und Transaktionen, die nicht Autorisierungen sind

acquirer bank – a bank which collects from merchants the transactions that are submitted to the interchange system and which pays the respective amounts to the merchants on the basis of a merchant agreement

cf.: acquirer, acquiring bank, acquiring institution, acquiring member, collecting bank

opp.: card issuer, card issuing bank, cardholder bank, issuer, issuer bank, issuing bank, issuing institution, issuing member

vertragsunternehmensabrechnende Bank

acquirer batch processing – the processing of all batch functions related to the merchant database

opp.: issuer batch processing

see also: acquirer back-office processing

Stapelverarbeitung von vertragsunternehmensbezogenen Daten und Transaktionen

acquirer country – the country in which the acquirer carries on its business

opp.: issuer country

Land der vertragsunternehmensabrechnenden Bank

acquirer country code – a code in the transaction data defining the acquirer country

opp.: issuer country code

see also: country code

Code des Landes, in dem die vertragsunternehmensabrechnende Bank domiziliert ist

acquirer economics – revenue, cost and margin situation of an acquirer

opp.: issuer economics

see also: card economics

Ertrags-, Aufwands- und Gewinnsituation einer vertragsunternehmensabrechnenden Bank

acquirer host – the computer system of an acquirer that processes authorizations

cf.: acquirer host system (AHS), AHS (acquirer host system)

opp.: IHS (issuer host system), issuer host, issuer host system (IHS), primary, primary processing centre

Autorisierungscomputer der vertragsunternehmensabrechnenden Bank

*Autorisierungs-
computer der ver-
trangsunterneh-
mensabrechnenden
Bank*

acquirer host system (AHS) – the host computer system of an acquirer forwarding authorization requests to the issuer or authorizing on behalf of the issuer
cf.: acquirer host, AHS (acquirer host system)
opp.: IHS (issuer host system), issuer host, issuer host system (IHS), primary, primary processing centre

*Identifikationsnum-
mer der vertrags-
unternehmensab-
rechnenden Bank*

acquirer identification code (AIC) – a code used to identify the acquirer of a transaction
cf.: AIC (acquirer identification code)

*Reduktion der
Interchange Fee,
Reduktion des In-
terbankenentgelts*

acquirer interchange discount (AID) – a reduction of the interchange fee for every transaction which is authorized and submitted to the interchange system if made within a very short time
cf.: AID (acquirer interchange discount)
see also: interchange fee

*Fähigkeit einer ver-
tragsunternehmens-
abrechnenden Bank,
ihren finanziellen
Verpflichtungen
nachzukommen*

acquirer liability – the capability of an acquirer to fulfil its financial obligations
opp.: issuer liability
see also: liability, liability shift

*Unternehmen, das
EDV-Dienstleistun-
gen im Auftrag der
vertragsunterneh-
mensabrechnenden
Bank erbringt*

acquirer processor – a processor providing IT service for an acquirer
opp.: issuer processor
see also: processor

*Transaktions-
referenznummer*

acquirer reference data – a unique number assigned to a transaction by the acquirer used during the entire life cycle of a transaction
cf.: acquirer reference number

*Transaktions-
referenznummer*

acquirer reference number – a unique number assigned to a transaction by the acquirer used during the entire life cycle of a transaction
cf.: acquirer reference data

acquirer site – the place where the acquirer host system (AHS) is located

cf.: acquirer authorization centre

Genehmigungszen-
trale der vertrags-
unternehmensab-
rechnenden Bank

acquiring – the collection of transactions from merchants which are submitted to the interchange system and the payment of the respective amounts to the merchants on the basis of a merchant agreement

cf.: acquiring business, merchant acquiring business, merchant business

opp.: card issuance, card issuing business, issuing, issuing business

Geschäft im Zusam-
menhang mit der
Vertragsunterneh-
mensabrechnung,
Vertragsunterneh-
mensgeschäft

acquiring bank – a bank which collects from merchants the transactions that are submitted to the interchange system and which pays the respective amounts to the merchants on the basis of a merchant agreement

cf.: acquirer, acquirer bank, acquiring institution, acquiring member, collecting bank

opp.: card issuer, card issuing bank, cardholder bank, issuer, issuer bank, issuing bank, issuing institution, issuing member

vertragsunterneh-
mensabrechnende
Bank

acquiring business – all card business activities concerning the collection of transactions from merchants which are submitted to the interchange system and the payment of the respective amounts to the merchants on the basis of a merchant agreement

cf.: acquiring, merchant acquiring business, merchant business

opp.: card issuance, card issuing business, issuing, issuing business

Geschäft im Zusam-
menhang mit der
Vertragsunterneh-
mensabrechnung,
Vertragsunterneh-
mensgeschäft

acquiring institution – a bank which collects from merchants the transactions that are submitted to the interchange system and which pays the respective amounts to the merchants on the basis of a merchant agreement

cf.: acquirer, acquirer bank, acquiring bank, acquiring member, collecting bank

opp.: card issuer, card issuing bank, cardholder bank, issuer, issuer bank, issuing bank, issuing institution, issuing member

vertragsunterneh-
mensabrechnende
Bank

Lizenz für das Ver-
tragsunternehmens-
geschäft; Lizenz,
Vertragsunternehmen
abzurechnen

acquiring licence – the right granted by a licensor to a licensee to acquire merchants

opp.: issuing licence

see also: licence

vertragsunterneh-
mensabrechnende
Bank

acquiring member – a bank which collects from merchants the transactions that are submitted to the interchange system and which pays the respective amounts to the merchants on the basis of a merchant agreement

cf.: acquirer, acquirer bank, acquiring bank, acquiring institution, collecting bank

opp.: card issuer, card issuing bank, cardholder bank, issuer, issuer bank, issuing bank, issuing institution, issuing member

eingesetzte Karte

active card – a card which is used

opp.: inactive card

Karteneinsatz-
kontrolle

activity checking – manual or automated control of the data contained in the activity file

see also: activity file

Karteneinsatzdaten

activity data – the data that reflects all transaction-related information

opp.: primary data

see also: cardholder activity data, merchant activity data

Transaktionsentgelt

activity fee – a fee charged per transaction

cf.: transaction fee

Karteneinsatzdatei

activity file – a file which contains the authorization data and/or all received but not yet settled transactions of cards

see also: activity checking

Karten(inhaber)-
Limits

activity limits – the parameters (e.g. maximum amount and/or number of transactions that can be authorized within a defined period) set by the issuer either for individual accounts in the account detail file or for a range of accounts in the account range file which are checked during authorization processing cf.: account limits, account parameters, activity parameters, authorization limits, authorization parameters, card limits

see also: account detail parameters, account range parameters

activity parameters – the limits (e.g. maximum amount and/or number of transactions that can be authorized within a defined period) set by the issuer either for individual accounts in the account detail file or for a range of accounts in the account range file which are checked during authorization processing

cf.: account limits, account parameters, activity limits, authorization limits, authorization parameters, card limits

see also: account detail parameters, account range parameters

Karten(inhaber)-Limits

activity pattern – the cardholder behaviour which can be in line or deviate from the usual spending profile

cf.: cardholder spending behaviour, cardholder spending pattern, spending pattern

Zahlungsverhalten des Karteninhabers

ad valorem fee – a fee based on a percentage of the amount of the transaction

cf.: percentage fee

opp.: fixed fee, flat fee

Prozententgelt, wertabhängiges Entgelt

additional card – a card issued to either a member of the primary cardholder's family or a staff member of a company to whom a primary card has been issued

cf.: secondary card

opp.: primary card

see also: extra card

Zusatzkarte

additional cardholder – the cardholder who has the additional card when more than one card is issued to a family or a company member

cf.: secondary cardholder

opp.: primary cardholder

Zusatzkarten-inhaber

Zusatzleistung   **add-on service** – any additional service provided by a card

Berichtigung   **adjustment** – a correction of a data entry

Zusatzinformation zu einer Transaktion   **administrative data** – the data of an administrative message
see also: administrative message

Nachricht mit Zusatzinformation zu einer Transaktion   **administrative message** – a message concerning additional data requested by / given through a party involved in a transaction
see also: administrative data

Vorauszahlung   **advance payment** – payment effected in advance to obtain goods or services at a later date
cf.: pre-payment

Hinweis   **advice** – a message notifying a party of action taken

Benachrichtigung über den Stand des Abrechnungskontos des Mitglieds eines Zahlungssystems   **advisement** – the information about a member's net settlement position

Bank, die nicht direkt, sondern über eine andere Bank Mitglied eines Zahlungssystems ist   **affiliate** – a bank participating in the card business via a principal licensee
cf.: affiliate licensee, affiliate member, sublicense
opp.: principal, principal licensee, principal member

Sub-Lizenz   **affiliate licence** – a licence which allows a bank to participate in the card activities of a payment system via a principal licensee
cf.: sublicence
opp.: principal licence

Bank, die nicht direkt, sondern über eine andere Bank Mitglied eines Zahlungssystems ist   **affiliate licensee** – a bank participating in the card business via a principal licensee
cf.: affiliate, affiliate member, sublicense
opp.: principal, principal licensee, principal member

affiliate member – a bank participating in the card business via a principal licensee
cf.: affiliate, affiliate licensee, sublicense
opp.: principal, principal licensee, principal member

Bank, die nicht direkt, sondern über eine andere Bank Mitglied eines Zahlungssystems ist

affinity card – a credit card issued by a member with a special design and distributed through a third party institution
cf.: co-branded card, third-party card

Karte, die von einer Bank mit speziellem Design ausgegeben und über einen Dritten vertrieben wird

agent bank – a bank which sells credit cards on behalf of another bank

Bank, die Kreditkarten nicht im eigenen Namen verkauft

AHS (acquirer host system) – the host computer system of an acquirer forwarding authorization requests to the issuer or authorizing on behalf of the issuer
cf.: acquirer host, acquirer host system (AHS)
opp.: IHS (issuer host system), issuer host, issuer host system (IHS), primary, primary host system

Autorisierungscomputer der vertragsunternehmensabrechnenden Bank

AID (acquirer identification code) – a code used to identify the acquirer of a transaction
cf.: acquirer identification code (AID)

Identifikationsnummer der vertragsunternehmensabrechnenden Bank

AID (acquirer interchange discount) – a reduction of the interchange fee for every transaction which is authorized and submitted to the interchange system within a very short time
cf.: acquirer interchange discount (AID)
see also: interchange fee

Reduktion der Interchange Fee, Reduktion des Interbankenentgelts

airline card – a credit card issued by an airline which can only be used in the issuer's environment

Kundenkarte einer Fluglinie

airline itinerary data – the information concerning specific data on airline tickets

Flugticketdaten

airport lounges access – a service granted by some card organizations for certain cardholders providing free access to selected airport lounges

Zutritt zu Airport-Lounges

mißbräuchlicher Karteneinsatz, der Sofortmaßnahmen erfordert

alert case – a card usage which indicates fraudulent intentions and which requires immediate action

alphanumerischer Code

alphanumeric code – a code made up of alphanumeric characters

opp.: numeric code

den Magnetstreifen verändern, den Magnetstreifen verfälschen

alter the magnetic stripe, to – to change the data on the magnetic stripe

Verfälschung

alteration – the illegal falsification of a card

see also: altered card, altered magnetic stripe, altered signature panel

verfälschte Karte

altered card – a card which has been falsified either by changing the embossed figures, the signature or the magnetic stripe

see also: alteration, altered magnetic stripe, altered signature

verfälschter Magnetstreifen

altered magnetic stripe – the falsification of the magnetic stripe of a card

see also: alteration, altered card

gefälschte Unterschrift

altered signature – the falsification of the signature on a card

see also: alteration, altered card

Ersatzgenehmigungssystem bei Systemausfall

alternate – a back-up issuer processing facility for authorizations when the primary processing system is not available

cf.: alternate processing system, back-up processing system, down-option processing system, dynamic stand-in processing system, permanent stand-in processing system, stand-in processing system

see also: IHS (issuer host system), issuer host, issuer host system (IHS), primary, primary processing system

alternate authorization – an authorization performed by a pre-determined alternate processing system used whenever the issuer is unable to respond

cf.: back-up authorization, down-option authorization, dynamic stand-in authorization, permanent stand-in authorization, stand-in authorization

opp.: primary authorization

Genehmigung bei einem System- ausfall durch ein Ersatzsystem

alternate limits – the authorization parameters set by the issuer for the alternate processing system in case the primary processing system is unable to respond

cf.: alternate parameters, back-up limits, back-up parameters, down-option limits, down-option parameters, dynamic stand-in limits, dynamic stand-in parameters, fall-back limits, fall-back parameters, permanent stand-in limits, permanent stand-in parameters, stand-in limits, stand-in parameters

von der karten- ausgebenden Bank festgelegte Limits für das Ersatz- system

alternate parameters – the authorization parameters set by the issuer for the alternate processing system in case the primary processing system is unable to respond

cf.: alternate limits, back-up limits, back-up parameters, down-option limits, down-option parameters, dynamic stand-in limits, dynamic stand-in parameters, fall-back limits, fall-back parameters, permanent stand-in limits, permanent stand-in parameters, stand-in limits, stand-in parameters

von der karten- ausgebenden Bank festgelegte Limits für das Ersatz- system

alternate processing – the performance of authorizations by a pre-determined alternate processing system used whenever the issuer is unable to respond

cf.: back-up processing, down-option processing, dynamic stand-in processing, permanent stand-in processing, stand-in processing

opp.: primary processing

Genehmigungs- verfahren durch ein Ersatzsystem bei einem Systemausfall

alternate processing system – a back-up issuer processing facility for authorizations when the primary processing system is not available

Ersatzgenehmi- gungssystem bei Systemausfall

cf.: alternate, back-up processing system, down-option processing system, dynamic stand-in processing system, permanent stand-in processing system, stand-in processing system

see also.: IHS (issuer host system), issuer host, issuer host system (IHS), primary, primary processing system

*Ort des Ersatzge-
nehmigungssystems*

alternate site – the place where the alternate processing system is located

opp.: primary site

see also: alternate processing system

*Transaktion, die
bei einem System-
ausfall von einem
Ersatzgenehmi-
gungssystem auto-
risiert wird*

alternate transaction – a transaction which is authorized by an alternate processing system

cf.: back-up transaction, down-option transaction, dynamic stand-in transaction, permanent stand-in transaction, stand-in transaction

opp.: primary transaction

see also: alternate processing system

American Express

American Express – a corporation active in bank business, card business and travel agency business

see also: American Express card

*American Express-
Karte*

American Express card – a card issued by a unit of American Express

see also: American Express

ANSI

American National Standards Institute (ANSI) – the US member of ISO which has ratified numerous American standards used in the card industry

cf.: ANSI (American National Standards Institute)

see also: CEN (Comité Européen de Normalisation), Comité Européen de Normalisation (CEN), International Organization for Standardization (ISO), ISO (International Organization for Standardization)

American Standard Code for Information Interchange (ASCII) – the protocol used by numerous computers for information interchange
cf.: ASCII (American Standard Code for Information Interchange)

ASCII

ancillary charge – a fee which is levied in addition to the standard fee
cf.: supplementary charge, surcharge
see also: surcharge, to; surcharging

Aufschlag, Zusatzentgelt

annual fee – a fee to be paid annually by the cardholder
see also: card charges

Jahresentgelt

annual percentage rate (APR) – the rate of interest expressed as equivalent simple interest per annum
cf.: APR (annual percentage rate)

Jahreszinssatz

ANSI (American National Standards Institute) – the US member of ISO which has ratified numerous American standards used in the card industry
cf.: American National Standards Institute (ANSI)
see also: CEN (Comité Européen de Normalisation), Comité Européen de Normalisation (CEN), International Organization for Standardization (ISO), ISO (International Organization for Standardization)

ANSI

APACS (Association for Payment and Clearing Services) – British clearing institution
cf.: Association for Payment and Clearing Services (APACS)

APACS

application fraud – fraud committed by submitting an untrue card application form

Kartenbetrug, der auf einen unrichtigen Kartenantrag zurückgeht

apply for a card, to – to fill in a card application form in order to obtain a card
see also: card application, card application form, card application processing

eine Karte beantragen

A

Autorisierungscode, Autorisierungs-nummer, Genehmi-gungscode, Geneh-migungsnummer

approval code – a code given by the issuer (or its agent) when an authorization request has been approved

Kartenantrags-genehmigung

approval of a card application – the acceptance of the card application by the issuer
opp.: refusal of a card application

Autorisierung, Genehmigung

approval of an authorization request – an affirmative response of the issuer to the acquirer which is forwarded by the acquirer to the merchant or cash advance location to permit a card transaction
cf.: authorization
opp.: refusal of an authorization request

Verfahren zur Bewilligung von Kartenanträgen

approval processing – the procedure to approve card applications

einen Kartenantrag annehmen

approve a card application, to – to accept a card application
opp.: refuse a card application, to

eine Genehmi-gungsanfrage bewilligen

approve an authorization request, to – to provide an affirmative response to an authorization request
cf.: authorize, to
opp.: decline an authorization request, to; deny an authorization request, to; refuse an authorization request, to

Jahreszinssatz

APR (annual percentage rate) – the rate of interest expressed as equivalent simple interest per annum
cf.: annual percentage rate (APR)

außergerichtliches Vermitteln in einem Streitfall

arbitrate a dispute, to – to settle a difference of opinion on a specific case out of court
see also: arbitration, arbitration procedure

arbitration – the settlement of a difference of opinion on a specific case out of court
see also: arbitrate a dispute, to; arbitration procedure

außergerichtliche Vermittlung in einem Streitfall

arbitration fee – a fee to be paid by the plaintiff in order to initiate an arbitration procedure

Entgelt, das bei Verlangen nach einem Schieds-gerichtsverfahren vom Antragsteller zu bezahlen ist

arbitration procedure – the process of settling a difference of opinion on a specific case out of court
see also: arbitrate a dispute, to; arbitration

Vorgangsweise bei der außergericht-lichen Vermittlung in einem Streitfall

ASCII (American Standard Code for Information Interchange) – the protocol used by numerous computers for information interchange
cf.: American Standard Code for Information Interchange (ASCII)

ASCII

assessment – the fees paid by a member to a payment system to support its activities
cf.: assessment fee

Entgelt zur Erhaltung und Weiterentwick-lung eines Zahlungs-systems

assessment fee – the amounts paid by a member to a payment system to support its activities
cf.: assessment

Entgelt zur Erhaltung und Weiterentwick-lung eines Zahlungs-systems

Association for Payment and Clearing Services (APACS) – British clearing institution
cf.: APACS (Association for Payment and Clearing Services)

APACS

asymmetric cryptography – a set of cryptographic techniques in which two different keys - the private and the public key - are used for encrypting and decrypting data
cf.: public key cryptography
opp.: symmetric cryptography
see also: cryptography, private key, public key

asymmetrische Verschlüsselung, Verschlüsselung mit öffentlichem und privatem Schlüssel

Geldausgabe-
automat

ATM (automated teller machine) – a cardholder-operated automatic machine activated by a card and a PIN and whose primary purpose is to dispense cash

cf.: automated teller machine (ATM), cash dispenser

Akzeptanz an
Geldausgabe-
automaten

ATM acceptance – the honouring of an inserted card by an ATM

see also: acceptance, merchant acceptance

Akzeptanzdichte
von Geldausgabe-
automaten

ATM acceptance level – the density of an ATM network based on the number of available ATMs

cf.: ATM coverage

see also: acceptance level, coverage

Genehmigung für
einen Bargeldbezug
an einem Geld-
ausgabeautomaten

ATM authorization – an affirmative response of the issuer to a bank's ATM to permit a card transaction

see also: electronic authorization, terminal authorization

Bargeldbezugs-
karte

ATM card – a card which can only be used to obtain cash at ATMs

cf.: ATM-only card

Bargeldbezug
an einem Geld-
ausgabeautomaten

ATM cash advance transaction – a transaction by which cash is obtained at an ATM

cf.: ATM transaction, ATM cash disbursement transaction, automated teller transaction

opp.: merchant transaction, purchase transaction, sales transaction

see also: cash advance transaction

Bargeldbezug
an einem Geld-
ausgabeautomaten

ATM cash disbursement transaction – a transaction by which cash is obtained at an ATM

cf.: ATM transaction, ATM cash advance transaction, automated teller transaction

opp.: merchant transaction, purchase transaction, sales transaction

see also: cash advance transaction

ATM coverage – the density of an ATM network depending on the number of available ATMs

cf.: ATM acceptance level

see also: acceptance level, coverage

Akzeptanzdichte von Geldausgabeautomaten

ATM density – the penetration of ATMs in a defined area

cf.: ATM penetration

see also: merchant density, merchant penetration, POS (terminal) density, POS (terminal) penetration

Geldausgabeautomatendichte

ATM deployment – the installation of an ATM

Installation eines Geldausgabeautomaten

ATM directory – a list of all available ATMs in a given area

cf.: ATM location directory

see also: directory, merchant directory, merchant location directory, travel directory

Geldausgabeautomatenverzeichnis

ATM function – a function embedded in a given card so that this card can also be used to obtain cash

Bargeldbezugsfunktion

ATM limits – the maximum and the minimum amount which can be withdrawn from an ATM

cf.: maximum ATM withdrawal amount, minimum ATM withdrawal amount

Geldausgabeautomatenlimits

ATM location directory – a list of all available ATMs in a given area

cf.: ATM directory

see also: directory, merchant directory, merchant location directory, travel directory

Geldausgabeautomatenverzeichnis

ATM locator – an electronic file of available ATMs (in a given area)

see also: ATM directory, ATM location directory

elektronisches Verzeichnis von Geldausgabeautomaten (einer Region)

ATM network – a linked system of ATMs maintained by a network operator

Geldausgabeautomatennetz

Ausfall eines Geld-ausgabeautomaten-systems

ATM network breakdown – the failure of an ATM network

see also: network breakdown, POS (terminal) network breakdown

Geldausgabe-automatenbetreiber

ATM network operator – a bank or a third party which establishes and operates a series of ATMs connected to a host computer

Geldausgabe-automatendichte

ATM penetration – the density of ATMs in a defined area

cf.: ATM density

see also: merchant density, merchant penetration, POS (terminal) density, POS (terminal) penetration

Geldausgabe-automatenbeleg

ATM receipt – a piece of paper printed out by an ATM documenting a performed transaction

see also: receipt, terminal receipt

Auszeichung eines Geldausgabe-automaten

ATM signage – the decalization of an ATM

see also: POS signage, signage

Bargeldbezug an einem Geldaus-gabeautomaten

ATM transaction – a transaction by which cash is obtained at an ATM

cf.: ATM cash advance transaction, ATM cash disbursement transaction, automated teller transaction

opp.: merchant transaction, purchase transaction, sales transaction

see also: cash advance transaction

Bargeld-bezugskarte

ATM-only card – a card which can only be used to obtain cash at ATMs

cf.: ATM card

Stornoquote

attrition rate – the percentage of cancelled cards with respect to the total number of cards

Transaktionsreihen-folgeüberprüfung, Transaktionsnachver-folgung, Transaktions-verknüpfung

audit trail – (a method which results from) linked transactions according to a sophisticated tracing system by rewriting the magnetic stripe and/or the chip

see also: audit, to; auditability

audit, to – the check the linkage of transactions
see also: audit trail, auditability

Transaktionsreihen-folge überprüfen, Transaktionsreihen nachverfolgen, Transaktionsreihe verknüpfen

auditability – the ability to check the linkage of transactions
see also: audit, to, audit trail

Transaktionsnachvollziehbarkeit, Transaktionsreihenfolge-überprüfung, Transaktionsnachvollzug, Transaktionsverknüpfungsüberprüfung

authentication – the procedure to check the genuineness

Echtheitserkennung, Feststellung der Echtheit

authorization – an affirmative response of the issuer to the acquirer which is forwarded by the acquirer to the merchant or cash advance location to permit a card transaction
cf.: approval of an authorization request
opp.: authorization request, refusal of an authorization request
see also: cash authorization, electronic authorization, merchant authorization, retail authorization, sales authorization, telephone authorization, voice authorization

Autorisierung, Genehmigung

authorization call – an authorization request of a merchant or a cash advance office by telephone to permit a card transaction
see also: authorization request

Autorisierungs-anruf, Genehmigungsanruf

authorization centre –
1) the site where the merchants call for authorization codes and which routes the authorization requests to the issuer (acquirer authorization centre);
2) the site where the authorizations actually take place by the issuer (issuer authorization centre)
see also: acquirer authorization centre, issuer authorization centre

Autorisierungs-zentrale, Genehmigungs-zentrale

*Autorisierungs-
nummer, Genehmi-
gungsnummer*

authorization code – a code given by the issuer or a substitute and sent via the acquirer to the merchant as a confirmation of an authorization

*Autorisierungs-
entscheidung,
Genehmigungs-
entscheidung*

authorization decision – a positive or negative response to an authorization request

*Autorisierungs-
entgelt, Genehmi-
gungsentgelt*

authorization fee – the fee which has to be paid to the payment system by the issuer and/or acquirer for an authorization

*Autorisierungs-
dateien, Genehmi-
gungsdateien*

authorization files – the files containing the authorization frames which include e.g. the account detail file, the account range file, the preferred file and the stoplist file

*Karten(inhaber)-
Limits*

authorization limits – the parameters (e.g. maximum amount and/or number of transactions that can be authorized within a defined period) set by the issuer either for individual accounts in the account detail file or for a number of accounts in the account range file which are checked during authorization processing

cf.: account limits, account parameters, activity limits, activity parameters, authorization parameters, card limits

see also: account detail parameters, account range parameters

*Autorisierungs-
anfrage oder
-anwort, Genehmi-
gungsanfrage oder
-antwort*

authorization message – the message between the acquirer and the issuer or vice versa concerning authorization requests or approvals / refusals of the authorization requests

see also: authorization request, authorization response

*Autorisierungs-
nummer, Genehmi-
gungsnummer*

authorization number – a numeric / alphanumeric confirmation number accompanying the approval of an authorization

*Karten(inhaber)-
Limits*

authorization parameters – the limits (e.g. maximum amount and/or number of transactions that can be authorized within a defined period) set by the issuer either for individual accounts in the account detail file or for a range of accounts in the account range file which are checked during authorization processing

cf.: account limits, account parameters, activity limits, activity parameters, authorization limits, card limits

see also: account detail parameters, account range parameters

authorization processing – all procedures relating to an authorization that have to be executed in order to handle a voice or electronic request

see also: electronic request, voice request

Autorisierungs-abwicklung, Genehmigungs-abwicklung

authorization request – a request by a merchant or a cash advance location to permit a card transaction

opp.: approval of an authorization request, authorization, refusal of an authorization request

see also: electronic request, telephone request, voice request

Autorisierungs-anfrage, Genehmigungsanfrage

authorization response – the answer to an authorization request

opp.: authorization request

see also: authorization, authorization code, authorization denial

Antwort auf eine Autorisierungs-anfrage / Genehmigungsanfrage

authorization routing – the path taken by an authorization request from the merchant to the acquirer, from there to the issuer and by the respective authorization response back again

see also: authorization request, authorization response

Routing einer Autorisierungs-anfrage / Genehmigungsanfrage und ihrer Antwort

authorization service – a service to provide the merchants and ATMs / cash advance offices with authorizations

see also: authorization system

Autorisierungs-dienst, Genehmigungsdienst

authorization system – a setup to provide the merchants and ATMs / cash advance offices with authorizations

see also: authorization service

Autorisierungs-system, Genehmigungssystem

*Geschwindigkeits-
überprüfung von
Autorisierungen/
Genehmigungen*

authorization velocity monitoring – the supervision of the speed with which authorizations are made in order to secure a proper authorization service

*eine Autorisie-
rungsanfrage/
Genehmigungs-
anfrage bewilligen*

authorize, to – to provide an affirmative response to an authorization request

cf.: approve an authorization request, to

opp.: decline an authorization request, to; deny an authorization request, to; refuse an authorization request, to

*zugelassener
Kartenproduzent*

authorized contractor – a company authorized by the respective card organization to produce card plastics

*genehmigte
Transaktion*

authorized transaction – a transaction that was approved by the issuer

opp.: unauthorized transaction

Clearingzentrale

automated clearing house (ACH) – a centre for the automated clearing of payment transactions

cf.: ACH (automated clearing house)

*automatisierte Da-
tenerfassung*

automated data capturing – the process of capturing paper-based data through electronic reading devices

*Geldausgabe-
automat*

automated teller machine (ATM) – a cardholder-operated automatic machine activated by a card and a PIN and whose primary purpose is to dispense cash

cf.: ATM (automated teller machine), cash dispenser

*Bargeldbezug an
einem Geldaus-
gabeautomaten*

automated teller transaction – a transaction by which cash is obtained at an ATM

cf.: ATM transaction, ATM cash advance transaction, ATM cash disbursement transaction

opp.: merchant transaction, purchase transaction, sales transaction

see also: cash advance transaction

*automatische
Abbuchung*

automatic debiting – a scheme where debits are effected through one-off or standing orders

average transaction value – the average value of a transaction

durchschnittlicher Transaktionsbetrag

B2B card (business-to-business card) – a card designated to be used for commercial purposes
cf.: business-to-business card (B2B card)
see also: procurement card, purchasing card

Karte für kommerzielle Einkäufe

B2B payment (business-to-business payment) – a payment for the purchase of products or services of a business company from another business company
cf.: business-to-business payment (B2B payment)
opp.: person-to-person payment (P2P payment), P2P payment (person-to-person payment)

Zahlung eines Unternehmens an ein anderes Unternehmen

back-up authorization – an authorization performed by a pre-determined alternate processing system used whenever the issuer is unable to respond
cf.: alternate authorization, down-option authorization, dynamic stand-in authorization, permanent stand-in authorization, stand-in authorization
opp.: primary authorization

Genehmigung bei einem Systemausfall durch ein Ersatzsystem

back-up limits – the authorization parameters set by the issuer for the alternate processing system in case the primary processing system is unable to respond
cf.: alternate limits, alternate parameters, back-up parameters, down-option limits, down-option parameters, dynamic stand-in limits, dynamic stand-in parameters, fall-back limits, fall-back parameters, permanent stand-in limits, permanent stand-in parameters, stand-in limits, stand-in parameters

von der kartenausgebenden Bank festgelegte Limits für das Ersatzsystem

back-up parameters – the authorization parameters set by the issuer for the alternate processing system in case the primary processing system is unable to respond

von der kartenausgebenden Bank festgelegte Limits für das Ersatzsystem cf.: alternate limits, alternate parameters, back-up limits, down-option limits, down-option parameters, dynamic stand-in limits, dynamic stand-in parameters, fall-back limits, fall-back parameters, permanent stand-in limits, permanent stand-in parameters, stand-in limits, stand-in parameters

Genehmigungs-verfahren durch ein Ersatzsystem bei einem System-ausfall

back-up processing – the performance of authorizations by a pre-determined alternate processing system used whenever the issuer is unable to respond

cf.: alternate processing, down-option processing, dynamic stand-in processing, permanent stand-in processing, stand-in processing

opp.: primary processing

Ersatzgenehmi-gungssystem bei Systemausfall

back-up processing system – a back-up issuer processing facility for authorizations when the primary processing system is not available

cf.: alternate, alternate processing system, down-option processing system, dynamic stand-in processing system, permanent stand-in processing system, stand-in processing system

see also: IHS (issuer host system), issuer host, issuer host system (IHS), primary, primary processing system

Transaktion, die bei einem System-ausfall von einem Ersatzgenehmi-gungssystem auto-risiert wird

back-up transaction – a transaction which is authorized by a back-up processing system

cf.: alternate transaction, down-option transaction, dynamic stand-in transaction, permanent stand-in transaction, stand-in transaction

opp.: primary transaction

see also: alternate processing system

Konten mit wertberichtigten Forderungen

bad accounts – accounts with bad debts

Kontostands-abfrage

balance check – a transaction enabling a cardholder to determine the balance of his / her account

cf.: balance inquiry

balance display – a facility which shows the opening balance of an electronic purse before a transaction takes place and the closing balance after a transaction has taken place

Anzeigenfeld für das auf einer elektronischen Geldbörse gespeicherte Guthaben

balance inquiry – a query performed to check the account balance
cf.: balance check

Kontostandsabfrage

balance reader – a device to show the balance of an electronic purse
cf.: value checker

Wertanzeiger, Guthabenanzeiger

bank card – a) a card issued by a bank; b) a credit card issued by a bank providing extended credit

Bankkarte; Bankkreditkarte mit festgelegtem Kreditrahmen

bank card association – an association formed by a group of banks using a common processing centre for their card business

Bankenvereinigung zum gemeinsamen Betrieb eines Kartenabrechnungsrechenzentrums

bank cheque – a bank-specific cheque
cf.: bank proprietary cheque

Bankscheck

bank counter transaction – a transaction performed at the bank's teller
cf.: branch counter transaction

Transaktion am Bankschalter

bank identification number (BIN) – a number designating a bank
cf.: bank identifier code (BIC), BIC (bank identifier code), BIN (bank identification number)

Bankleitzahl

bank identifier code (BIC) – a code designating a bank
cf.: bank identification number (BIN), BIC (bank identifier code), BIN (bank identification number)

Bankleitzahl

bank note – a piece of paper stating a certain amount of money in a given denomination and used as legal tender
see also: coin

Banknote

Bankkundenkarten

bank proprietary card – a card issued by a bank with one or more service functions which can only be used in the issuer's environment
cf.: bank-owned card

Bankscheck

bank proprietary cheque – a bank-specific cheque
cf.: bank cheque

Geldtransfer, Über-weisung

bank transfer – the transfer of money from one bank account to another
cf.: money transfer
see also: money order, payment order

Bevölkerungsteil mit Bank-verbindung

banked population – the number of persons or the percentage of a population holding a bank account
opp.: unbanked population

Bankscheck

banker's cheque – a cheque drawn on a bank
see also: bank cheque, bank proprietary cheque, cheque

Bankkundenkarte

bank-owned card – a card issued by a bank with one or more service functions which can only be used in the issuer's environment
cf.: bank proprietary card

Offline-Verarbeitung

batch mode processing – data processing carried out in off-line operations
cf.: off-line processing

Inhaberscheck

bearer cheque – a cheque which is paid to whoever presents it
see also: cheque

Karteneinsatzbeob-achtung in Hinblick auf aus dem üblichen Rahmen fallende Transaktionen

behavioural scoring – the process of checking whether current payment transactions contradict a previous spending pattern
cf.: behavioural screening

Karteneinsatzbeob-achtung in Hinblick auf aus dem üblichen Rahmen fallende Transaktionen

behavioural screening – the process of checking whether current payment transactions contradict a previous spending pattern
cf.: behavioural scoring

below floor limit fraud – a fraud that was perpetrated be-   *Betrugsfall unter*
cause the transaction amount was less than the floor limit   *der Genehmigungs-*
and therefore an authorization request was not made   *grenze*

cf.: under floor limit fraud

opp.: above floor limit fraud

below floor limit transaction – a transaction that does   *Transaktion unter*
not require the merchant to call his authorization centre for   *der Genehmigungs-*
authorization because the transaction amount is below the   *grenze*
merchant floor limit

cf.: under floor limit transaction

opp.: above floor limit transaction

beneficiary – the payee of a given amount of money   *Begünstigter*

beneficiary bank – a bank receiving a credit for one of its   *begünstigte Bank*
accounts

opp.: paying bank

betting transaction – a transaction to pay bets   *Zahlung von Wett-*
einsätzen

BIC (bank identifier code) – a code designating a bank   *Bankleitzahl*

cf.: bank identifier code (BIC), bank identification number
(BIN), BIN (bank identification number)

bilateral agreement – an arrangement between an ac-   *Vereinbarung*
quirer and an issuer on financial clearing and settlement out-   *zwischen zwei*
side of the normal clearing and settlement procedure   *Mitgliedern eines*
Zahlungssystems
see also: bilateral clearing, bilateral settlement

bilateral clearing – an arrangement between an acquirer   *direktes Clearing*
and an issuer on transaction clearing outside of the normal   *zwischen zwei*
clearing and settlement procedure   *Mitgliedern eines*
Zahlungssystems
opp.: centralized clearing

see also: bilateral agreement, bilateral settlement

bilateral settlement – an arrangement between an ac-   *direkte Abrechnung*
quirer and an issuer on financial settlement outside of the   *zwischen zwei Mit-*
normal clearing and settlement procedure   *gliedern eines*
Zahlungssystems
opp.: centralized settlement

see also: bilateral agreement, bilateral clearing

B

bilateral vereinbartes Entgelt, das von der vertragsunterneh-mensabrechnenden Bank an die karten-ausgebende Bank bezahlt wird

bilaterally (agreed) interchange fee – an interchange fee which is agreed between a specific acquirer and a specific issuer

opp.: default interchange fee, fall-back interchange fee, multilateral (agreed) interchange fee (MIF), MIF (multilaterally [agreed] interchange fee)

see also: interchange fee

Rechnung legen

bill, to – to print the open amounts on a statement which is transmitted to the cardholder

Rechnungslegung

billing – a procedure by which the open amounts are printed on a statement which is transmitted to the cardholder

Abrechnungsbetrag

billing amount – the total of the cardholder's statement which has to be paid

cf.: cardholder billing amount

Abrechnungs-währung

billing currency – the currency in which the cardholder is billed

cf.: cardholder billing currency

Abrechnungszyklus

billing cycle – the specific card number ranges which are billed at different dates

Abrechnungsdatum

billing date – the date at which the cardholder statement is made out

Abrechnungs-zeitraum

billing interval – the period between two billing dates

cf.: billing period

Abrechnungs-möglichkeiten

billing options – the possibilities for billing more than one card either individually or centrally

see also: central billing, individual billing

Abrechnungs-zeitraum

billing period – the period between two billing dates

cf.: billing interval

Bankleitzahl

BIN (bank identification number) – a number designating a bank

cf.: bank identifier code (BIC), bank identification number (BIN), BIC (bank identifier code)

BIN range – a defined series of bank identification numbers

definierter Teil des Bankleitzahlenverzeichnisses

BIN table – a table of bank identification numbers

Bankleitzahlentabelle

biometric authentication – any method of verifying the identity of a person by measuring an individual biological characteristic
see also: biometrics, biometric techniques

biometrische Identitätsfeststellung

biometric techniques – the techniques of verifying an individual based on physical or behavioural characteristics unique for a given individual
cf.: biometrics
see also: biometric authentication, finger scanning, fingerprint verification, retina scanning, voice recognition

biometrische Identifizierungsverfahren

biometrics – the techniques of verifying an individual based on physical oder or behavioural characteristics unique for a given individual
cf.: biometric techniques
see also: biometric authentication, finger scanning, fingerprint verification, retina scanning, voice recognition

biometrische Identifizierungsverfahren

bit density – the number of bits per unit of length of a data media

Bit-Dichte

blacklist – a printout containing card numbers which are not to be honoured
cf.: hot card list, restricted card list, stoplist, warning, warning bulletin, warning notice bulletin
see also: blacklist file, hot card file, negative file, stoplist file

Sperrliste

blacklist file – a data file containing card numbers which are not to be honoured
cf.: hot card file, negative file, stoplist file
see also: blacklist, hot card list, restricted card list, stoplist, warning bulletin

Sperrdatenbestand

eine Karten-
nummer sperren

blacklist, to – to put a card number on the blacklist
cf.: stoplist, to

gesperrte Karte

blacklisted card – a card that has been put on the blacklist
cf.: hot card, pick-up card

nicht unterschriebene
Karte

blank card – a card without a signature

leeres Scheckformu-
lar, nicht ausgefüllter
Scheck

blank cheque – a cheque form which is not filled in

Mischentgelt, Entgelt
als Ergebnis einer
Mischkalkulation

blended fee – a fee obtained from a mixed calculation
see also: blended rate

Mischprozentsatz,
Prozentsatz als Er-
gebnis einer Misch-
kalkulation

blended rate – a percentage rate obtained from a mixed
calculation
see also: blended fee

eine Karte
blockieren

block a card, to – to set a card to a status which prevents
the cardholder from making transactions when authorization
requests are made

blockierte Karte

blocked card – a card which is prevented from making
transactions when authorization requests are made
cf.: blocked card number

blockierte Karten-
nummer

blocked card number – a card number which is barred
from making transactions when authorization requests are
made
cf.: blocked card

vertrauenswürdiger
Karteninhaber

bonafide cardholder – a trustworthy cardholder

vertrauenswürdiger
Dritter

bonafide third party – a trustworthy third party

geplatzer Scheck,
nicht eingelöster
Scheck

bounced cheque – a cheque that was not honoured
opp.: honoured cheque
see also: covered cheque

branch counter transaction – a transaction performed at the bank's teller
cf.: bank counter transaction

Transaktion am Bankschalter

brand – the identity of a payment product
see also: brand awareness, brand choice, brand logo, brand loyalty, brand mark, brand recognition, brand value, brand visibility

Marke

brand awareness – the extent to which a branded card is recognized by the general public

Markenbekanntheit

brand choice – the result of a decision-making process where a specific branded card is given preference over another

Markenwahl (beim Kaufentscheid)

brand logo – the combination of name, symbol and colour that visually characterizes the identity of a branded card
cf.: brand mark

Markenlogo

brand loyalty – the attitude of cardholders to use and renew the respective branded cards continuously

Markentreue

brand mark – the combination of name, symbol and colour that visually characterizes the identity of a branded card
cf.: brand logo

Markenlogo

brand recognition – the ability to recognize a specific branded card

Marken-wiedererkennung

brand value – the value created by a brand

Markenwert

brand visibility – the conspicuousness of a brand

Markensichtbarkeit

broad card – a card which is issued to a considerable proportion of the population
cf.: mainstream card, mass card
opp.: gold card, premier card, premium card, prestige card, privilege card, up-market card, up-scale card

Massenkarte

Beweislast

burden of proof – the need to furnish evidence

Wechselstube

bureau de change – an authorized agent of a bank to exchange money, to encash cheques and to give cash advances
cf.: change bureau, exchange bureau, exchange office, foreign exchange bureau

Firmenkarte

business card – a card which is issued to the staff of a business unit for payment of business expenses
cf.: company card, corporate card
opp.: private card
see also: purchasing card

Geschäfts-bedingungen für Karteninhaber

business conditions – terms and conditions of a card issuer under which a cardholder may use that card
cf.: card business conditions, disclosure

Geschäftstag

business day – a day during which an entity is open to provide full business operations

Karte für kommerzielle Einkäufe

business-to-business card (B2B card) – a card designated to be used for commercial purposes
cf.: B2B card (business-to-business card)
see also: procurement card, purchasing card

Zahlung eines Unternehmens an ein anderes Unternehmen

business-to-business payment (B2B payment) – a payment for the purchase of products or services of a business company from another business company
cf.: B2B payment (business-to-business payment)
opp.: person-to-person payment (P2P payment), P2P payment (person-to-person payment)

Transaktion, bei der das Vertragsunternehmen die vertragsunternehmensabrechnende Bank kontaktieren muß

call me transaction – a transaction where the automated authorization service gives the response that the merchant should contact the acquirer / the acquirer should contact the issuer directly

Aufforderung eines elektronischen Genehmigungssystems zu einer telefonischen Genehmigungsanfrage

call referral – a request by an automated authorization system that the merchant has to call the acquirer to obtain an authorization
see also: call me transaction, referral, referral call

calling card – a card which can be used for telephone purposes only

cf.: phone card, telephone card

Telefonkarte

CAM (card authentication method) – a method to ensure the authenticity of a card

cf.: card authentication, card authentication method (CAM)

opp.: merchant authentication

see also: cardholder verification, cardholder verification method (CVM), CVM (cardholder verification method)

Feststellung der Kartenechtheit, Kartenechtheits-erkennung

cancel a card, to – to terminate the agreement between cardholder and issuer

eine Karte stornieren

cancel a transaction, to – to invalidate a transaction that has already been carried out by a merchant or a cash advance office

eine Transaktion stornieren

cancellation number – a number provided by a hotel to verify a cardholder's notification to cancel a guaranteed reservation

Storno-Codezahl

cancellation of a card – the termination of a card according to the business conditions

cf.: card cancellation, card termination, termination of a card

Storno einer Karte

cancellation of a transaction – the invalidation of a transaction that has already been carried out by a merchant or a cash advance office

Storno einer Transaktion

capture date – the date on which a transaction is captured and as a result of this processed by the acquirer

Erfassungsdatum, Verarbeitungs-datum

card – a piece of plastic used for payment

Karte

card acceptor – a legal entity with which there is an agreement to accept cards as a means of payment for goods or services when properly presented

cf.: acceptor, ME (member establishment, merchant establishment), member establishment (ME), merchant, merchant establishment (ME), retailer, SE (service establishment), service establishment (SE)

Kartenakzeptant, Vertrags-unternehmen

Kartenkonto — **card account** – an account on which card transactions and payments by the cardholder are entered

Kartennummer — **card account number** – a unique series of digits on the card created by the issuer to identify the issuer and the card-holder

cf.: account number, card number, PAN (primary account number), primary account number (PAN)

see also: non-standard account number, non-standard card account number, non-standard card number, standard account number, standard card account number, standard card number

definierter Teil einer Karten-nummernserie — **card account range** – a defined segment of an account number series

cf.: card range

see also: account range

Kartenaktivierung — **card activation** – actions taken by an issuer to increase the number of card transactions

see also: card activation programme

Kartenaktivie-rungsprogramm — **card activation programme** – a programme implemented by an issuer to increase the number of card transactions

cf.: card usage programme

see also: card activation

Kartenantrag — **card application** – the completion of a card application form in order to obtain a card

see also: apply for a card, to; card application form, card application processing

Kartenantrags-formular — **card application form** – a form which must be filled in by the card applicant

see also: apply for a card, to; card application, card application processing

Kartenantrags-bearbeitung — **card application processing** – the process of checking the card application form, entering its data and issuing the card

see also: apply for a card, to; card application, card application form

card authentication – a method to ensure the authenticity of a card

cf.: CAM (card authentication method), card authentication method (CAM)

opp.: merchant authentication

see also: cardholder verification, cardholder verification method (CVM), CVM (cardholder verification method)

Feststellung der Kartenechtheit, Kartenechtheits-erkennung

C

card authentication method (CAM) – a method to ensure the authenticity of a card

cf.: CAM (card authentication method), card authentication

opp.: merchant authentication

see also: cardholder verification, cardholder verification method (CVM), CVM (cardholder verification method)

Feststellung der Kartenechtheit, Kartenechtheits-erkennung

card authenticity – the genuineness of a card

Kartenechtheit

card base – all cards of an issuer

cf.: card portfolio

Kartenbestand, Kartenportfolio

card branding – the marketing measures to develop and maintain a favourable brand image for a given card

Marketingmaßnahmen, um eine Karte zum Markenartikel zu machen

card business – all activities concerning

1) the issuance of cards and the collection of the amounts paid with the cards from the cardholders (card issuing business, issuing business) and

2) the processing and settlement of merchant and cash advance transactions (acquiring business, merchant acquiring business, merchant business)

see also: acquiring business, card issuing business, issuing business, merchant acquiring business, merchant business

Kartengeschäft

card business conditions – terms and conditions of a card issuer under which a carholder may use that card

cf.: business conditions, disclosure

Geschäfts-bedingungen für Karteninhaber

card cancellation – the termination of a card according to the business conditions

cf.: cancellation of a card, card termination, termination of a card

Storno einer Karte

C

Karteneinzug

card capture – the pick-up of a card
cf.: card pick-up, card recovery, card retention, confiscation of a card

Kartenträger-
(papier)

card carrier – the supporting paper used to transport the card in an envelope

einem Karteninha-
ber digital zuge-
ordneter öffent-
licher Schlüssel

card certificate – the digital assignment of a public key to a card to be used for electronic commerce
opp.: merchant certificate
see also: certificate

Entgelte im Zu-
sammenhang mit der
Ausgabe und Ver-
wendung von Karten

card charges – the fees the cardholder has to pay
see also: annual fee, cash advance fee, entrance fee, exchange rate mark-up, item charge, joining fee, transaction charge, transaction fee

Kartendaten

card data – the data associated with a card or a card base

Kartengestaltung,
Kartendesign

card design – the visual appearance of the front and the reverse side of the card
see also: card design specifications

Kartengestaltungs-
vorschriften, Karten-
designvorschriften

card design specifications – the rules with which all the manufactured cards must comply
see also: card design

Kartenverkaufs-
automat

card dispensing machine – a vending machine used for dispensing pre-paid cards
cf.: card vending machine

Strategie einer
Bank, sowohl
MasterCard- als
auch Visa-Karten
auszugeben

card duality – a strategy of a bank to conduct issuing activities with both MasterCard and Visa
opp.: merchant duality
see also: duality

Kartenfälschung

card duplication – the illegal reproduction of a card
cf.: counterfeiting a card
see also: alteration of a card

card economics – revenue, cost and margin situation of the card business

see also: acquirer economics, issuer economics

Ertrags-, Aufwands- und Gewinnsituation des Kartengeschäfts

D

card embossing – the affixation of data to a card in the form of raised characters through a special machine

Kartenprägung

card encoding – the recording of data concerning details of the card on the magnetic stripe of the card

Kartencodierung

card expiry – the date embossed on the card after which the card must not be honoured

cf.: expiration date, expiry date

Ablaufdatum, Gültigkeitsende

card face – the side of a card which contains the logo of the card system and the embossed / printed data of the card

cf.: card front, front side

opp.: card reverse, reverse side

Kartenvorderseite

card family – a group of cards with / without the same logo in a payment family

Kartenfamilie

card fee – a fee to be paid by the cardholder

see also: annual fee, card charges

Kartenentgelt

card file – a set of related data concerning a number of cards (e.g. account detail file, account range file, preferred file, stoplist file)

Kartendatei

card fraud – the misuse of a card / the card data by a criminal cardholder or a fraudster (dishonest finder, thief, forger)

cf.: fraudulent card use

opp.: collusive fraud, fraudulent merchant activity, merchant fraud

see also: fraud

Kartenbetrug

card front – the side of a card which contains the logo of the card system and the embossed / printed information

cf.: card face, front side

opp.: card reverse, reverse side

Kartenvorderseite

card imprint – the information visibly transferred from an embossed card to a sales slip

Kartenabdruck (auf einem Beleg)

C

Karten-
personalisierung

card initialization – the personalization of a card plastic
cf.: card personalization

Geschäft im Zu-
sammenhang mit
der Karten-
ausgabe, Karten-
inhabergeschäft

card issuance – all activities concerning the issuance of
cards, the receipt of cardholder transactions from the members / merchants, the guaranteeing of the payments and the
collection of the respective amounts from the cardholders
cf.: card issuing business, issuing, issuing business
opp.: acquiring business, merchant acquiring business

kartenausgebende
Bank, Karten-
emittent

card issuer – a bank which issues cards, receives the
cardholder transactions from the members / merchants, guarantees the payment and collects the respective amounts from
the cardholders
cf.: card issuing bank, cardholder bank, issuer, issuer bank,
issuing bank, issuing institution, issuing member, paying
bank
opp.: acquirer, acquirer bank, acquiring bank, acquiring institution, acquiring member, beneficiary bank

kartenausgebende
Bank, Karten-
emittent

card issuing bank – a bank which issues cards, receives
the cardholder transactions from the members / merchants,
guarantees the payment and collects the respective amounts
from the cardholders
cf.: card issuer, cardholder bank, issuer, issuer bank, issuing
bank, issuing institution, issuing member, paying bank
opp.: acquirer, acquirer bank, acquiring bank, acquiring institution, acquiring member, beneficiary bank

Geschäft im
Zusammenhang
mit der Karten-
ausgabe, Karten-
inhabergeschäft

card issuing business – all activities concerning the issuance of cards, the receipt of cardholder transactions from
the members / merchants, the guaranteeing of the payments
and the collection of the respective amounts from the cardholders
cf.: card issuance, issuing, issuing business
opp.: acquiring business, merchant acquiring business

Kartenlebenszyklus

card life cycle – the time span in which a card is renewed

card limits – the parameters (e. g. maximum amount and/or number of transactions that can be authorized within a defined period) set by the issuer either for individual accounts in the account detail file or for a number of accounts in the account range file which are checked during authorization processing

cf.: account limits, account parameters, activity limits, activity parameters, authorization limits, authorization parameters

see also: account detail parameters, account range parameters

Karten(inhaber)-Limits

card manufacturer – the producer of plastic cards
see also: card production

Kartenhersteller

card marketing – all measures aimed at increasing the card base, promoting cardholder transactions and preventing card terminations

opp.: merchant marketing

Karten(inhaber)-marketing

card misuse – the illegal use of a card

Kartenmißbrauch

card not received fraud – fraud which took place with a card that the cardholder claimed he / she did not receive

Betrug mit einer Karte, die der Karteninhaber nicht erhalten hat

card number – a unique series of digits on the card created by the issuer to identify the issuer and the cardholder

cf.: account number, card account number, PAN (primary account number), primary account number (PAN)

see also: non-standard account number, non-standard card account number, non-standard card number, standard account number, standard card account number, standard card number

Kartennummer

card organization – a business set-up which operates a (worldwide) card system, either consisting of an association of members or established as a single entity

see also: Amercian Express, Diner Club, JCB, MasterCard, Visa

Kartenorganisation

card payment – the payment with a card

Kartenzahlung

kartengesteuertes Zahlungssystem, Kartenzahlungssystem	**card payment system** – a payment system based on cards cf.: card-based payment system see also: payment system
Karten-durchdringung	**card penetration** – the percentage of cards issued in relation to (a share of) the population
Karten-personalisierung	**card personalization** – the initialization of a card plastic with cardholder-related data cf.: card initialization
Kartentelefon	**card phone** – a telephone which can be activated by using a card
Karteneinzug	**card pick-up** – the capture of a card cf.: card capture, card recovery, card retention, confiscation of a card
Kartenrohling	**card plastic** – a piece of plastic without embossed or printed data
Kartenbestand, Kartenportfolio	**card portfolio** – all cards of an issuer cf.: card base
Kartentransaktion, bei der die Karte körperlich vorliegt	**card present transaction** – a transaction whereby the card is presented for payment opp.: card not present transaction
Karteninhaber-Preispolitik	**card pricing** – the fixing of the fees, charges and interest rates applied in connection with cards cf.: cardholder pricing opp.: merchant pricing
Kartenherstellung	**card production** – the manufacturing of plastic cards see also: card manufacturer
Zahlungen von Käufen mit Karte	**card purchases** – the payment of purchases with a card
definierter Teil einer Kartennummernserie	**card range** – a defined segment of a card number series

card recognition – the process of recognizing a card   *Kartenerkennung*

card recovery – the retrieval of a misused or counterfeit card   *Karteneinzug*

cf.: card capture, card pick-up, card retention, confiscation of a card

card registration – a service rendered to cardholders where a cardholder's identification cards are registered   *Karten-registrierung*

card renewal process – the process of issuing card renewals   *Kartenerneuerung*

see also: card renewals

card renewals – the cards that are renewed after the expiration of the previous ones   *Erneuerungskarten*

see also: card renewals process

card replacement – the issuance of a card instead of another one   *Kartenersatz*

see also: emergency card replacement

card retention – the withdrawal of a card from circulation   *Karteneinzug*

cf.: card capture, card pick-up, card recovery, confiscation of a card

see also: card retention reward

card retention reward – the reward paid for the retrieval of a card   *Karteneinzugs-prämie*

cf.: merchant reward, pick-up reward

see also: card retention

card reverse – the rear side of a card   *Kartenrückseite*

cf.: reverse side

opp.: card face, card front, front side

card risk – the total risk arising from the issuance of a card   *Kartenrisiko*

see also: card risk management

card risk management – the process of managing the total risk inherent to the issuance of a card   *Kartenrisikomanagement, Kartenrisikosteuerung, Risikomanagement im Zusammenhang mit Karten*

see also: card risk

C

Kartenausgabe-
programm

card scheme – a program to issue cards with specific features

Kartenfolge-
nummer

card sequence number – the number defining the sequence of issued cards

Kartenzahlungs-
verweigerung

card suppression – an attempt by merchants to deny acceptance of the card

Kartensystem

card system – the set-up created by a card organization to run a (worldwide) card business
see also: American Express, Diners Club, JCB, Master-Card, Visa

Storno einer Karte

card termination – the cancellation of a card according to the business conditions
cf.: cancellation of a card, card cancellation, termination of a card

Kartentransaktion

card transaction – one use of a card for purchasing goods / services or for obtaining a cash advance

Kartenbenützung,
Kartennutzung,
Kartenverwendung

card usage – the process of using a card to purchase goods / services or for obtaining cash advances
see also: card usage programme, card user

Kartenaktivie-
rungsprogramm

card usage programme – a programme implemented by an issuer to increase the number of card transactions
cf: card activation programme
see also: card usage

Kartenbenützer,
Kartennutzer,
Kartenverwender

card user – a person performing a card transaction
see also: card usage

Kartengültigkeits-
feststellung

card validation – the process of checking the card validity
see also: card validity

Kartenverifizierung-
scode, Code zur
Feststellung der
Kartenechtheit

card validation code (CVC) – an algorithmically-derived code provided on the magnetic stripe to ensure that the original card is presented
cf.: card verification value (CVV), CVC (card validation code), CVV (card verification value)

card validity – a period during which the card is valid and which is explicitly stated on the card
see also: card validation

Kartengültigkeit

card vending machine – a vending machine used for dispensing pre-paid cards
cf.: card dispensing machine

Kartenverkaufs-automat

card verification value (CVV) – an algorithmically-derived code provided on the magnetic stripe of a card to protect it against alteration
cf.: card validation code (CVC), CVC (card validation code), CVV (card verification value)

Kartenverifizie-rungscode, Code zur Feststellung der Kartenechtheit

card-based payment system – a payment system which is based on cards
cf.: card payment system
see also: payment system

kartengesteuertes Zahlungssystem, Kartenzahlungssystem

card-guaranteed cheque – a cheque which is guaranteed by the simultaneous presentation of a cheque-guarantee card
see also: cheque, cheque guarantee card

kartengarantierter Scheck

cardholder – a person to whom a card has been issued

Karteninhaber

cardholder account maintenance – the updates carried out so as to ensure a correct cardholder database
opp.: merchant account maintenance

Karteninhaber-Datenbestands-pflege

cardholder activated POS terminal – a POS terminal that does not require any assistance by a cashier (e.g. at parking garages, toll ways, vending machines)
cardholder activated terminal (CAT), CAT (cardholder activated terminal), unattended POS terminal

Selbstbedienungs-terminal mit Kartenzahlungsfunktion, unbedientes POS-Terminal

cardholder activity data – the data that reflects all transaction-related cardholder information
opp.: cardholder primary data, merchant activity data
see also: activity data, cardholder history, transaction history

Karteninhaber-Umsatzdaten, Transaktionen eines Karteninhabers

Geschäftsbedin-
gungen für
Karteninhaber

cardholder agreement – a contract between a cardholder and an issuer covering the terms and conditions under which a card can be used
cf.: business conditions, card business conditions

kartenausgebende
Bank, Karten-
emittent

cardholder bank – a bank which issues cards, receives the cardholder transactions from the members / merchants, guarantees the payment and collects the respective amounts from the cardholders
cf.: card issuer, card issuing, issuer, issuer bank, issuing bank, issuing institution, issuing member, paying bank
opp.: acquirer, acquirer bank, acquiring bank, acquiring institution, acquiring member, beneficiary bank

Gesamtheit aller
Karten einer karten-
ausgebenden Bank

cardholder base – the entirety of all cards of an issuer

Karteninhaber-
Umsatz-
beobachtung

cardholder behaviour monitoring – the process of regularly checking the cardholders' spending behaviour
opp.: merchant behaviour monitoring

Abrechnungsbetrag

cardholder billing amount – the total of the cardholder's statement which has to be paid
cf.: billing amount

Abrechnungs-
währung

cardholder billing currency – the currency in which the cardholder is billed
cf.: billing currency

Karteninhaber-
reklamation

cardholder complaint – the objection of a cardholder, mostly concerning the acceptance of the card, the billing of wrong amounts, and the use of incorrect exchange rates
cf.: complaint

Karteninhaber-
datenbestand

cardholder database – all cardholder data stored in a computer file
opp.: merchant database

Karteninhaber-
daten

cardholder file – the details of a cardholder record stored in a computer
opp.: merchant file

cardholder history – the total of data reflecting all transaction-related cardholder information

cf.: transaction history

opp.: merchant history

see also: cardholder activity data, cardholder history file

Karteninhaber-Umsatzdaten, Transaktionen eines Karten-inhabers

cardholder history file – the file containing all transaction-related data

opp.: merchant history file

see also: cardholder activity data, cardholder history, transaction history

Umsatzdaten-bestand der Karteninhaber

cardholder loyalty – the willingness of a cardholder to keep his / her card

Karteninhaberbindung, Karteninhabertreue

cardholder pricing – the fixing of fees, charges and interest rates applied in connection with cards

cf.: card pricing

opp.: merchant pricing

Karteninhaber-Preispolitik

cardholder primary data – the data that is entered into the computer when the card application is received and that is infrequently updated

opp.: cardholder activity data, merchant primary data, primary data

Karteninhaber-Stammdaten

cardholder spending behaviour – the cardholder spending pattern which can be in line or deviate from the usual spending profile

cf.: activity pattern, cardholder spending pattern, spending pattern

Zahlungsverhalten des Karteninhabers

cardholder spending pattern – the cardholder behaviour which can be in line or deviate from the usual spending profile

cf.: activity pattern, cardholder spending behaviour, spending pattern

Zahlungsverhalten des Karteninhabers

cardholder statement – the bill sent to the cardholder

cf.: statement

see also: monthly statement

Karteninhaber-abrechnung

*Feststellung der
Karteninhaber-
echtheit,
Karteninhaber-
echtheitsnachweis*

cardholder verification – a method to ensure that the cardholder presenting the card is the lawful cardholder

cf.: cardholder verification method (CVM), CVM (cardholder verification method)

see also: CAM (card authentication method), card authentication, card authentication method (CAM)

*Feststellung der
Karteninhaber-
echtheit,
Karteninhaber-
echtheitsnachweis*

cardholder verification method (CVM) – a method to ensure that the cardholder presenting the card is the lawful cardholder

cf.: cardholder verification, CVM (cardholder verification method)

see also: CAM (card authentication method), card authentication, card authentication method (CAM)

*von einem Kartenin-
haber initiierte La-
dung einer elektroni-
schen Geldbörse*

cardholder-initiated load(ing) – a loading transaction of an electronic purse initiated by the cardholder

cf.: manual load(ing)

opp.: card-initiated load(ing)

*von einer Karte initi-
ierte Ladung einer
elektronischen Geld-
börse*

card-initiated load(ing) – a loading transaction offered by an electronic purse if the value is below a threshold

opp.: cardholder initiated load(ing), manual load(ing)

*Transaktion, bei
der die Karte nicht
körperlich vorliegt*

card-not-present transaction – a transaction where the card is not present at the mechant such as a mail order or a telephone order

see also: mail order, telephone order

*Kartentransaktion,
bei der die Daten von
einem POS-Terminal
gelesen werden*

card-read transaction – a transaction where card data is read (from magnetic stripe or chip) by a terminal

*direkte Übertragung
eines Betrages von
einer elektronischen
Geldbörse auf eine
andere*

card-to-card transfer – the direct switch of value from an electronic purse of a card to an electronic purse of another one

Bargeld

cash – legal tender (bank notes and coins) issued by a central bank

Cash – brand name of the Swiss electronic purse

Cash, die elektronische Geldbörse der Schweiz

cash access – a card feature which allows the cardholder to obtain cash

Bargeldbezugsmöglichkeit

cash advance – the procedure to obtain cash with a card
cf.: cash disbursement

Bargeldauszahlung

cash advance accommodation fee – a fee paid by the issuer to the acquirer
cf.: cash advance interchange fee, cash advance service fee, cash disbursement accommodation fee, cash disbursement interchange fee, cash disbursement service fee
see also: negative interchange fee

Interchange-Bargeldauszahlungsentgelt, Interbank-Bargeldauszahlungsentgelt

cash advance draft – the paper used to document the cash advance by a card
cf.: cash advance slip, cash draft, cash slip
opp.: charge slip, sales draft, sales receipt, sales slip, sales voucher
see also: transaction information paper

Bargeldauszahlungsbeleg

cash advance fee – a fee paid by the cardholder to the issuer for obtaining cash
see also: card charges

Bargeldauszahlungsentgelt

cash advance interchange fee – a fee paid by the issuer to the acquirer
cf.: cash advance accommodation fee, cash advance service fee, cash disbursement accommodation fee, cash disbursement interchange fee, cash disbursement service fee
see also: negative interchange fee

Interchange-Bargeldauszahlungsentgelt, Interbank-Bargeldauszahlungsentgelt

cash advance limit – the maximum amount that may be taken in cash by the cardholder in a given period
cf.: cash limit
opp.: retail limit, sales limit
see also: domestic cash advance limit, international cash advance limit

Bargeldbezugslimit

Bargeld- *auszahlungsstelle*	**cash advance location** – a (bank) location which provides cash advances cf.: cash advance office, cash advance outlet
Bargeld- *auszahlungsstelle*	**cash advance office** – a (bank) location which provides cash advances cf.: cash advance location, cash advance outlet
Bargeld- *auszahlungsstelle*	**cash advance outlet** – a (bank) location which provides cash advances cf.: cash advance location, cash advance office
Interchange- *Bargeldauszah-* *lungsentgelt,* *Interbank-Bargeld-* *auszahlungsentgelt*	**cash advance service fee** – a fee paid by the issuer to the acquirer cf.: cash advance accommodation fee, cash advance interchange fee, cash disbursement accommodation fee, cash disbursement interchange fee, cash disbursement service fee see also: negative interchange fee
Bargeld- *auszahlungsbeleg*	**cash advance slip** – the paper used to document the cash advance by a card cf.: cash advance draft, cash draft, cash slip opp.: charge slip, sales draft, sales receipt, sales slip, sales voucher see also: transaction information paper
Bargeldauszahlung	**cash advance transaction** – a transaction by which cash is obtained opp.: merchant transaction, payment transaction, purchase transaction, retail transaction, sales transaction
Autorisierung *einer Bargeld-* *auszahlung,* *Genehmigung* *einer Bargeld-* *auszahlung*	**cash authorization** – an affirmative response of the issuer to the acquirer which is forwarded by the acquirer to the cash advance location to permit a cash advance transaction opp.: merchant authorization, retail authorization, sales authorization see also: authorization

cash cheque – a cheque presented to a bank for obtaining cash

opp.: retail cheque

see also: cheque

Scheck, mit dem Bargeld bezogen wird

cash disbursement – the procedure to obtain cash with a card

cf.: cash advance

Bargeldauszahlung

cash disbursement accommodation fee – a fee paid by the issuer to the acquirer

cf.: cash advance accommodation fee, cash advance interchange fee, cash advance service fee, cash disbursement interchange fee, cash disbursement service fee

see also: negative interchange fee

Interchange-Bargeldauszahlungsentgelt, Interbank-Bargeldauszahlungsentgelt

cash disbursement interchange fee – a fee paid by the issuer to the acquirer

cf.: cash advance accommodation fee, cash advance interchange fee, cash advance service fee, cash disbursement accommodation fee, cash disbursement service fee

see also: negative interchange fee

Interchange-Bargeldauszahlungsentgelt, Interbank-Bargeldauszahlungsentgelt

cash disbursement service fee – a fee paid by the issuer to the acquirer

cf.: cash advance accommodation fee, cash advance interchange fee, cash advance service fee, cash disbursement accommodation fee, cash disbursement interchange fee

see also: negative interchange fee

Interchange-Bargeldauszahlungsentgelt, Interbank-Bargeldauszahlungsentgelt

cash dispenser – a cardholder-operated automatic machine activated by a card and a PIN and whose primary purpose is to dispense cash

cf.: ATM (automated teller machine), automated teller machine (ATM)

Geldausgabeautomat

cash draft – the paper used to document the cash advance by a card

cf.: cash advance draft, cash advance slip, cash slip

opp.: charge slip, sales draft, sales receipt, sales slip, sales voucher

see also: transaction information paper

Bargeldauszahlungsbeleg

Bargeldbezugslimit

cash limit – the maximum amount that may be taken in cash by the cardholder in a given period
cf.: cash advance limit
opp.: retail limit, sales limit
see also: domestic cash advance limit, international cash advance limit

Ladung einer elektronischen Geldbörse gegen Bargeld

cash load(ing) – a transaction whereby an electronic purse / issuer's float account is loaded against cash

Barzahlung bei Lieferung

cash on delivery – payment in cash when the delivery is received

Bargeldzahlung

cash payment – a payment effected by using cash
opp.: cashless payment

Örtlichkeit, bei der Bargeld bezogen werden kann

cash point – a place where you can obtain cash with a card either in a cash advance location or at an ATM
see also: ATM, cash advance location, cash advance office, cash advance outlet

Zahlungen von Käufen mit Bargeld

cash purchases – the payment of purchases with cash
opp.: card purchases

erneuter Einsatz von Bargeld

cash recycling – the recirculation of legal tender (bank notes or coins)

Handelskasse, Registrierkasse

cash register – a device at a POS which records amounts
see also: ECR (electronic cash register), electronic cash register (ECR)

Bargeldauszahlungsbeleg

cash slip – the paper used to document the cash advance by a card
cf.: cash advance draft, cash advance slip, cash draft
opp.: charge slip, sales draft, sales receipt, sales slip, sales voucher
see also: transaction information paper

C

cash substitution – the use of cashless payments instead of legal tender (banknotes and coins)

Bargeldersatz

cash withdrawal – a procedure to obtain cash with a cheque

Bargeldbezug

cash-back transaction – a transaction at a member establishment whereby the charged amount is higher than the original payment and the difference is refunded in cash

Kartentransaktion, bei der mehr verrechnet wird, als die Zahlung ausmacht, und die Differenz bar ausbezahlt wird

cashless payment – a payment effected without using cash

bargeldlose Zahlung

cashless society – a society in which goods and services are paid by cashless means

bargeldlose Gesellschaft

CAT (cardholder activated terminal) – a POS terminal that does not require any assistance by a cashier (e.g. at parking garages, toll ways, vending machines)
cf.: cardholder activated POS terminal, cardholder activated terminal (CAT), unattended POS terminal

Selbstbedienungsterminal mit Kartenzahlungsfunktion, unbedientes POS-Terminal

CEN (Comité Européen de Normalisation) – the European standardization committee
cf.: Comité Européen de Normalisation (CEN)

CEN

central acquiring – a multi-national merchant supplying all its transactions from various countries to one central acquirer
opp.: central issuing
see also: cross-border acquiring, global acquiring, international acquiring

grenzüberschreitendes Vertragsunternehmensgeschäft mit zentraler Abrechnung

central billing – a method whereby secondary cards / company cards are settled through a primary card
opp.: individual billing
see also: billing options

zentrale Kartenabrechnung

central issuing – an issuer supplying cards to a multi-national company with employees as cardholders posted in various countries

grenzüberschreitendes Karteninhabergeschäft mit zentraler Abrechnung

C

opp.: central acquiring

see also: cross-border issuing, global issuing, international issuing

zentrale PIN-Prüfung

central PIN checking – the verification of PINs at a central site

zentraler Computer eines Zahlungssystems

central site – the computer of a payment system organization routing data between acquirers and issuers in the respective network

zentrales Clearing

centralized clearing – the process where centrally at a computer centre transaction data is received from the acquirers and redistributed to the issuers

opp.: bilateral clearing

zentrale Abrechnung

centralized settlement – the process where payment is centrally effected on the basis of a centralized clearing

opp.: bilateral settlement

Transaktion bei einem Unternehmen, das in mehr als einem Land Niederlassungen hat, die von einer vertragsunternehmensabrechnenden Bank zentral abgerechnet werden

centrally acquired transaction – a transaction from an international merchant operating in more than one country acquired by a central acquirer

see also: central acquirer

Spezifikationen für eine grenzüberschreitende elektronische Geldbörse, CEPS

CEPS (Common Electronic Purse Specifications) – the specifications needed to implement a globally interoperable electronic purse

cf.: Common Electronic Purse Specifications (CEPS)

Gesellschaft, die für die Spezifikationen für eine grenzüberschreitende elektronische Geldbörse zuständig ist; CEPSCo

CEPSCo – the company founded to manage the Common Electronic Purse Specifications (CEPS)

ein digital zugeordneter öffentlicher Schlüssel

certificate – the digital assignment of a public key used for electronic commerce

see also: card certificate, merchant certificate

certificate authority – an authority delivering public keys so that participants in a system can be recognized as genuine ones

*Zertifizierungs-
stelle*

C

change bureau – an authorized agent of a bank to exchange money, to encash cheques and to give cash advances
cf.: bureau de change, exchange bureau, exchange office, foreign exchange bureau

Wechselstube

CHAPS (Clearing House Automated Payment System) – British automated clearing house
cf.: Clearing House Automated Payment System (CHAPS)

CHAPS

character height – the height of the embossed characters on a card

Zeichenhöhe

character spacing – the spacing of the embossed characters on a card

Zeichenabstand

charge card – a credit card usually with high spending limit and monthly payment without revolving credit
cf.: deferred debit card, delayed debit card
see also: credit card, current-account linked card, debit card, deferred debit card, delayed debit card, immediate payment card, pay later product, pay now product

*Kreditkarte mit ge-
wöhnlich hohem
Verfügungsrahmen
und monatlicher
Rechnungslegung
ohne Kreditrahmen*

charge slip – paper used to document the payment by card
cf.: sales draft, sales receipt, sales slip, sales voucher
opp.: cash advance draft, cash advance slip, cash draft, cash slip
see also: transaction information document

*Leistungsbeleg,
Verkaufsbeleg,
Zahlungsbeleg,
Kartenzahlungs-
beleg*

charge volume – the turnover charged to cardholders

*Karteninhaber-
umsatz*

chargeback – a transaction record which is returned to the acquiring member by the issuing member because of deficient transaction

Rückbelastung

chargeback cycle – the sequence of performing a chargeback

*Rückbelastungs-
verfahren, Rück-
belastungszyklus*

Rückbelastungs-auseinandersetzung	**chargeback dispute** – a procedure concerning a disagreement between acquirer and issuer as to whether there is a chargeback reason or not
Rückbelastungs-beleg	**chargeback draft** – an instrument of payment used by a member to collect money from another member with respect to a chargeback
Datum, ab dem eine Rückbelastung möglich ist	**chargeback effective date** – the date as of when the liability for a transaction with a stoplisted card is transferred from the issuer to the acquirer
Rückbelastungs-formular	**chargeback form** – a form which states the reasons pertaining to the chargeback
Rückbelastungs-zeitraum	**chargeback period** – the period in which a member may charge a transaction record back
Rückbelastungsver-arbeitung	**chargeback processing** – the processing of any dispute which may occur between the acquirer and the issuer and which results in a financial message
Rückbelastungs-grund	**chargeback reason** – the reason why a member may charge a transaction record back
Nummer des Rück-belastungsgrunds	**chargeback reason code** – a code identifying the specific reason for a chargeback
Rückbelastungs-datensatz	**chargeback record** – all computerized data pertaining to a chargeback case
Abschreibungsquote	**charge-off rate** – the rate of write-offs of bad debts
eine PIN überprüfen	**check a PIN, to** – to verify the correctness of a PIN see also: check a signature, to
eine Unterschrift überprüfen	**check a signature, to** – to verify the correctness of a signature see also: check a PIN, to
Prüfziffer	**check digit** – a part of the card number which is the result of a check digit routine

check digit routine – a calculation which is performed on the cardholder's card number and which results in a check digit

Prüfziffern-verfahren

C

checking account – an account used for handling payment transactions
cf.: current account, demand deposit account, giro account, sight deposit account

Girokonto

check-out page – the page in a website where the payment data are entered
cf.: payment page

Zahlungsseite bei einem Internet-Shop

cheque – a piece of paper that can be used for cash withdrawals and for the payment of goods / services
see also: bank cheque, bank proprietary cheque, banker's cheque, cash cheque, retail cheque

Scheck

cheque acceptor – a person / institution accepting cheques

Scheckempfänger

cheque bearer – the person who holds the cheque

Scheckinhaber

cheque book – a booklet containing detachable blank cheques

Scheckbuch, Scheckheft

cheque card – a card which guarantees a cheque up to a given amount under certain rules
cf.: cheque guarantee card

Scheckkarte, Scheckgarantiekarte

cheque encashment – the exchange of a cheque for cash
cf.: encashment

Scheckeinlösung

cheque encashment fee – a fee charged for cashing the cheque amount

Scheckeinlösungs-entgelt

cheque form – a form that must be filled in to make it a cheque

Scheckformular

cheque guarantee card – a card which guarantees a cheque up to a given amount under certain rules
cf.: cheque card

Scheckkarte, Scheckgarantiekarte

C

garantierter Scheck-
höchstbetrag

cheque guarantee limit – the maximum amount of a cheque which is subject to a guarantee

Scheckrecht

cheque law – the law which governs all aspects of cheque usage

Schecknummer

cheque number – a number which appears in the reading zone of a cheque providing the cheque with a unique number in connection with a given current account

Scheckerfassung, -auf-
bewahrung und -ein-
zug bei/durch Einlöse-
oder Clearingstelle

cheque truncation – a method by which a cheque is not physically transmitted to the issuer, but kept and stored by the acquirer

Chip

chip – a piece of silicon etched with an electronic circuit

Geldausgabeautomat
mit einem (zusätz-
lichen) Chipleser

chip ATM – an ATM which contains a chip reader and is able to process chip transactions
see also: chip terminal, magnetic stripe ATM

Chipkarte, Karte
mit Mikrochip

chip card – a card which contains a microchip
cf.: IC card (integrated circuit card), integrated circuit card (IC card), MC card (microcircuit card), microcircuit card (MC card)
see also: controller card, magnetic stripe card, memory card, processor card, smart card

chipimplantierendes
Unternehmen; Unter-
nehmen, das Chips in
Karten implantiert

chip embedder – an entity that implants chips into cards

komplette Chip-
transaktion

chip full grade (transaction) – a chip transaction whereby all relevant data obtained from the chip is used in authorization request and response messages
opp.: chip partial grade (transaction)

Chiphersteller

chip manufacturer – an entity that produces chips

Umstieg von
Magnetstreifen-
technologie auf
Chiptechnologie

chip migration – the changeover from magnetic stripe technology to chip technology

chip operating system – a special software for micro-processor cards which gives the chip computer-like functions

Chip-Betriebs-system

C

chip partial grade (transaction) – a chip transaction whereby a subset of the data obtained from the chip is used in the authorization request and response

opp.: chip full grade (transaction)

partielle Chip-transaktion

chip rollout – the issue of chip cards and the installation of chip terminal

Ausgabe von Chipkar-ten und Installation von Chip-Terminals

chip specifications – the data outlining the details of a chip

opp.: magnetic stripe specifications

see also: magnetic stripe specifications, POS (terminal) specifications

Chipspezifikationen

chip terminal – a POS terminal which contains a chip reader

see also: Chip ATM, magnetic stripe terminal

Chipterminal, POS-Terminal mit einem (zu-sätzlichen) Chipleser

chip transaction – a transaction whereby transaction data is captured directly from the chip of the card

opp.: magnetic stripe transaction

Chiptransaktion

Chipknip – brand name of the Dutch electronic purse

Chipknip, die elek-tronische Geldbörse der Niederlande

Cirrus – a licensed ATM card system with the licences being granted by Cirrus International

opp.: Plus

see also: Cirrus card, Cirrus International

Cirrus

Cirrus card – an ATM card issued by a licensee of Cirrus which can be used at all ATMs connected to the Cirrus net-work

opp.: Plus card

see also: Cirrus, Cirrus International

Cirrus-Karte

Cirrus International – an international ATM card organ-ization which is the licensor for Cirrus cards and wholly owned by MasterCard International

Cirrus International

C

opp.: Plus International
see also: Cirrus, Cirrus card

Kundenkreditkarte von Handels- und Dienstleistungsunternehmen einer Stadt

city card – a local card system where cards are issued by major retailers and accepted by all of them

Clearing

clearing – the process carried out in a computer centre where transaction data are supplied by the acquirers and then redistributed to the issuers in order to settle transactions
cf.: clearing processing

Clearingstelle

clearing centre – an institution processing the clearing data supplied by the acquirers and redistributing it to the issuers in order to settle transactions
cf.: clearing institution

Clearingdaten

clearing data – the information supplied to a clearing centre by the acquirers, with the data being redistributed to the issuers in order to settle transactions
cf.: clearing message

Clearingentgelt

clearing fee – a fee to be paid to the clearing centre for the clearing

Clearing-Datenbestand

clearing file – a compilation of clearing data

Clearingfunktion

clearing function – a process carried out in a computer centre which receives electronic files from different acquirer processing centres, sorts them and forwards them to different issuer processing centres
cf.: store-and-forward function

CHAPS

Clearing House Automated Payment System (CHAPS) – British automated clearing house
cf.: CHAPS (Clearing House Automated Payment System)

Clearingstelle

clearing institution – a computer centre processing the clearing data supplied by the acquirers and redistributing it to the issuers in order to settle transactions
cf.: clearing centre

clearing message – the information supplied to a clearing centre by the acquirers, with the data being redistributed to the issuers in order to settle transactions

cf.: clearing data

Clearingdaten

clearing processing – the process carried out in a computer centre where transaction data are supplied by the acquirers and then redistributed to the issuers in order to settle transactions

cf.: clearing

Clearing

clearing system – a system of a card organization in which transaction data supplied by the acquirers are processed in a computer centre and then redistributed to the issuers in order to settle transactions

Clearingsystem

closed (electronic) purse system – an electronic purse that is only issued within a specific group of people and can only be used within a closed-off system

opp.: open (electronic) purse system

see also: IEP (inter-sector electronic purse), inter-sector electronic purse (IEP)

geschlossene elektronische Geldbörse

closing balance – the balance of an electronic purse after a transaction

opp.: opening balance

Betrag auf einer elektronischen Geldbörse nach einer Transaktion

co-branded card – credit card issued by a member with a special design and distributed through a third party institution

cf.: affinity card, third party card

Karte, die von einer Bank mit speziellem Design ausgegeben und über einen Dritten vertrieben wird

coin – a piece of metal stating a certain amount of money in a given denomination and used as legal tender

see also: bank note

Münze

collect, to – to acquire transactions from merchants which are submitted to the interchange system and to pay the respective amounts to the merchants on the basis of a merchant agreement

cf.: acquire, to

see also. contract merchants, to

Vertragsunternehmen abrechnen

vertragsunterneh-mensabrechnende Bank

collecting bank – a bank which collects from merchants the transactions that are submitted to the interchange system and which pays the respective amounts to the merchants on the basis of a merchant agreement

cf.: acquirer, acquirer bank, acquiring bank, acquiring institution, acquiring member

opp.: card issuer, card issuing bank, cardholder bank, issuer, issuer bank, issuing bank, issuing institution, issuing member

Zahlungsersuchen

collection letter – a letter asking for payment if this was denied within the normal procedure

Kartenbetrug durch mitmachendes / mit-eingeweihtes Ver-tragsunternehmen

collusive fraud – a fraud case in which a merchant cooperates / participates

cf.: fraudulent merchant activity, merchant fraud

bei Kartenbetrug mit-machendes / mit-eingeweihtes Ver-tragsunternehmen

collusive merchant – a merchant cooperating / participating in a fraud case

see also: merchant collusion

gemeinsame Sperr-liste von Master-Card und Visa

combined warning bulletin – a stoplist published jointly by MasterCard und Visa to advise US merchants not to honour the cards on it

Karte, die sowohl Debit- als auch Kreditkarte ist

combo card – a card with both credit and debit functions on it

CEN

Comité Européen de Normalisation (CEN) – the European standardization committee

cf.: Comité Européen de Normalisation (CEN)

see also: American National Standards Institute (ANSI), ANSI (American National Standards Institute), International Organization for Standardization (ISO), ISO (International Organization for Standardization)

Flottenkarte, Fuhrparkkarte

commercial road transport card (CRT card) – a card which is not issued to a cardholder but to a specific vehicle to pay for vehicle-related goods / services

cf.: CRT card (commercial road transport card), fleet card

see also: truck card

commission – rate of the transaction amount to be paid by the merchant
cf.: commission rate, discount, discount rate, merchant service charge (MSC), MSC (merchant service charge), percentage discount, service charge, service fee

Disagio, Kommission, Umsatzprovision

commission rate – rate of the transaction amount to be paid by the merchant
cf.: commission, discount, discount rate, merchant service charge (MSC), MSC (merchant service charge), percentage discount, service charge, service fee

Disagio, Kommission, Umsatzprovision

Common Electronic Purse Specifications (CEPS) – the specifications needed to implement a globally interoperable electronic purse
cf.: CEPS (Common Electronic Purse Specifications)

CEPS

company card – a card which is issued to the staff of a company for payment of company expenses
cf.: business card, corporate card
opp.: private card
see also: purchasing card

Firmenkarte

complaint – the objection of a cardholder mostly concerning the acceptance of the card, the billing of wrong amounts, and the use of incorrect exchange rates
cf.: cardholder complaint

Karteninhaber-reklamation

compliance – the procedure a member of a card system has to use with another member to resolve a complaint if it cannot be resolved through the normal procedure

Schlichtungs-verfahren

compliance case – a concrete dissent between members of a payment scheme which was not solved through the normal procedure

Schlichtungsfall

confidentiality – the security to be protected against unauthorized disclosure

Vertraulichkeit

Hotelreservie-rungs-Codezahl

confirmation number – a number provided by a hotel to verify a cardholder's guaranteed reservation

eine Karte einziehen

confiscate a card, to – to retrieve a misused or counterfeit card
cf.: pick-up a card, to; recover a card, to; retain a card, to

eingezogene Karte

confiscated card – a card that has been retrieved
cf.: recovered card, retained card

Karteneinzug

confiscation of a card – the retrieval of a misused or counterfeit card
cf.: card capture, card pick-up, card recovery, card retention

Anschlußentgelt

connection fee – a fee to be paid by acquirers and issuers for the connection to an international authorization, clearing and settlement system

konsolidierte Abrechnung

consolidated settlement – a kind of settlement whereby credits and debits are offset and the difference is paid

Konsumentenkredit, Verbraucherkredit, Privatkredit

consumer credit – a loan granted to consumers for purchasing goods or services

Konsumentenschutz, Verbraucherschutz

consumer protection – the protection of consumers by state authorities or non-governmental organizations

kontaktlose Akzeptanz

contactless acceptance – the acceptance of a card without inserting a card into a payment terminal

kontaktlose Zutrittskontrolle

contactless access control – the access to a facility without inserting a card into an access terminal

kontaktlose Chipkarte

contactless chip card – a microprocessor card whereby the coupling between the electronic elements in the card and the external interface does not need pyhsical contact
cf.: non-contact card
opp.: contact-type chip card

kontaktlose elektronische Geldbörse

contactless purse – an electronic purse whereby payment is effected without inserting it into a payment terminal
see also: proximity payment, vicinity payment

contact-type chip card – a microprocessor card whereby coupling between the electronic elements in the card and
the external interface needs physical contact
opp.: contactless chip card

kontaktbehaftete
Chipkarte

contract merchants, to – to have merchants sign an
agreement concerning the acquiring of transactions
see also: acquire, to; collect, to

Vertragsunternehmen
akquirieren

contracted network – a network based on contracts between an acquirer and a commercial business

Akzeptanznetz auf der
Grundlage von Verträ-
gen mit Unternehmen

controller card – a card which contains a processor microchip
cf.: processor card, smart card
opp.: memory card
see also: chip card, IC card (integrated circuit card), integrated circuit card (IC card), MC card (microcircuit card),
microcircuit card (MC card)

Karte mit Prozessor-
chip, Prozessorkarte

convenience card – a credit card which is used by the
cardholder mainly for convenient use

Kreditkarte, die vor-
wiegend aus Bequem-
lichkeit verwendet wird

conversion – the exchange of an amount from one currency into another
cf.: currency conversion

Umrechnung,
Währungs-
umrechnung

conversion date – the date on which the conversion rate
is applied
cf.: exchange date

Tag, an dem eine
Währung in eine
andere Währung um-
gerechnet wurde

conversion error – a mistake made in the conversion of
an amount from one currency into another

Umrechnungsfehler

conversion rate – the rate applied in the exchange of one
currency into another
cf.: exchange rate

Wechselkurs

copy request – the demand for a copy of a transaction receipt by the issuer from the acquirer

Anfrage
um eine Kopie

co-residing application – an additional function implemented on a chip which is contained on a card

zusätzliche Funktion
auf dem Chip einer
Zahlungskarte

Firmenkarte

corporate card – a card which is issued to the staff of a corporation for payment of corporation expenses

cf.: business card, company card

opp.: private card

see also: purchasing card

Verzichtserklärung auf Firmenhaftung bei Firmenkarten

corporate liability waiver – a declaration of an issuer to waive the liability of the corporation for transactions effected through a corporate card privately by the cardholder in case of misuse

Korrespondenz-bank

correspondent bank – a bank that holds an account for another bank

see also: correspondent bank clearing

Clearing durch eine Korrespon-denzbank

correspondent bank clearing – a clearing performed through a correspondent bank

see also: correspondent bank

Fälschen einer Karte

counterfeit a card, to – to produce a card illegally

cf.: duplicate a card, to; fake a card, to; forge a card, to; skim a card, to

fälschungsanfällige Region

counterfeit area – a region with above-average counterfeit transactions

Fälschungsfall

counterfeit case – a case where a counterfeit(ed) card is illegally used for obtaining goods and services

Verlust durch Kar-tenfälschung(en)

counterfeit loss – the amounts paid by a member due to the use of a counterfeit card

fälschungsanfälliges Vertragsunternehmen

counterfeit merchant – a merchant with above-average counterfeit transactions

Verhaltensmuster bei einer Fälschung

counterfeit pattern – a pattern consistently employed in counterfeit cases

Fälschungs-vorsorge

counterfeit prevention – the measures implemented for avoiding counterfeit losses

fälschungsanfällige Branche

counterfeit sector – a business sector with above-average counterfeit transactions

counterfeit(ed) card – an illegally produced card   *gefälschte Karte*
cf.: duplicated card, fake(d) card, false card, forged card

counterfeiting of a card – the illegal production of a   *Kartenfälschung*
card
cf.: duplication of a card
see also: alteration

countervalue – the value of an amount in another currency   *Gegenwert*

country code – a code used to identify a particular   *Landescode*
country
see also: acquirer country code, issuer country code

country risk – a risk associated with a given country   *Länderrisiko*

coverage – the density of a merchant / ATM network de-   *Akzeptanzdichte*
pending on the number of available merchants / ATMs
cf.: acceptance level
see also: ATM acceptance level, ATM coverage, merchant
acceptance level, merchant coverage

covered cheque – a cheque which has been made out   *gedeckter Scheck*
with a value that lies within the disposable amount
see also: bounced cheque, honoured cheque

credit an account, to – to enter amounts to the credit of   *einem Konto*
an account   *gutschreiben*

credit card – a card for purchasing goods and services   *Kreditkarte*
and for obtaining cash advances with regular billing and
with / without extended credit
see also: charge card, current account linked card, debit
card, deferred debit card, delayed debit card, immediate payment card, pay later product, pay now product

credit card transaction – a transaction with a credit card   *Kreditkarten-*
                                                                         transaktion

credit ceiling – the limit imposed on or granted to an ac-   *Betrag, bis zu dem*
count   *ein Kredit ausgenützt*
                                                                         werden kann

credit draft – the paper used to document the refund of   *Gutschriftsbeleg*
money from a merchant to a cardholder

cf.: credit slip

opp.: charge slip, sales draft, sales receipt, sales slip, sales voucher

see also: transaction information document

*Betrag eines ein-
geräumten Kredits*

credit facility – the amount which is made available for credit purposes

*Kartenfunktion, die
eine Teilzahlung
ermöglicht*

credit function – a card function allowing payment in instalments

see also: debit function, deferred debit function

Kreditlimit

credit limit – the amount of credit a cardholder may obtain with a credit card

cf.: credit line

Kreditlimit

credit line – the amount of credit a cardholder may obtain with a credit card

cf.: credit limit

Kreditmanagement

credit management – the management of the outstanding amounts in order to minimize losses

Kreditauskunft

credit reference – the information on outstanding credits and credit behaviour of the borrower

Kreditrisiko

credit risk – the risk that a debtor fails to meet his / her payment obligations

Kreditprüfung

credit scoring – the process by which the credit worthiness is checked

Gutschriftsbeleg

credit slip – the paper used to document the refund of money from a merchant to a cardholder

cf.: credit draft

opp.: charge slip, sales draft, sales receipt, sales slip, sales voucher

see also: transaction information document

Gutschrift

credit transaction – a transaction which reverses the full or partial amount of a previous transaction

cf.: refund transaction

opp.: cash advance transaction, merchant transaction, payment transaction, purchase transaction, retail transaction, sales transaction

C

credit with recourse, to – to credit an amount to an account subject to final payment

mit „Eingang vorbehalten" gutschreiben, mit Vorbehalt gutschreiben

credit worthiness – the financial standing of a cardholder

Kreditwürdigkeit

credit write-offs – the depreciations made for possible credit losses

Abschreibung voraussichtlich uneinbringlicher Forderungen

cross-border acquiring – an acquiring business where bank and merchant are situated in different countries
cf.: central acquiring, global acquiring, international acquiring
opp.: cross-border issuing

grenzüberschreitendes Vertragsunternehmensgeschäft

cross-border business – the card business of an acquirer / issuer where the bank and the merchant / cardholder are situated in different countries
cf.: global business, international business

grenzüberschreitendes Kartengeschäft

cross-border fraud – a fraud case which does not occur in the issuer's country
cf.: international fraud

grenzüberschreitender Betrug

cross-border issuing – an issuing business where bank and cardholder are situated in different countries
cf.: global issuing, international issuing
opp.: cross-border acquiring, global acquiring, international acquiring
see also: central issuing

grenzüberschreitende Kartenausgabe

cross-border merchant – a merchant situated in another country than the acquirer

Vertragsunternehmen, das seinen Geschäftsbetrieb in einem anderen Land als die vertragsunternehmensabrechnende Bank hat

grenzüberschrei- *tende Zahlung*	**cross-border payment** – a payment where the payer and the payee are situated in different countries
grenzüberschrei- *tende Transaktion,* *internationale* *Transaktion*	**cross-border transaction** – a transaction where the acquirer of a transaction is situated in another country than the issuer or the card cf.: international transaction, inter-country transaction
grenzüberschrei- *tende Überweisung*	**cross-border transfer** – a money transfer where the payer and the payee are situated in different countries
grenzüberschrei- *tende Verwendung*	**cross-border usage** – a transaction whereby a card is used in a country other than the one where it was issued
grenzüberschrei- *tender Umsatz*	**cross-border volume** – the gross volume which is generated with cards in countries other than the one where they were issued
Verrechnungs- *scheck*	**crossed cheque** – a cheque issued for credit to an account only
Flottenkarte, *Fuhrparkkarte*	**CRT card (commercial road transport card)** – a card which is not issued to a cardholder but to a specific vehicle to pay for vehicle-related goods / services cf.: commercial road transport card (CRT card), fleet card see also: truck card
Kryptogramm, ver- *schlüsselte Information*	**cryptogram** – a coded message between two parties with guaranteed confidentiality and undeniability
kryptographischer *Schlüssel*	**cryptographic key** – a specific value to control the cryptographic transformation performed by a mathematical algorithm that is used to encrypt or decrypt a message, to create or verify a digital signature or to authenticate the integrity and/or origin of a message
Verschlüsselungs- *technik*	**cryptography** – the application of mathematical algorithms to transform information to make it unintelligible
Währungscode	**currency code** – a code to identify the currency of a transaction

currency conversion – the exchange of one currency into another
cf.: conversion, currency exchange

Währungs-umrechnung

C

currency denomination – the display of a specific currency on legal tender, other means of payment or any type of documents

Währungsangabe

currency exchange – the conversion of one currency into another
cf.: conversion, currency conversion

Währungs-umrechnung

currency exponent – a code to identify the number of digits behind the decimal point in a currency

Währungsexponent

current account – an account used for handling payment transactions
cf.: checking account, demand deposit account, giro account, sight deposit account

Girokonto

current account linked card – a card whose transactions are debited from a current account
cf.: debit card, immediate payment card
see also: charge card, credit card, deferred debit card, delayed debit card, pay later product, pay now product

Debitkarte

customer loyalty – the consistency with which customers remain with a commercial business

Kundentreue

cut-off time – the time until a transaction is accepted for clearing / settlement

Zeitpunkt, bis zu dem Transaktionen für Clearing und Settlement akzeptiert werden

CVC (card validation code) – an algorithmically-derived code provided on the magnetic stripe to ensure that the original card is presented
cf.: card validation code (CVC), card verification value (CVV), CVV (card verification value)

Kartenverifizierungscode, Code zur Feststellung der Kartenechtheit

CVM (cardholder verification method) – a method to ensure that the cardholder presenting the card is the lawful cardholder
cf.: cardholder verification, cardholder verification method (CVM)
see also: CAM (card authentication method), card authentication, card authentication method (CAM)

Feststellung der Karteninhaberechtheit, Karteninhaberechtheitsnachweis

Kartenverifizie-rungscode, Code zur Feststellung der Kartenechtheit

CVV (card verification value) – an algorithmically-derived code provided on the magnetic stripe to ensure that the original card is presented
cf.: card validation code (CVC), CVC (card validation code), CVV (card verification value)

Datenerfassung

data capture – the entry of data into a computer system

Datenerfassungs-terminal

data capture terminal – a terminal which captures transactions off-line only

Schlüssel zur Verschlüsselung von Daten

data encrypting key – a standard key which is used to encrypt PIN numbers for their electronic transmission and to authenticate messages

Datenverschlüssel-ungsnorm, DES

Data Encryption Standard (DES) algorithm – a standardized symmetric cryptosystem widely used in PIN generation
cf.: DES (Data Encryption Standard) algorithm
see also: triple DES (3DES), RSA algorithm

Daten-unversehrtheit

data integrity – the fact that data has not been altered or truncated

Datengeheimhaltung, Datenvertraulichkeit

data privacy – the protection of data from third pary access

Debitkarte

debit card – a card whose transactions are (instantly) debited from a current account
cf.: current account linked card, immediate payment card
see also: charge card, credit card, deferred debit card, delayed debit card, pay later product, pay now product

Debitkarten-transaktion

debit card transaction – a transaction with a debit card
opp.: credit card transaction

Kartenfunktion, die zur Belastung eines Girokontos führt

debit function – a card function that leads to the (instant) deduction of an amount from a current account
see also: credit function, deferred debit function

Klebeetikette

decal – a polyethylene foil which is covered on the reverse side with an adhesive material and shows the logo of a card system
cf.: sticker

decal, to – to attach a decal   *auszeichnen*

decalization – the process of attaching a decal   *Auszeichnung*
cf.: decalling, merchant decalization, merchant decalling

decalling – the process of attaching a decal   *Auszeichnung*
cf.: decalization, merchant decalization, merchant decalling

decipher, to – to reverse the process of encryption to re-   *entschlüsseln*
cover the original information
cf.: decrypt, to
opp.: encipher, to; encrypt, to

decipherment – the reversal of the process of encryption   *Entschlüsselung*
to recover the original information
cf.: decryption
opp.: encipherment, encryption

decline an authorization request, to – to give a nega-   *eine Autorisierungs-*
tive response to an authorization request   *anfrage / Genehmi-*
cf.: deny an authorization request, to; refuse an authoriza-   *gungsanfrage ab-*
tion request, to   *lehnen*
opp.: approve an authorization request, to; authorize, to

decline fee – a fee paid by the issuer to the acquirer /   *Ablehnungsentgelt*
ATM bank if a retail / ATM transaction was refused

decline of an authorization request – a negative re-   *Ablehnung einer*
sponse to an authorization request   *Autorisierungs-*
cf.: refusal of an authorization request   *anfrage / Genehmi-*
opp.: approval of an authorization request, authorization   *gungsanfrage*

decrypt, to – to reverse the process of encryption to re-   *entschlüsseln*
cover the original information
cf.: decipher, to
opp.: encipher, to; encrypt, to

decryption – the reversal of the process of encryption to   *Entschlüsselung*
recover the original information
cf.: decipherment
opp.: encipherment, encryption

Standleitung

dedicated line – a communications system where data are transmitted between two endpoints which are permanently connected

cf.: leased line, private line

D

Entgelt, das von der vertragsunternehmensabrechnenden an die kartenausgebende Bank bei Fehlen einer bilateralen Vereinbarung bezahlt wird

default interchange fee – a charge paid by acquirers to issuers in the case that there is no bilaterally agreed charge for payments which is applied to most interchange transactions

cf.: fall-back interchange fee, MIF (multi-laterally [agreed] interchange fee), multi-laterally (agreed) interchange fee (MIF)

opp.: bilaterally (agreed) interchange fee

see also: interchange fee

eingegebener Wert, der so lange gilt, bis er verändert wird

default value – the settings that are automatically set up in a system as long as they are not modified

Aufschub, Verzögerung

deferment – the time-lag between the use of the card and the billing date

cf.: delay

Karte, deren Umsätze mit Verzögerung vom Girokonto des Karteninhabers abgebucht werden

deferred debit card – a card by which the cardholder need not settle every transaction separately but where the balance of all transactions are charged at a defined billing date so that there is a delay between the usage of the card and the billing date

cf.: charge card, delayed debit card

see also: credit card, current-account linked card, debit card, immediate payment card, pay later product, pay now product

Kartenfunktion, die zu einer verzögerten Belastung des Girokontos führt

deferred debit function – a card function that leads to the deduction of an amount from a current account with a delay

cf.: delayed debit function

see also: credit function, debit function

verzögerte Vertragsunternehmensbezahlung

deferred payment – merchant payment which is not effected promptly, but with a certain delay

cf.: delayed payment

delay – the time-lag between the use of the card and the billing date

cf.: deferment

Aufschub,
Verzögerung

delayed debit card – a card by which the cardholder need not settle every transaction separately but where the balance of all transactions are charged at a defined billing date so that there is a delay between the usage of the card and the billing date

cf.: charge card, deferred debit card

see also: credit card, current-account linked card, debit card, immediate payment card, pay later product, pay now product

Karte, deren Um-
sätze mit Verzöge-
rung vom Giro-
konto des Karten-
inhabers abgebucht
werden

delayed debit function – a card function that leads to the deduction of an amount from a current account with a delay

cf.: deferred debit function

see also: credit function, debit function

Kartenfunktion, die
zu einer verzöger-
ten Belastung des
Girokontos führt

delayed payment – merchant payment which is not effected promptly, but with a certain delay

cf.: deferred payment

verzögerte Ver-
tragsunterneh-
mensbezahlung

delinquency processing – the processing of misused cards

Bearbeitung nicht
ordnungsgemäß
verwendeter Karten

delinquent card account – a card account with an unsettled overdue amount

Kartenkonto mit un-
reguliertem Sollsaldo

demand deposit account – an account used for handling payment transactions

cf.: checking account, current account, giro account, sight deposit account

opp.: deposit account, savings account

Girokonto

denial of an authorization request – a negative response of the issuer to the acquirer which is forwarded by the acquirer to the merchant or cash advance location to prohibit a card transaction

cf.: refusal of an authorization request

opp.: approval of an authorization request

see also: authorization, authorization code, authorization decision, authorization response, authorization request

Ablehnung einer
Genehmigungs-
anfrage

Bearbeitung von abgelehnten Kartenanträgen	**denial processing** – the processing of a refused card application
Ablehnung einer Genehmigungsanfrage	**deny an authorization request, to** – to provide a negative response to an authorization request cf.: decline an authorization request, to; refuse an authorization request, to opp.: approve an authorization request, to; authorize, to
Sparkonto	**deposit account** – a bank account for savings purposes cf.: savings account
Datenverschlüsselungsnorm, DES	**DES (Data Encryption Standard) algorithm** – a standardized symmetric private key cryptosystem widely used in PIN generation cf.: Data Encryption Standard (DES) algorithm see also: triple DES (3DES), +RSA algorithm
Kartenmarkt, der sich entwickelt	**developing card market** – a card market in the process of being developed cf.: emerging card market opp.: mature card market, saturated card market
digitale Unterschrift, digitale Signatur	**digital signature** – a cryptographically produced sequence of characters which proves the authenticity of the person signing see also: electronic signature
Diners Club	**Diners Club** – a licensed card system with the licences being granted by Diners Club International see also: Diners Club card, Diners Club International
Diners Club-Karte	**Diners Club card** – a card issued by a licensee of Diners Club International see also: Diners Club, Diners Club International
Diners Club International	**Diners Club International** – an international card organization which is licensor for the Diners Club card see also: Diners Club, Diners Club card
Girokontobelastung, Lastschrift	**direct debit(ing)** – payment method whereby a giro account is debited directly

directory – a list of data, usually sorted alphabetically or alpha-numerically   *Verzeichnis*

see also: ATM directory, ATM location directory, merchant directory, merchant location directory, travel directory

disburse, to – to pay out an amount   *auszahlen*

disbursement – paying out of an amount   *Barauszahlung*

disclosure – the terms and conditions of a card issuer under which a cardholder may use that card   *Geschäftsbedin-gungen für*

cf.: business conditions, card business conditions   *Karteninhaber*

discount – rate of the transaction amount to be paid by the merchant   *Disagio, Kommission, Umsatzprovision*

cf.: commission, commission rate, discount rate, merchant service charge (MSC), MSC (merchant service charge), percentage discount, service charge, service fee

discount broker – a person/institution that wishes to negotiate terms and conditions in the name of several (potential) member establishments   *Person/Institution, die im Namen mehrerer (potentieller) Vertrags-unternehmen Kondi-tionen vereinbaren möchte*

discount rate – rate of the transaction amount to be paid by the merchant   *Disagio, Kommission, Umsatzprovision*

cf.: commission, commission rate, discount, merchant service charge (MSC), MSC (merchant service charge), percentage discount, service charge, service fee

discount scheme – a customer loyalty programme with discounts   *Kundenbindungs-programm mit Preisnachlässen*

Discover – a card system of Dean Witter, Discover & Co   *Discover*

Discover card – a card issued by Dean Witter, Discover & Co   *Discover-Karte*

disposable card – a non-reloadable pre-paid card   *nicht wiederauflad-bare Wertkarte*

cf.: non-rechargeable card, non-reloadable card

opp.: rechargeable card, reloadable card

dispute – a difference of opinion between two parties   *Auseinander-setzung*

see also: arbitration, compliance

Name, der anders ist als die Firma des Unternehmens, unter dem ein Geschäft betrieben wird

doing-business-as name – the business name used by a merchant

nicht-grenzüberschreitendes Kartengeschäft

domestic business – a business of an acquirer / issuer where the bank and the merchant / cardholder are situated in the same country
opp.: cross-border business, international business
see also: global business

nur im Inland verwendbare Karte

domestic card – a card designated for national use only
opp.: international card
see also: local card

Bargeldbezug mit einer inländischen Karte im Inland

domestic cash advance – a cash advance is domestic if the principal office of the issuer and the location disbursing the cash advance are located within the same country
opp.: international cash advance

inländisches Bargeldbezugslimit

domestic cash advance limit – the maximum amount that may be taken in cash by the cardholder in his country within a given period
cf.: domestic cash limit
opp.: domestic retail limit, domestic sales limit, international cash advance limit
see also: cash advance limit, cash limit

inländisches Bargeldbezugslimit

domestic cash limit – the maximum amount that may be taken in cash by the cardholder in his country within a given period
cf.: domestic cash advance limit
opp.: domestic retail limit, domestic sales limit, international cash advance limit
see also: cash advance limit, cash limit

nur im Inland einsetzbare elektronische Geldbörse

domestic electronic purse – an electronic purse which can only be used in the issuing country
opp.: global electronic purse, international electronic purse

Vertragsunternehmens-Genehmigungsgrenze

domestic floor limit – the limit above which an authorization must be requested by the merchant from the acquirer cf.: floor limit, local floor limit, merchant floor limit

see also: international floor limit, intra-European floor limit

domestic interchange – (the exchange of) transaction data between acquirers and issuers within a country

opp.: international interchange

see also: European interchange, interchange, intra-European interchange, non-European interchange

(Datenaustausch der) inländische(n) Umsätze

D

domestic interchange fee – a charge paid by acquirers to issuers which is applied to most domestic transactions

opp.: international interchange fee, MIF (multi-laterally [agreed] interchange fee), multi-laterally (agreed) interchange fee (MIF)

see also: European interchange fee, interchange fee, interregional interchange fee, intra-European interchange fee, non-European interchange fee

Entgelt, das von der vertragsunternehmensabrechnenden Bank an die kartenausgebende Bank bei nationalen Transaktionen bezahlt wird

domestic payment scheme – a payment system that does not provide any cross-border transactions

opp.: international payment scheme

see also: payment scheme

Zahlungssystem, das keine grenzüberschreitenden Transaktionen vorsieht

domestic retail limit – the maximum amount that can be spent on goods / services by the cardholder in his country within a given period

cf.: domestic sales limit

opp.: domestic cash advance limit, domestic cash limit, international retail limit, international sales limit

see also: retail limit, sales limit

inländisches Zahlungslimit

domestic rules – the rules of a domestic payment scheme

opp.: international rules

Regeln eines Zahlungssystems für Transaktionen, die nicht grenzüberschreitend sind

domestic sales limit – the maximum amount that can be spent on goods / services by the cardholder in his country within a given period

inländisches Zahlungslimit

cf.: domestic retail limit

opp.: domestic cash advance limit, domestic cash limit, international retail limit, international sales limit

see also: retail limit, sales limit

inländische
Transaktion

domestic transaction – a transaction with a card effected in the issuing country

cf.: intra-country transaction

inaktive Karte

dormant card – a valid card which is not used

Markenpolitik, die
auf zwei Marken
auf einer Karte
ausgerichtet ist

double branding – the marking of a card with two brands

opp.: single branding

see also: multiple branding

Doppelbelastung

double charging – a charge levied twice for a single transaction

Doppelumrechnung,
zweifache Wäh-
rungsumrechnung

double currency conversion – a currency conversion whereby the original currency is converted first into an intermediate currency and from that into the target currency

see also: currency conversion

Herunterladung

down-line loading – the transmission of data to a computer via a network

cf.: downloading

herunterladen

download, to – to transmit data to a computer via a network

Herunterladung

downloading – the transmission of data to a computer via a network

cf.: down-line loading

Genehmigung bei
einem System-
ausfall durch ein
Ersatzsystem

down-option authorization – an authorization performed by a pre-determined alternate processing system used whenever the issuer is unable to respond

cf.: alternate authorization, back-up authorization, dynamic stand-in authorization, permanent stand-in authorization, stand-in authorization

opp.: primary authorization

down-option limits – the authorization parameters set by the issuer for the alternate processing system in case the primary processing system is unable to respond

cf.: alternate limits, alternate parameters, back-up limits, back-up parameters, down-option parameters, dynamic stand-in limits, dynamic stand-in parameters, fall-back limits, fall-back parameters, permanent stand-in limits, permanent stand-in parameters, stand-in limits, stand-in parameters

von der karten-ausgebenden Bank festgelegte Limits für das Ersatz-system

D

down-option parameters – the authorization parameters set by the issuer for the alternate processing system in case the primary processing system is unable to respond

cf.: alternate limits, alternate parameters, back-up limits, back-up parameters, down-option limits, dynamic stand-in limits, dynamic stand-in parameters, fall-back limits, fall-back parameters, permanent stand-in limits, permanent stand-in parameters, stand-in limits, stand in-parameters

von der karten-ausgebenden Bank festgelegte Limits für das Ersatzsys-tem

down-option processing – the performance of authorizations by a pre-determined alternate processing system which is used whenever the issuer is unable to respond

cf.: alternate processing, back-up processing, dynamic stand-in processing, permanent stand-in processing, stand-in processing

opp.: primary processing

Genehmigungs-verfahren durch ein Ersatzsystem bei einem System-ausfall

down-option processing system – a back-up issuer processing facility for authorizations when the primary processing system is not available

cf.: alternate, alternate processing system, back-up processing system, dynamic stand-in processing system, permanent stand-in processing system, stand-in processing system

see also: IHS (issuer host system), issuer host, issuer host system (IHS), primary, primary processing system

Ersatzgenehmi-gungssystem bei Systemausfall

down-option transaction – a transaction which is authorized by a down-option processing system

cf.: alternate transaction, back-up transaction, dynamic stand-in transaction, permanent stand-in transaction, stand-in transaction

opp.: primary transaction

see also: alternate processing system

Transaktion, die bei einem System-ausfall von einem Ersatzgenehmi-gungssystem autorisiert wird

einen Scheck
ausstellen

draw a cheque, to – to issue a cheque

bezogene Bank

drawee bank – the bank holding the cheque issuer's account

Geldausgabe-
automat, der vom
Auto aus bedient
werden kann

drive-through-ATM – an ATM that can be operated from a car

see also: in-bank ATM, in-branch ATM, indoor ATM, lobby ATM, off-premises ATM, off-site ATM, outdoor ATM, through-the-wall ATM,

vertragsunterneh-
mensabrechnende
Bank, die sowohl
MasterCard- als
auch Visa-Transak-
tionen abrechnet

dual acquirer – an acquirer for both MasterCard and Visa transactions

opp.: single acquirer

Marketing einer kar-
tenausgebenden Bank
sowohl für Master-
Card- als auch für
Visa-Karten

dual card marketing – marketing by an issuer for both MasterCard and Visa cards

opp.: single card marketing

Karte mit zwei Chips:
einer für kontaktbe-
haftete und einer für
kontaktlose Zwecke

dual interface (chip) card – a card with 2 chips: one for contact and one for contactless purposes

cf.: hybrid (chip) card

Bank, die sowohl
MasterCard- als
auch Visa-Karten
ausgibt

dual issuer – an issuer of both MasterCard and Visa cards

opp.: single issuer

Zahlungstransaktion,
die erst dann komplett
ist, wenn zwei Nach-
richten zusammen-
geführt worden sind

dual message transaction – a transaction that is only complete when two messages are merged

opp.: single message transaction

zweistufige
Transaktion

dual messaging – the processing of an ATM or a POS transaction in two passes comprising authorization request and confirmation response in the first pass and clearing in the second pass

opp.: single messaging

duality – a strategy according to which a bank carries on business both in the MasterCard and Visa spheres

Strategie einer Bank, im MasterCard- und im Visa-Geschäft aktiv zu sein

D

due amount – the sum that becomes payable at a certain date

Fälligkeitsbetrag

due date – the date at which an amount becomes payable

Fälligkeitstag

duplicate a card, to – to produce a card illegally
cf.: counterfeit a card, to; fake a card, to; forge a card, to; skim a card, to

Fälschen einer Karte

duplicated card – an illegally produced card
cf.: counterfeit(ed) card, fake(d) card, false card, forged card
opp.: genuine card, original card

gefälschte Karte

duplication of a card – the illegal reproduction of a card
cf.: counterfeiting of a card
see also: alteration of a card

Kartenfälschung

dynamic off-line CAM – a card authentication method whereby the chip signs dynamically variable data using an asymmetric algorithm and a private key and the terminal verifies the digital signature with a public key
see also: dynamic on-line CAM

dynamisches Offline-Verfahren zur Feststellung der Kartenechtheit

dynamic on-line CAM – a card authentication method whereby the chip signs dynamically variable data using an asymmetric algorithm and a private key and the issuer verifies the digital signature with the same private key
see also: dynamic off-line CAM

dynamisches Online-Verfahren zur Feststellung der Kartenechtheit

dynamic signature verification – an electronic on-line system which is reliably capable of detecting the correctness of a signature

Unterschriftsprüfungsverfahren

dynamic stand-in processing system – a back-up issuer processing facility for authorizations when the primary processing system is not available

Ersatzgenehmigungssystem bei Systemausfall

cf.: alternate, alternate processing system, back-up processing system, down-option processing system, permanent stand-in processing system, stand-in processing system

see also: IHS (issuer host system), issuer host, issuer host system (IHS), primary, primary processing system

Genehmigung bei einem System-ausfall durch ein Ersatzsystem

dynamic stand-in authorization – an authorization performed by a pre-determined alternate processing system used whenever the issuer is unable to respond

cf.: alternate authorization, back-up authorization, down-option authorization, permanent stand-in authorization, stand-in authorization

opp.: primary authorization

von der karten-ausgebenden Bank festgelegte Limits für das Ersatz-system

dynamic stand-in limits – the authorization parameters set by the issuer for the alternate processing system in case the primary processing system is unable to respond

cf.: alternate limits, alternate parameters, back-up limits, back-up parameters, down-option limits, down-option parameters, dynamic stand-in parameters, fall-back limits, fall-back parameters, permanent stand-in limits, permanent stand-in parameters, stand-in limits, stand-in parameters

von der karten-ausgebenden Bank festgelegte Limits für das Ersatz-system

dynamic stand-in parameters – the authorization parameters set by the issuer for the alternate processing system in case the primary processing system is unable to respond

cf.: alternate limits, alternate parameters, back-up limits, back-up parameters, down-option limits, down-option parameters, dynamic stand-in limits, fall-back limits, fall-back parameters, permanent stand-in limits, permanent stand-in parameters, stand-in limits, stand-in parameters

Genehmigungs-verfahren durch ein Ersatzsystem bei einem System-ausfall

dynamic stand-in processing – the performance of authorizations by a pre-determined alternate processing system which is used whenever the issuer is unable to respond

cf.: alternate processing, back-up processing, down-option processing, permanent stand-in processing, stand-in processing

opp.: primary processing

D
E

dynamic stand-in transaction – a transaction which is authorized by a dynamic stand-in processing system
cf.: alternate transaction, back-up transaction, down-option transaction, permanent stand-in transaction, stand-in transaction
opp.: primary transaction
see also: alternate processing system

Transaktion, die bei einem System- ausfall von einem Ersatzgenehmi- gungssystem auto- risiert wird

e-business – the purchase / sale of goods / services on electronic / virtual marketplaces
cf.: e-commerce, electronic commerce, virtual commerce
see also: electronic marketplace, virtual marketplace

Kauf / Verkauf von Waren / Dienstleis- tungen im Internet / in der virtuellen Welt

ECBS (European Committee for Banking Standards) – a European committee that defines banking standards
cf.: European Committee for Banking Standards (ECBS)

Europäisches Ko- mitee für Banken- standards, ECBS

e-commerce – the purchase / sale of goods / services on electronic / virtual marketplaces
cf.: e-business, electronic commerce, virtual commerce
see also: electronic marketplace, virtual marketplace

Kauf / Verkauf von Waren / Dienstleis- tungen im Internet / in der virtuellen Welt

ECR (electronic cash register) – a cash register which records amounts by electronic means
cf.: electronic cash register (ECR)
see also: cash register

elektronische Handelskasse, elektronische Registrierkasse

ECR integration – the connection of the electronic cash register to the POS terminal

Handelskassenan- bindung, Registrier- kassenanbindung

EDI (electronic data interchange) – a system of data interchange by electronic means
cf.: electronic data interchange (EDI)
see also: EDIFACT (Electronic Standard for Administra- tion, Commerce and Transport)

Datenfern- übertragung, elektronischer Datenaustausch

EDIFACT (Electronic Standard for Administration, Commerce and Transport) – international standard for electronic data interchange of commercial transactions
cf.: Electronic Standard for Administration, Commerce and Transport (EDIFACT)

EDIFACT

see also: EDI (electronic data interchange), electronic data interchange (EDI)

EEPROM,
Speicherart auf
einem Chip

EEPROM (electrical erasable programmable ROM) – a chip where data is stored by using an electrical erasable programmable read-only memory

see also: EPROM (erasable programmable ROM), PROM (programmable ROM), RAM (random access memory), ROM (read-only memory)

Zeitgang des Risiko-
übergangs bei einer
Kartensperre

effective date – the date from which the entry of a card in the stoplist is valid

elektronischer Geld-
transfer

EFT (electronic funds transfer) – an electronic movement of funds that eliminates the need for paper

cf.: electronic funds transfer (EFT)

elektronische
Zahlung am POS
mit zugehörigem
Datentransfer

EFTPOS (electronic funds transfer at the point-of-sale) – a system to accept EFTPOS cards and to initiate electronic funds transfers via a POS terminal located in a merchant outlet

cf.: electronic funds transfer at the point-of-sale (EFTPOS)

Karte, die bei einem
POS-Terminal ein-
gesetzt werden kann

EFTPOS card – a card which can be used at an EFTPOS terminal

Kassenterminal mit
Zahlungsfunktion,
POS-Terminal

EFTPOS terminal – an electronic device that accepts financial data at a point of sale and transmits the data to a computer centre for authorization, clearing and settlement

cf.: POS terminal

see also: integrated POS terminal

elektronische
Genehmigung,
elektronische
Autorisierung

electronic authorization – an affirmative response of the issuer to the acquirer which is forwarded by the acquirer to the merchant or cash advance location by electronic means to permit a card transaction

opp.: telephone authorization, voice authorization

see also: ATM authorization, authorization, terminal authorization

elektronischer
Rechnungsversand,
elektronische Rech-
nungsübermittlung

electronic bill presentment – a bill which is presented by electronic means

electronic cash – 1) a general term used for electronic means of payment, 2) the payment system of the German banking industry with debit card and code

1) generelle Bezeichnung für elektronische Zahlungsmittel 2) Zahlungssystem der deutschen Kreditwirtschaft mit Debitkarte und Code

E

electronic cash register (ECR) – a cash register which records amounts by electronic means
cf.: ECR (electronic cash register)
see also: cash register

elektronische Handelskasse, elektronische Registrierkasse

electronic commerce – the purchase / sale of goods / services on a virtual market place
cf.: e-business, e-commerce, virtual commerce
see also: electronic market place, virtual market place

elektronischer Kauf / Verkauf von Waren / Dienstleistungen

electronic counterfeiting – a fraudulent alteration of data contained on the magnetic stripe of a card

Magnetstreifen-(ver)fälschung

electronic data interchange (EDI) – a system of data interchange by electronic means
cf.: EDI (electronic data interchange)
see also: EDIFACT (Electronic Standard for Administration, Commerce and Transport)

Datenfernübertragung, elektronischer Datenaustausch

electronic draft capture – the electronic capture of sales slips by the acquirer

elektronische Belegerfassung

electronic funds transfer (EFT) – an electronic movement of funds that eliminates the need for paper
cf.: EFT (electronic funds transfer)

elektronischer Geldtransfer

electronic funds transfer at the point-of-sale (EFT-POS) – a system to accept EFTPOS cards and to initiate electronic funds transfers via a POS terminal located in a merchant outlet
cf.: EFTPOS (electronic funds transfer at the point-of-sale)

elektronische Zahlung am POS mit zugehörigem Datentransfer

electronic market place – the virtual market where products / services are offered electronically
cf.: virtual marketplace
opp.: physical marketplace
see also: electronic commerce, virtual commerce

elektronischer Markt, virtueller Markt

elektronisches Geld	**electronic money** – stored monetary value on a technical device (e.g. card or hard drive)
elektronische Geld-börse ohne nachvoll-ziehbare Transaktionen	**electronic money card** – an electronic purse with no audit trail
elektronische Zahlung(en)	**electronic payment(s)** – payment(s) effected by electronic devices
elektronische Geldbörse	**electronic purse** – a chip on a card pre-loaded with a money value which can be used for low value payments in an offline environment

E

see also: pay before product, pre-paid card, pre-payment card, stored value card, traveller's cheque

elektronisch über-mittelter Trans-aktionsdatensatz

electronic record – the data pertaining to a transaction which is transmitted electronically

opp.: paper record

see also: record

elektronische Autorisierungs-anfrage / Genehmi-gungsanfrage

electronic request – a request by a merchant or cash advance location by electronic means to permit a card transaction

opp.: telephone request, voice request

see also: authorization request

EDIFACT

Electronic Standard for Administration, Commerce and Transport (EDIFACT) – international standard for electronic data interchange of commercial transactions

cf.: EDIFACT (Electronic Standard for Administration, Commerce and Transport)

see also: EDI (electronic data interchange), electronic data interchange (EDI)

elektronische Mauteinhebung

electronic toll collection (ETC) – the collection of toll data by electronic means

cf.: ETC (electronic toll collection)

elektronische Transaktion

electronic transaction – a transaction carried out by avoiding paper drafts (e.g. a transaction at a POS terminal with PIN)

opp.: paper-based transaction

see also: terminal transaction

electronic transmission – the use of magnetic tapes or telecommuncations to forward payment data
opp.: physical transmission

*beleglose Daten-
übermittlung*

electronic value – the amount on an electronic purse

elektronischer Wert

embed, to – to implement a chip into a plastic card

einbringen

E

emboss, to – to affix data to a card in the form of raised characters through a special machine

prägen

embossed card – a card whereby the visible card data in letters and numbers are elevated by technical means
opp.: non-embossed card

*hochgeprägte
Karte*

embossing and encoding system – a system that allows the personalization of a card and the recording of the magnetic tracks of the magnetic stripe with the relevant data
see also: embossing machine, encoding machine

*Präge- und
Codierungssystem*

embossing machine – a device to emboss data on cards
see also: embossing and encoding system, encoding machine

Prägemaschine

emergency card replacement – the issuance of a card to travelling cardholders whose cards were lost or stolen
see also: card replacement

*Ersatzkarten-
ausstellung*

emergency cash advance – a cash advance made without presentment of a card by travelling cardholders whose cards were lost or stolen

*Bargeldauszahlung
ohne Karten-
vorlage*

emerging card market – a card market in the process of being developed
cf.: developing card market
opp.: mature card market, saturated card market

*Kartenmarkt,
der sich entwickelt*

EMV standards – the specifications developed for chip cards by MasterCard and Visa and managed by EMVCo
see also: EMVCo

EMV-Standard

EMVCo – the company founded to manage to EMV specifications for chip cards
see also: EMV standards

*Gesellschaft, die für die
Spezifikationen für Chip-
karten von MasterCard
und Visa zuständig ist;
EMVCo*

E

einen Scheck einlösen

encash a cheque, to – to issue and present a cheque for obtaining cash

Scheckeinlösung

encashment – the exchange of a cheque for cash
opp.: cheque encashment

verschlüsseln

encipher, to – to effect encryption
cf.: encrypt, to
opp.: decipher, to; decrypt, to

Verschlüsselung

encipherment – a transformation of information, based on a key, to make the information unintelligible to unauthorized persons
cf.: encryption
opp.: decipherment, decryption

codieren

encode, to – to record information concerning details of the card on the magnetic stripe side of the card

Codiermaschine

encoding machine – a device to record data on the magnetic stripes of cards
see also: embossing and encoding system, embossing machine

verschlüsseln

encrypt, to – to effect encryption
cf.: encipher, to
opp.: decipher, to; decrypt, to

Verschlüsselung

encryption – a transformation of information, based on a key, to make the information unintelligible to unauthorized persons
cf.: encipherment
opp.: decipherment, decryption

Schlüssel, der im Rahmen eines Verschlüsselungsverfahrens verwendet wird

encryption key – a mathematical value which is used in an algorithm to protect data within a network
see also: key

Abnahmeverfahren zur Überprüfung der Kartenakzeptanz

end-to-end acceptance test – a test performed to check the proper acceptance of a card from one end of the system to the other to ensure it functions correctly
cf.: end-to-end quality audit

end-to-end quality – the quality determined as a result of a test/audit performed from one end of a system to the other

Qualität unter Berücksichtigung aller Systemkomponenten

end-to-end quality audit – an audit performed to check the proper acceptance of a card from one end of a system to the other to ensure it functions correctly
cf.: end-to-end acceptance test

Abnahmeverfahren zur Überprüfung der Kartenakzeptanz

enter the PIN, to – to key in the PIN

PIN eingeben

entrance fee – a single payment by the cardholder to receive a card
cf.: joining fee

Beitrittsentgelt

entry date – the date of the entry of a card number in the stoplist
cf.: listing date

Eingabedatum einer Kartennummer in die Sperrliste

entry fee – the fee to be paid to enter a card number on a stoplist
cf.: insertion fee, stoplist entry fee, stoplist insertion fee
see also: stoplist storage fee, storage fee

Sperrlisten-Eintragungsentgelt

envelope stuffer – a leaflet added to the cardholder statements

Beilage zu Karteninhaberabrechungen

EPROM (erasable progammable ROM) – a chip where data is stored by using an erasable programmable read-only memory
see also: EEPROM (electrical erasable programmable ROM), PROM (programmable ROM) RAM (random access memory), ROM (read-only memory)

EPROM, Speicherart auf einem Chip

e-purse card – a card containing an electronic purse

*eine Karte, die
a) ausschließlich als elektronische Geldbörse dient, oder
b) die mit der Funktion einer elektronischen Geldbörse ausgestattet ist*

elektronische
Mauteinhebung

ETC (electronic toll collection) – the collection of toll data by electronic means
cf.: electronic toll collection (ETC)

Transaktion im Internet/in der virtuellen Welt

e-transaction – transaction in the Internet/in the virtual world
see also: m-transaction

eurocheque

eurocheque – a cheque issued under the rules of the eurocheque system until end of 2001
see also: cash cheque, cheque, eurocheque card, retail cheque

eurocheque-Karte

eurocheque card – a cheque guarantee card issued under the rules of the eurocheque system until end of 2001
see also: eurocheque

Auslaufen des eurocheques

eurocheque phase-out – the day the eurocheque died: December 31st, 2001

(Datenaustausch) grenzüberschreitende(r) europäische(r) Umsätze

European interchange – (the exchange of) transactions between different countries in Europe
cf.: intra-European interchange
opp.: non-European interchange
see also: domestic interchange, interchange, international interchange

Entgelt, das von der vertragsunternehmensabrechnenden Bank an die kartenausgebende Bank bei grenzüberschreitenden europäischen Transaktionen bezahlt wird

European interchange fee – a charge paid by acquirers to issuers which is applied to most European cross-border transactions
cf.: intra-European interchange fee
opp.: inter-regional interchange fee, non-European interchange fee
see also: domestic interchange fee, international interchange fee, interchange fee

Europäisches Kommitee für Bankenstandards, ECBS

European Committee for Banking Standards (ECBS) – a European committee that defines banking standards
cf.: ECBS (European Committee for Banking Standards)

der Hinweis, a) dass bei der beauftragten Autorisierung nicht in der üblichen Art und Weise vorgegangen wurde, oder b) warum eine Karte auf der Stoppliste steht

exception indicator – a code defined by the issuer to indicate
a) an exceptional action to be taken by the on-behalf authorization service or
b) the reason why the card has been stoplisted

exception processing – the processing of transactions that are handled outside the usual procedures

Verarbeitung von Transaktionen nicht in der üblichen Art und Weise

exchange bureau – an authorized agent of a bank to exchange money, to encash cheques and to give cash advances
cf.: bureau de change, change bureau, exchange office, foreign exchange bureau

Wechselstube

E

exchange date – the date on which the exchange rate is applied
cf.: conversion date

Tag, am dem eine Währung in eine andere Währung umgerechnet wurde

exchange difference – the difference between the buying and the selling rates
see also: exchange earnings, exchance profit, exchange rate mark-up, foreign exchange earnings

Wechselkursdifferenz, Wechselkursspanne

exchange earnings – the revenues gained from currency exchange
cf.: foreign exchange earnings
see also: exchange difference, exchance profit, exchange rate mark-up

Erträge aus der Konvertierung fremder Währungen

exchange office – an authorized agent of a bank to exchange money, to encash cheques and to give cash advances
cf.: bureau de change, change bureau, exchange bureau, foreign exchange bureau

Wechselstube

exchange profit – the profits gained from currency exchange
see also: exchange earnings, exchance profit, exchange rate mark-up, foreign exchange earnings

Wechselkursgewinn

exchange rate – the rate applied in the conversion of one currency into another
cf.: conversion rate

Wechselkurs

exchange rate mark-up – a percentage added to the exchange rate on transactions in foreign currencies
see also: card charges, exchange earnings, exchance profit, foreign exchange earnings

Aufschlag zum Wechselkurs

Wechselkursrisiko   **exchange risk** – the risk that fluctuations of foreign exchange rates could lead to losses
cf.: foreign exchange risk

Exklusiv-Lizenz-nehmer für das Vertragsunter-nehmensgeschäft   **exclusive acquirer** – the only acquirer within a given territory as a consequence of an exclusive licence agreement

Expertensystem   **expert system** – a sophisticated software system by which cardholder and merchant behaviour is monitored to detect fraudulent transactions
see also: neural network system, parameters system

Ablaufdatum, Gültigkeitsende   **expiration date** – the date embossed on the card after which the card must not be honoured
cf.: card expiry, expiry date

abgelaufene Karte   **expired card** – a card whose validity has already expired

Ablaufdatum, Gültigkeitsende   **expiry date** – the date embossed on the card after which the card must not be honoured
cf.: card expiry, expiration date

Kommastelle   **exponent value** – a mathematical nomenclature determining the decimal point

Hotelservice, aufgrunddessen ein Kreditkarteninhaber ohne Rechnung abreisen kann   **express checkout** – a service by which a cardholder can check out of a hotel without signing the sales slip at departure and by authorizing the merchant to charge his account by signing a specific form in advance

ausgenützter Kredit   **extended credit** – the amount outstanding which need not be paid instantly

Zweitkarte   **extra card** – a second card issued to a primary cardholder to allow him to separate different kinds of transactions
opp.: primary card
see also: additional card, secondary card

face-to-face transaction – a payment transaction which takes place by presenting a card at the point of sale

cf.: walk-in transaction

opp.: non-face-to-face transaction, remote transaction, signature-on-file transaction

Zahlung, die durch Vorlage einer Karte am POS erfolgt

E

facsimile document – a legible microfilm copy or another reproduction of the original slip

cf.: facsimile draft, substitute document, substitute draft

Ersatzbeleg

facsimile draft – a legible microfilm copy or another reproduction of the original slip

cf.: facsimile document, substitute document, substitute draft

Ersatzbeleg

fake a card, to – to produce a card illegally

cf.: counterfeit a card, to; duplicate a card, to; forge a card, to; skim a card, to

Fälschen einer Karte

fake(d) ATM – a device set up so as to resemble a genuine ATM to collect card data and PINs for fraud purposes

cf.: fake(d) POS terminal, fake(d) terminal

Geldausgabe-automatenattrappe

fake(d) card – an illegally produced card

cf.: counterfeit(ed) card, duplicated card, false card, forged card

opp.: genuine card, original card

gefälschte Karte

fake(d) POS terminal – a device set up so as to resemble a genuine POS terminal to collect card data and PINs for fraud purposes

cf.: fake(d) terminal

opp.: genuine terminal

see also: fake(d) ATM, fake(d) terminal

Attrappe eines POS-Terminals

F

Attrappe eines
POS-Terminals

fake(d) terminal – a device set up so as to resemble a genuine POS terminal to collect card data and PINs for fraud purposes
cf.: fake(d) POS terminal
opp.: genuine terminal
see also: fake(d) ATM

Interchange-Bargeld-
auszahlungsentgelt,
das bei Fehlen eines
bilateral vereinbarten
Bargeld-
auszahlungsentgelts
verrechnet wird

fall-back cash advance accommodation fee – a charge paid by issuers to ATM acquirers in the case that there is no bilaterally agreed charge for cash advances

Entgelt, das von
der vertragsunter-
nehmensabrech-
nenden an die kar-
tenausgebende
Bank bei Fehlen
einer bilateralen
Vereinbarung be-
zahlt wird

fall-back interchange fee – a charge paid by acquirers to issuers in the case that there is no bilaterally agreed charge for payments which is applied to most interchange transactions
cf.: default interchange fee, MIF (multi-laterally [agreed] interchange fee), multi-laterally (agreed) interchange fee (MIF)
opp.: bilaterally (agreed) interchange fee
see also: interchange fee

von der karten-
ausgebenden Bank
festgelegte Limits
für das Ersatz-
system

fall-back limits – the authorization parameters set by the issuer for the alternate processing system in case the primary processing system is unable to respond
cf.: alternate limits, alternate parameters, back-up limits, back-up parameters, down-option limits, down-option parameters, dynamic stand-in limits, dynamic stand-in-parameters, fall-back parameters, permanent stand-in limits, permanent stand-in parameters, stand-in limits, stand-in parameters

von der karten-
ausgebenden Bank
festgelegte Limits
für das Ersatz-
system

fall-back parameters – the authorization parameters set by the issuer for the alternate processing system in case the primary processing system is unable to respond
cf.: alternate limits, alternate parameters, back-up limits, back-up parameters, down-option limits, down-option parameters, dynamic stand-in limits, dynamic stand-in parameters, fall-back limits, permanent stand-in limit, permanent stand-in parameter, stand-in limit, stand-in parameter

fall-back solution – the technology used in cases where the normally used technology has failed

Ersatzlösung

fall-back technology – the solution used where the normally used technology has failed

Ersatztechnologie

false application – an application where false information has been used to illegally obtain a card

cf.: fraudulent application

Kartenantrag mit falschen Karteninhaberdaten

false card – an illegally produced card

cf.: counterfeit(ed) card, duplicated card, fake(d) card, forged card

opp.: genuine card, original card

gefälschte Karte

false cardholder – a cardholder who has illegally obtained a card

unrechtmäßiger Karteninhaber

fast food application – an off-line POS solution catering to the special needs of the fast food industry which generally has low maximum transaction amounts

see also: quick payment service (QPS), QPS (quick payment service), rapid payment service (RPS), RPS (rapid payment service)

offline POS-Lösung für Schnellimbisse

file – a collection of data records

Datenbestand

file maintenance – the update of files to keep them up to date

Datenpflege, Datenbestandspflege

file transfer – a method for the secure transmission of electronic files between two hosts

Datentransfer, Datenübertragung

financial transaction card – a card which allows financial transactions like cashless payments and cash withdrawals

cf.: payment card

Zahlungskarte

fine-line printing – a special kind of printing on payment instruments so as to avoid their illegal copying and alteration

Guillochendruck

finger scanning – a biometric technique to verify the cardholder authentication

cf.: fingerprint verification

see also: biometric techniques, biometrics

Fingerabdruckprüfung

Fingerabdruck-prüfung

fingerprint verification – a biometric technique to verify the cardholder authentication
cf.: finger scanning
see also: biometric techniques, biometrics

Fixbetragsentgelt, stückanzahlabhängiges Entgelt

fixed fee – a fee with a fixed amount per transaction
cf.: flat fee
opp.: ad valorem fee, percentage fee

vorgeschlagener Ladebetrag

fixed load(ing) amount – the base amount proposed for the load(ing) of an electronic purse

Fixbetragsentgelt, stückanzahl-abhängiges Entgelt

flat fee – a fee with a fixed amount per transaction
cf.: fixed fee
opp.: ad valorem fee, percentage fee

Flottenkarte, Fuhrparkkarte

fleet card – a card which is not issued to a cardholder but to a specific vehicle to pay for vehicle-related goods / services
cf.: commercial road transport card (CRT card), CRT card (commercial road transport card)
see also: truck card

Float

float – the value of the pool account because of the time-lag between loading of the electronic purses and payment with the electronic purses
see also: float account, funds pool account, pool account, purse pool account, underlying account

Float-Konto, Pool-Konto eines elektronischen Geldbörsensystems

float account – an account where the issuer of an electronic purse scheme holds the float
cf.: funds pool account, pool account, purse pool account, underlying account

Float-Management

float management – the management of the float which is held on the pool account
see also: float account, funds pool account, pool account, purse pool account, underlying account

Vertragsunter-nehmens-Genehmi-gungsgrenze

floor limit – a maximum amount above which a particular transaction requires an authorization
cf.: domestic floor limit, local floor limit, merchant floor limit
see also: international floor limit, intra-European floor limit

floor limit management – a dynamic adjustment of floor limits and the random determination of a percentage of under floor limit transactions which require an on-line authorization

Variation von Genehmigungsanteil und -grenze

foreign currency transaction – a transaction which is effected in a foreign currency

Zahlungstransaktion im fremder Währung

foreign exchange bureau – an authorized agent of a bank to exchange money, to encash cheques and to give cash advances
cf.: bureau de change, change bureau, exchange bureau, exchange office

Wechselstube

foreign exchange earnings – the revenues gained from currency exchange
cf.: exchange earnings
see also: exchange difference, exchance profit, exchange rate mark-up

Erträge aus der Konvertierung fremder Währungen

foreign exchange risk – the risk that fluctuations of foreign exchange rates could lead to losses
cf.: exchange risk

Wechselkursrisiko

forge a card, to – to produce a card illegally
cf.: counterfeit a card, to; duplicate a card, to; fake a card, to; skim a card, to

Fälschen einer Karte

forged card – an illegally produced card
cf.: counterfeit(ed) card, duplicated card, fake(d) card, false card
opp.: genuine card, original card

gefälschte Karte

fraud – the misuse of a card / the card data by the criminal cardholder or a third party
see also: card fraud, merchant fraud

Betrug

fraud case – the entirety of all misuses with a specific card

Betrugsfall

fraud detection – efforts made to uncover fraud

Betrugsaufdeckung

Betrugsverluste	**fraud loss** – a loss caused by the misuse of a card
Verhalten bei Kartenbetrug	**fraud pattern** – the pattern indicating that a card is misused cf.: fraudulent behaviour, fraudulent pattern
Betrugsvorbeugung	**fraud prevention** – all measures implemented for avoiding fraud cases
Betrugsprofil	**fraud profile** – a card usage pattern indicating a fraud case
Kartenantrag mit falschen Karten-inhaberdaten	**fraudulent application** – an application where false information has been used to illegally obtain a card cf.: false application
Verhalten bei Kartenbetrug	**fraudulent behaviour** – a behaviour indicating that a card is misused cf.: fraud pattern, fraudulent pattern
Kartenbetrug	**fraudulent card use** – the illegal use of a card to obtain goods / services at a merchant location or cash at a bank location / ATM cf.: card fraud opp.: collusive fraud, fraudulent merchant activity, merchant fraud
Kartenbetrug durch mitmachendes / mit-eingeweihtes Vertragsunternehmen	**fraudulent merchant activity** – a fraud case in which a merchant cooperates / participates cf.: collusive fraud, merchant fraud opp.: card fraud, fraudulent card use
Verhalten bei Kartenbetrug	**fraudulent pattern** – the pattern indicating that a card is misused cf.: fraud pattern, fraudulent behaviour
Karteneinsatz-kontrollsystem	**fraudulent patterns detecting system** – a sophisticated computer system used for detecting specific fraudulent behaviour
betrügerischer Karteneinsatz	**fraudulent transaction** – a transaction which was made for fraudulent reasons
zinsenfreie Zeit, Zeit ohne Zinsen-berechnung	**free period** – the period within which the billed amount has to be paid by the cardholder cf.: funding period, grace period, interest free period

front side – the side of a card which contains the logo of the card system and the embossed / printed information
cf.: card face, card front
card reverse, reverse side

Kartenvorderseite

fulfillment – the supplying of the requested sales slip or a legible reproduction thereof

Leistungsbeleg-übermittlung

fully accountable card – an electronic purse with an audit trail
opp.: electronic money card

elektronische Geld-börse mit nachvollzieh-baren Transaktionen

fund an electronic purse, to – to transfer value from the cardholder's account to the electronic purse / issuer's float account
cf.: load an electronic purse, to
opp.: unload an electronic purse, to

eine elektronische Geldbörse laden

fund process – the transfer of value from the card-holder's account to the electronic purse / issuer's float account

Ladung einer elektronischen Geldbörse

funding period – the period within which the billed amount has to be paid by the cardholder
cf.: free period, grace period, interest free period

zinsenfreie Zeit, Zeit ohne Zinsen-berechnung

funds pool account – an account where the issuer of an electronic purse scheme holds the float
cf.: float account, pool account, purse pool account, under-lying account

Float-Konto, Pool-Konto eines elektronischen Geldbörsensystems

gambling transaction – a transaction performed in a game of chance
cf.: gaming transaction

Glücksspiel-transaktion

gaming transaction – a transaction performed in a game of chance
cf.: gambling transaction

Glücksspiel-transaktion

Geldkarte – brand name of the German electronic purse

Geldkarte, die elek-tronische Geldbörse in Deutschland

umfassend
einsetzbare Karte

general purpose card – a card which is issued to credit-worthy persons for worldwide use to obtain a comprehensive range of goods / services at merchant locations and cash at bank locations / ATMs

echte Karte,
Originalkarte

genuine card – a card issued to the genuine cardholder
cf.: original card
opp.: counterfeit(ed) card, duplicated card, fake(d) card, false card, forged card
see also: genuine cardholder

rechtmäßiger
Karteninhaber

genuine cardholder – the cardholder to whom the card was legally issued
cf.: lawful cardholder, legitimate cardholder, rightful cardholder, true cardholder

echtes Terminal

genuine terminal – a POS terminal lawfully installed for payment transactions
opp.: fake(d) terminal

Girokonto

giro account – an account used for handling payment transactions
cf.: checking account, current account, demand deposit account, sight deposit account

eine Transaktion über
einen höheren Betrag
durchführen und
die Differenz bar
auszahlen

give cash backs, to – to perform a payment transaction over a higher amount and to pay out the difference in cash

grenzüberschrei-
tendes Vertragsun-
ternehmensgeschäft

global acquiring – an acquiring business where bank and merchant are situated in different countries
cf.: cross-border acquiring, international acquiring
opp.: cross-border issuing
see also: central acquiring

grenzüber-
schreitendes
Kartengeschäft

global business – the card business of an acquirer / issuer where the bank and the merchant / cardholder are situated in different countries
cf.: cross-border business, international business

global electronic purse – an electronic purse that can be used worldwide

cf.: international electronic purse

opp.: domestic electronic purse

*weltweit einsetz-
bare elektronische
Geldbörse*

global issuing – an issuing business where bank and cardholder are situated in different countries

cf.: cross-border issuing, international issuing

opp.: cross-border acquiring, global acquiring, international acquiring

see also: central issuing

*grenzüberschreiten-
de Kartenausgabe*

G

gold card – a card which is issued in gold to persons of a higher income bracket and which is provided with a high spending limit and additional features

opp.: broad card, mainstream card, mass card

see also: preferred card, premier card, premium card, prestige card, privilege card, up-market card, up-scale card

*Goldkarte,
Karte mit hohem
Ausgaberahmen*

good faith attempt – a letter to find an amicable solution to a problem concerning the relation between two banks

cf.: good faith letter

*schriftliches
Ersuchen um
Kulanzlösung*

good faith letter – a letter to find an amicable solution to a problem concerning the relation between two banks

cf.: good faith attempt

*schriftliches
Ersuchen um
Kulanzlösung*

grace period – the period within which the billed amount has to be paid

cf.: free period, funding period, interest free period

zinsenfreie Zeit

Groupement de Cartes Bancaires – French payment systems organization

*Groupement de
Cartes Bancaires*

guaranteed cheque – a cheque that is guaranteed up to a defined amount under specific rules, including the presentation of a cheque guarantee card

opp.: non-guaranteed cheque

see also: cheque guarantee card

garantierter Scheck

garantierte
Zahlung

guaranteed payment – a transaction where the payment is guaranteed for the payee

cf.: guaranteed transaction

opp.: non-guaranteed payment

garantierte
Reservierung

guaranteed reservation – a reservation by transmitting a card number to ensure that a hotel room is kept available even after 6 p.m.

garantierte
Transaktion

guaranteed transaction – a transaction where the payment is guaranteed for the payee

cf.: guaranteed transaction

opp.: non-guaranteed payment

tragbares, meist
kabelloses POS-
Terminal

handheld POS terminal – a portable, mostly wireless POS terminal

cf.: mobile POS terminal

see also: wireless POS terminal

Entgelt für die Über-
mittlung eines Origi-
nal-Leistungsbelegs

hard copy fee – a fee for providing the hard copy of a sales slip for a retrieval request

Notfallservice

helpdesk – a service provided by a bank / card organization to support cardholders in emergency situations

Gebiet mit hohem
Risiko

high risk area – an area where fraud / counterfeit cases frequently occur

opp.: low risk area

Vertragsunterneh-
men mit hohem
Risiko

high risk merchant – a merchant where cards are misused and counterfeit cards are used frequently

opp.: low risk merchant

Niederlassung
eines Vertrags-
unternehmens mit
hohem Risiko

high risk outlet – an outlet of a merchant where cards are misused and counterfeit cards are used frequently

cf.: high risk point of sale

opp.: low risk outlet, low risk point of sale

Niederlassung
eines Vertrags-
unternehmens mit
hohem Risiko

high risk point of sale – an outlet of a merchant where cards are misused and counterfeit cards are used frequently

cf.: high risk outlet

opp.: low risk outlet, low risk point of sale

high risk postal area – an area in which the risk of interception and theft of a mailed card is high
opp.: low risk postal area

*Postbezirk mit hohem
Diebstahlsrisiko
bei postalischer
Kartenzustellung*

high traffic area – a region with a high number of transactions and/or a high turnover
cf.: high volume area
opp.: low traffic area, low volume area

*Gebiet mit hohem
Umsatz*

high value transaction – a transaction of a higher
amount
opp.: low value transaction

*größere
Kartentransaktion*

H

high volume area – a region with a high number of transactions and/or high turnover
cf.: high traffic area
opp.: low traffic area, low volume area

*Gebiet mit hohem
Umsatz*

high volume merchant – a merchant with a high number
of transactions and/or high turnover
opp.: low volume merchant

*Vertragsunter-
nehmen mit hohem
Umsatz*

high volume sector – a business sector with a high number of transactions and/or a high turnover
opp.: low volume sector

*Branche mit hohem
Umsatz*

hologram – a flat optical image which looks three-dimen-
sional
see also: hologram card, hologram technique

Hologramm

hologram card – a card bearing a hologram as a security
feature
see also: hologram, hologram technique

*Karte mit
Hologramm*

hologram technique – a method by which a hologram is
added to a card as a security feature
see also: hologram, hologram card

*Hologramm-
verfahren*

home banking – banking service a bank customer can access using a technical device as a communication link to the
bank's computer centre
cf.: e-banking, net-banking

*Erledigung der
Bankgeschäfte
von zu Hause aus*

eine Karte akzeptie-ren, eine Karte an-nehmen	**honour a card, to** – to accept a presented card cf.: accept a card, to
einen Scheck akzep-tieren, einen Scheck annehmen	**honour a cheque, to** – to accept a presented cheque cf.: accept a cheque, to
Regel, dass alle Kar-ten, die mit dem Logo eines Kartensystems versehen sind, vom Vertragsunternehmen akzeptiert werden müssen	**honour-all-cards rule** – a rule determining that all cards of a payment system must be accepted by a member establishment
eingelöster Scheck	**honoured cheque** – a cheque which is cashed or credited by the issuer's bank opp.: bounced cheque see also: covered cheque
Host-Verbindung	**host connection** – the facility that interfaces between a member host system and the card organization's network
Host-Computer	**host system** – the computer system of a member which is / is not linked to the card organization's network
gesperrte Karte	**hot card** – a card that has been put on the blacklist cf.: blacklisted card, pick-up card
Sperrdatenbestand	**hot card file** – a data file containing card numbers which are not to be honoured cf.: blacklist file, negative file, stoplist file see also: blacklist, hot card list, restricted card list, stoplist, warning bulletin
Sperrliste	**hot card list** – a printout containing card numbers which are not to be honoured cf.: blacklist, restricted card list, stoplist, warning, warning bulletin, warning notice bulletin see also: blacklist file, hot card file, negative file, stoplist file
Hybridkarte	**hybrid card** – a card with two card technologies: magnetic stripe and chip see also: hybrid terminal

H

hybrid chip card – a card with two chips: one for contact and one for contactless purposes

cf.: dual interface (chip) card

Karte mit zwei Chips: einer für kontakt-behaftete, einer für kontaktlose Zwecke

hybrid reader – a card reader in an ATM or a POS terminal capable of reading both the magnetic stripe and the chip

see also: card reader

Kartenleser, der sowohl den Magnet-streifen als auch den Chip einer Karte lesen kann

hybrid terminal – a terminal designed for two card technologies: magnetic stripe and chip

see also: hybrid card

Hybridterminal

IBAN (International Bank Account Number) – a number designating a bank account used internationally

cf.: International Bank Account Number (IBAN)

internationale Bankkontonummer

IC card (intergrated circuit card) – a card which contains a microchip

cf.: chip card, integrated circuit card (IC card), MC card (microcircuit card), microcircuit card (MC card)

see also: controller card, magnetic stripe card, memory card, processor card, smart card

Chipkarte, Karte mit Mikrochip

identification card – a card identifying its bearer

Ausweiskarte

identification check – the process of verifying a person's identity

Identitätsprüfung

identity theft – the fraudulent use of personal data to impersonate another person

Identitätsdiebstahl

IEP (inter-sector electronic purse) – an electronic purse that is issued to be used in an open system covering various branches of business

cf.: inter-sector electronic purse

see also: open (electronic) purse system, closed (electronic) purse system

branchenüber-greifende elektroni-sche Geldbörse

Autorisierungs-
computer / Geneh-
migungscomputer
der kartenaus-
gebenden Bank

IHS (issuer host system) – the processing system designated by the issuer as the preferred system to provide authorizations

cf.: issuer host, issuer host system (IHS), primary, primary
processing system

opp.: acquirer host, acquirer host system (AHS), AHS (acquirer host system)

see also: alternate, alternate processing system, back-up
processing system, down-option processing system, dynamic stand-in processing system

Bankleitzahl der
kartenausgebenden
Bank

IIN (issuer identification number) – a number designating an issuer

cf.: issuer identification number (IIN)

see also: bank identification number (BIN), BIN (bank
identification number)

Person / Institution,
die gegenüber der ver-
tragsunternehmens-
abrechnenden Bank
als Vertragsunter-
nehmen für Internet-
Handels- und Dienst-
leistungsunternehmen
auftritt, die selbst
keinen Vertrag mit
der vertragsunterneh-
mensabrechnenden
Bank haben

IMA (Internet merchant aggregator) – a person / institution acting as member establishment towards the acquirer
on behalf of Internet dealers and vendors that have no direct
contractual relationship with the acquirer

cf.: Internet merchant aggregator (IMA)

see also: discount broker

prompte Zahlung
des Vertragsunter-
nehmens

immediate payment – merchant payment effected on the
day or the day after the transaction is received by the acquirer

opp.: deferred payment, delayed payment

Debitkarte

immediate payment card – a card whose transactions
are (instantly) debited from a current account

cf.: current-account linked card, debit card

see also: charge card, credit card, deferred debit card, delayed debit card, pay later product, pay now product

Handprägegerät,
Imprinter

imprinter – a device used to imprint the card data and the
merchant or cash advance location data on a paper slip

imprinter transaction – a paper-based transaction carried out with an imprinter
see also: paper-based transaction

beleggebundene Transaktion mittels eines Handprägegeräts

impulse purchase – a sales transaction effected by a cardholder spontaneously

Spontankauf

in-bank ATM – an ATM located in a bank
cf.: in-branch ATM, indoor ATM
opp.: off-premises ATM, off-site ATM, outdoor ATM
see also: drive-through ATM, lobby ATM, through-the-wall ATM

Geldausgabeautomat in einer Bank (-filiale)

in-bank cash advance – a cash advance effected in a bank branch
cf.: in-bank cash withdrawal, in-branch cash advance, in-branch cash withdrawals

Bargeldbehebung in einer Bank (-filiale)

in-bank cash terminal – a terminal located in a bank branch at which cash advances can be made by using a payment card and the PIN
cf.: in-branch cash terminal

für die Abwicklung von Bargeldauszahlungen mit Karten geeignetes Terminal in einer Bank(-filiale)

in-bank cash withdrawals – a cash withdrawal effected in a bank branch
cf.: in-bank cash advance, in-branch cash advance, in-branch cash withdrawals

Bargeldabhebung in einer Bank (-filiale)

in-bank encashment – an encashment of a cheque in a bank branch
cf.: in-branch encashment

Scheckeinlösung in einer Bank (-filiale)

inbound data – the transaction data received by the issuer from the clearing system
cf.: inbound file, inbound traffic, inbound transactions, incoming data, incoming file, incoming traffic, incoming transactions
opp.: outbound data, outbound file, outbound traffic, outbound transactions, outgoing data, outgoing file, outgoing traffic, outgoing transactions

vom Clearingsystem an die kartenausgebende Bank übermittelte Umsätze

vom Clearing-system an die kartenausgebende Bank übermittelte Umsätze

inbound file – the transaction data received by the issuer from the clearing system

cf.: inbound data, inbound traffic, inbound transactions, incoming data, incoming file, incoming traffic, incoming transactions

opp.: outbound data, outbound file, outbound traffic, outbound transactions, outgoing data, outgoing file, outgoing traffic, outgoing transactions

vom Clearing-system an die kartenausgebende Bank übermittelte Umsätze

inbound traffic – the transaction data received by the issuer from the clearing system

cf.: inbound data, inbound file, inbound transactions, incoming data, incoming file, incoming traffic, incoming transactions

opp.: outbound data, outbound file, outbound traffic, outbound transactions, outgoing data, outgoing file, outgoing traffic, outgoing transactions

vom Clearing-system an die kartenausgebende Bank übermittelte Umsätze

inbound transactions – the transaction data received by the issuer from the clearing system

cf.: inbound data, inbound file, inbound traffic, incoming data, incoming file, incoming traffic, incoming transactions

opp.: outbound data, outbound file, outbound traffic, outbound transactions, outgoing data, outgoing file, outgoing traffic, outgoing transactions

Übertragung der Um-sätze vom Clearing-system an die karten-ausgebende Bank

inbound transmission – the process of transmitting the inbound data by the clearing centre to the issuer

cf.: incoming transmission

opp.: outbound transmission, outgoing transmission

Geldausgabe-automat in einer Bank(filiale)

in-branch ATM – an ATM located in a bank branch

cf.: in-bank ATM, indoor ATM

opp.: off-premises ATM, off-site ATM, outdoor ATM

see also: drive-through ATM, lobby ATM, through-the-wall ATM

Bargeldbehebung in einer Bank(filiale)

in-branch cash advance – a cash advance effected in a bank branch

cf.: in-bank cash advance, in-bank cash withdrawal, in-branch cash withdrawal

in-branch cash terminal – a terminal located in a bank branch at which cash advances can be made by using a payment card and the PIN
cf.: in-bank cash terminal

für die Abwicklung von Bargeldauszahlungen mit Karten geeignetes Terminal in einer Bank(filiale)

in-branch cash withdrawals – a cash withdrawal effected in a bank branch
cf.: in-bank cash advance, in-bank cash withdrawal, in-branch cash advance

Bargeldbehung in einer Bank(filiale)

in-branch encashment – an encashment of a cheque in a bank branch
cf.: in-bank encashment

Scheckeinlösung in einer Bank(filiale)

incoming data – the transaction data received by the issuer from the clearing system
cf.: inbound data, inbound file, inbound traffic, inbound transactions, incoming file, incoming traffic, incoming transactions
opp.: outbound data, outbound file, outbound traffic, outbound transactions, outgoing data, outgoing file, outgoing traffic, outgoing transactions

vom Clearing- system an die kartenausgebende Bank übermittelte Umsätze

incoming file – the transaction data received by the issuer from the clearing system
cf.: inbound data, inbound file, inbound traffic, inbound transactions, incoming data, incoming traffic, incoming transactions
opp.: outbound data, outbound file, outbound traffic, outbound transactions, outgoing data, outgoing file, outgoing traffic, outgoing transactions

vom Clearing- system an die kartenausgebende Bank übermittelte Umsätze

incoming traffic – the transaction data received by the issuer from the clearing system
cf.: inbound data, inbound file, inbound traffic, inbound transactions, incoming data, incoming file, incoming transactions
opp.: outbound data, outbound file, outbound traffic, outbound transactions, outgoing data, outgoing file, outgoing traffic, outgoing transactions

vom Clearing- system an die kartenausgebende Bank übermittelte Umsätze

vom Clearing-system an die kartenausgebende Bank übermittelte Umsätze

incoming transactions – the transaction data received by the issuer from the clearing system

cf.: inbound data, inbound file, inbound traffic, inbound transactions, incoming data, incoming file, incoming traffic

opp.: outbound data, outbound file, outbound traffic, outbound transactions, outgoing data, outgoing file, outgoing traffic, outgoing transactions

Übertragung der Umsätze vom Clearingsystem an die kartenausgebende Bank

incoming transmission – the process of transmitting the inbound data by the clearing centre to the issuer

cf.: inbound transmission

opp.: outbound transmission, outgoing transmission

laufende Belastung

incremental debit – continuous debiting of amounts

verfälschungssicherer Druck der Kartennummer auf der Rückseite der Karte

indent printing – the application of the card number with a special font on the reverse side of the card

Einzelabrechnung, individuelle Abrechnung

individual billing – a method whereby cards are settled individually by the cardholder

opp.: central billing

see also: billing options

Geldausgabeautomat in einer Bank(filiale)

indoor ATM – an ATM located in a bank

cf.: in-bank ATM, in-branch ATM

opp.: off-premises ATM, off-site ATM, outdoor ATM

see also: drive-through ATM, lobby ATM, through-the-wall ATM

Zahlungstransaktion während eines Fluges

in-flight transaction – a payment transaction performed during a flight

Marke, die in den kommunikativen Auftritt eines anderen Produkts / eines anderen Unternehmens eingefügt werden kann

ingredient brand – a brand incorporated in the products of another company

Sperrlisten-Eintragungsentgelt

insertion fee – the fee to be paid to enter a card number on a stoplist

cf.: entry fee, stoplist entry fee, stoplist insertion fee
see also: stoplist storage fee, storage fee

instalment payment – the repayment of a debt by partial amounts as agreed in advance

Ratenzahlung

in-store card – a plastic card issued by a merchant which can be used only in the issuer's environment
cf.: private label card, proprietary card, two-party card

Kundenkarte

integrated circuit card (IC card) – a card which contains a microchip
cf.: chip card, IC card (integrated circuit card), MC card (microcircuit card), microcircuit card (MC card)
see also: controller card, magnetic stripe card, memory card, processor card, smart card

Chipkarte, Karte mit Mikrochip

integrated POS terminal – a POS terminal that is integrated in the cashier terminal
opp.: stand-alone POS terminal
see also: POS terminal

integriertes POS-Terminal, mit der Handelskasse verbundenes POS-Terminal

integrity of a payment system – the correctness and the reliability of a payment system

Korrektheit und Zuverlässigkeit eines Zahlungssystems

intercept fraud – the fraud which occurs due to misuse of a card that was intercepted

Mißbrauch mittels Karten, die auf dem Postweg abgefangen wurden

intercept, to – to illegally take possession of a card sent by mail to the genuine cardholder

eine per Post versandte Karte abfangen

intercepted card – a card which is illegally taken possession of while being sent to the genuine cardholder by mail

eine unrechtmäßig auf dem Postweg abgefangene Karte

interchange – (the exchange of) transactions between acquirers and issuers
see also: domestic interchange, European interchange, interchange in, interchange out, international interchange, intra-European interchange, non-European interchange, non-interchange

(Datenaustausch der) Umsätze der vertragsunternehmensabrechnenden Bank mit der kartenausgebenden Bank

Studie über die Kosten von Interchange-Transaktionen

interchange cost study – a study that calculates / checks specific costs that issuers incur in particular for the payment guarantee, funding and processing of incoming transactions

Interchange-Kosten, Kosten für die vertragsunternehmensabrechnende und für die kartenausgebende Bank bei Interchange-Transaktionen

interchange costs – all fees and charges levied on interchange transactions

Entgelt, das von der vertragsunternehmensabrechnenden Bank an die kartenausgebende Bank bezahlt wird; Interchange Fee, Interbankenentgelt

interchange fee – a charge paid by acquirers to issuers which is applied to most interchange transactions

cf.: positive interchange fee

opp.: negative interchange fee

see also: domestic interchange fee, European interchange fee, intra-European interchange fee, inter-regional interchange fee, non-European interchange fee, international interchange fee, bilateral (agreed) interchange fee, MIF (multi-lateral [agreed] interchange fee), multi-lateral (agreed) interchange fee (MIF), default interchange fee, fallback interchange fee

(Datenaustausch der) Umsätze von Karten einer Bank bei Vertragsunternehmen einer anderen Bank

interchange in – (the exchange of) transactions effected by the issuer's cardholders at member establishments of another acquirer

opp.: interchange out

see also: interchange

Erträge, die für die kartenausgebende Bank bei Interchange-Transaktionen anfallen; Interchange-Erträge

interchange income – earnings gained through interchange transactions

cf.: interchange revenue

(Datenaustausch der) Umsätze der Vertragsunternehmen einer Bank mit Karten einer anderen Bank

interchange out – (the exchange of) transactions effected at an acquirer's member establishment by cardholders of other issuers

opp.: interchange in

see also: interchange

interchange rate indicator – a value submitted by the acquirer to identify the interchange rate type for a given transaction

Indikator, der angibt, welche Kategorie einer Interchange Fee zur Verrechnung kommen soll

interchange revenue – earnings gained through interchange transactions
cf.: interchange income

Erträge, die für die kartenausgebende Bank bei Interchange-Transaktionen anfallen; Interchange-Erträge

interchange structure – the turnover structure of an acquirer / issuer according to the various interchange fees

Gliederung der Umsätze eines Issuers / Acquirers nach den unterschiedlichen Interchange Fees

interchange system – the set-up established to enable transactions between acquirers and issuers

System zum Datenaustausch zwischen vertragsunternehmensabrechnenden und kartenausgebenden Banken

interchange transaction – a transaction where the acquirer and the issuer are different entities

Interchange-Transaktion, Transaktion mit der Karte einer Bank bei einem Vertragsunternehmen einer anderen Bank

inter-country transaction – a cross-border transaction
cf.: cross-border transaction, international transaction

grenzüberschreitende Transaktion, internationale Transaktion

interest free period – the period within which the billed amount has to be paid by the cardholder
cf.: free period, funding period, grace period

zinsenfreie Zeit

interest rate – the percentage of the unpaid amount to be paid by the cardholder

Zinssatz

interlocking circles – the two intertwining circles in the brands of MasterCard International
cf: intertwining circles

die beiden ineinandergreifenden Kreise in den Logos der Produkte von MasterCard International

grenzüberschrei-
tendes Karten-
geschäft

international business – the card business of an acquirer / issuer where the bank and the merchant / cardholder are situated in different countries
cf.: cross-border business, global business

weltweit einsetz-
bare elektronische
Geldbörse

international electronic purse – an electronic purse that can be used worldwide
cf.: global electronic purse
opp.: domestic electronic purse

grenzüberschrei-
tende Kartenaus-
gabe

international issuing – an issuing business where bank and cardholder are situated in different countries
cf.: cross-border issuing, global issuing
opp.: cross-border acquiring, global acquiring, international acquiring
see also: central issuing

grenzüberschrei-
tendes Vertrags-
unternehmens-
geschäft

international acquiring – an acquiring business where bank and merchant are situated in different countries
cf.: cross-border acquiring, global acquiring
opp.: cross-border issuing
see also: central acquiring

internationale
Bankkontonummer

International Bank Account Number (IBAN) – a number designating a bank account used internationally
cf.: IBAN (International Bank Account Number)

im In- und Ausland
verwendbare Karte

international card – a card designated for domestic and international use
opp.: domestic card
see also: local card

Bargeldbezug
mit einer Karte
im Ausland

international cash advance – a cash advance is international if the principal office of the issuer and the location disbursing the cash advance are not located within the same country
opp.: domestic cash advance

internationales
Bargeldbezugslimit

international cash advance limit – the maximum amount that may be taken in cash by the cardholder abroad in a given period cf.: international cash limit

opp.: domestic cash advance limit, international retail limit, international sales limit

see also: cash advance limit, cash limit

international cash limit – the maximum amount that may be taken in cash by the cardholder abroad in a given period   *internationales Bargeldbezugslimit*

cf.: international cash advance limit

opp.: domestic cash advance limit, international retail limit, international sales limit

see also: cash advance limit, cash limit

international floor limit – the limit above which an authorization must be requested by the acquirer from the issuer for all cards issued outside of a given country   *Genehmigungsgrenze bei grenzüberschreitenden Umsätzen*

see also: domestic floor limit, floor limit, intra-European floor limit, local floor limit, merchant floor limit

international fraud – a fraud case which does not occur in the issuer's country   *grenzüberschreitender Betrug*

cf.: cross-border fraud

international interchange – the exchange of transaction data between acquirers and issuers which are situated in different countries   *(Datenaustausch der) grenzüberschreitende(n) Umsätze*

see also: European interchange, interchange, international interchange, intra-European interchange, non-European interchange

international interchange fee – a charge paid by acquirers to issuers which is applied to most international transactions   *Entgelt, das von der vertragsunternehmensabrechnenden Bank an die kartenausgebende Bank bei internationalen Transaktionen bezahlt wird*

opp.: domestic interchange fee

see also: European interchange fee, interchange fee, interregional interchange fee, intra-European interchange fee, non-European interchange fee

international merchant – a merchant carrying on business in more than one country   *internationales Vertragsunternehmen*

ISO

International Organization for Standardization (ISO) – an international organization that issues standards in all areas, including computer technology and information processing

cf.: ISO (International Organization for Standardization)

see also: American National Standards Institute (ANSI), ANSI (American National Standards Institute), CEN (Comité Européen de Normalisation), Comité Européen de Normalisation (CEN)

internationales Zahlungssystem

international payment scheme – an international payment system

opp.: domestic payment scheme

see also: payment scheme

internationale Genehmigungsgrenze

international retail limit – the maximum amount that can be spent by the cardholder abroad in a given period

cf.: international sales limit

opp.: domestic retail limit, international cash advance limit, international cash limit

see also: retail limit, sales limit

Regeln eines Zahlungssystems (insbesondere) für grenzüberschreitende Transaktionen

international rules – rules of a payment system especially for cross-border transactions

opp: domestic rules

internationale Genehmigungsgrenze

international sales limit – the maximum amount that can be spent by the cardholder abroad in a given period

cf.: international retail limit

opp.: domestic retail limit, international cash advance limit, international cash limit

see also.: retail limit, sales limit

internationale Transaktionen

international traffic – the entirety of cross-border transactions

see also: cross-border transaction, international transaction, inter-country transaction

grenzüberschreitende, internationale Transaktion

international transaction – a transaction where the acquirer of a transaction is situated in another country than the issuer or the card

cf.: cross-border transaction, inter-country transaction

Internet merchant aggregator (IMA) – a person / institution acting as member establishment towards the acquirer on behalf of Internet dealers and vendors that have no direct contractual relationship with the acquirer

cf.: IMA (Internet merchant aggregator)

Person / Institution, die gegenüber der vertragsunternehmensabrechnenden Bank als Vertragsunternehmen für Internet-Handels- und Dienstleistungsunternehmen auftritt, die selbst keinen Vertrag mit der vertragsunternehmensabrechnenden Bank haben

interoperability – the possibility of using a card at the terminal points (POS terminals, ATMs) of another card system

systemüberschreitende Nutzungsmöglichkeit von Terminals

inter-regional business – business activities of an issuer / acquirer in countries outside of its region

Geschäftstätigkeit einer kartenausgebenden oder vertragsunternehmensabrechnenden Bank in Ländern außerhalb der eigenen Region

inter-regional interchange fee – a charge paid by acquirers to issuers which is applied to most non-European cross-border transactions

cf.: non-European interchange fee

opp.: European interchange fee, intra-European interchange fee

see also: domestic interchange fee, international interchange fee, interchange fee

Entgelt, das von der vertragsunternehmensabrechnenden Bank an die kartenausgebende Bank bei grenzüberschreitenden nichteuropäischen Transaktionen bezahlt wird

inter-sector electronic purse (IEP) – an electronic purse that is issued to be used in an open system covering various branches of business

cf.: IEP (inter-sector electronic purse)

see also: open (electronic) purse system, closed (electronic) purse system

branchenübergreifende elektronische Geldbörse

inter-system competition – competition between different payment schemes

Wettbewerb zwischen verschiedenen Zahlungssystemen

intertwining circles – the two interlocking circles in the brands of Mastercard International

cf: interlocking circles

die beiden ineinandergreifenden Kreise in den Logos der Produkte von Mastercard International

intra-country transaction – a transaction with a card effected in the issuing country

cf.: domestic transaction

inländische Transaktion

Bargeldbezug
mit einer Karte
im europäischen
Ausland

intra-European cash advance – a cash advance is intra-European if the principal office of the issuer and the location disbursing the cash advance are situated in different countries within Europe

see also: international cash advance

Genehmigungs-
grenze bei grenz-
überschreitenden
europäischen
Transaktionen

intra-European floor limit – the limit above which an authorization must be requested by a European acquirer from a European issuer

see also: domestic floor limit, floor limit, international floor limit, local floor limit, merchant floor limit

(Datenaustausch)
grenzüberschrei-
tende(r) europä-
ische(r) Umsätze

intra-European interchange – the exchange of transaction data between acquirers and issuers which are situated in different countries within Europe

cf.: European interchange

opp.: non-European interchange

see also: domestic interchange, interchange, international interchange

Entgelt, das von der
vertragsunterneh-
mensabrechnenden
Bank an die karten-
ausgebende Bank bei
grenzüberschreiten-
den europäischen
Transaktionen be-
zahlt wird

intra-European interchange fee – a charge paid by acquirers to issuers which is applied to most European cross-border transactions

cf.: European interchange fee

inter-regional interchange fee, non-European interchange fee

see also: domestic interchange fee, international interchange fee, interchange fee

grenzüberschrei-
tende europäische
Transaktionen

intra-European traffic – the entirety of cross-border transactions within Europe

grenzüberschreiten-
de Transaktionen
innerhalb einer
Region

intra-regional traffic – the entirety of cross-border transactions within a region

Wettbewerb innerhalb
eines Zahlungssystems

intra-system competition – competition within a payment scheme

iris scanning – a biometric technique to verify the card-holder authentication

see also: biometrics, biometric techniques

Regenbogenhaut-prüfung

irrevocability – the inability to revoke a transaction

opp.: revocability

Unwiderrufbarkeit

ISO (International Organization for Standardization) – an international organization that issues standards in all areas, including computer technology and information processing

cf.: International Organization for Standardization (ISO)

see also: American National Standards Institute (ANSI), ANSI (American National Standards Institute), CEN (Comité Européen de Normalisation), Comité Européen de Normalisation (CEN)

ISO

ISO standards – the standards agreed by the International Organization of Standardization which have been applied to information transmissions and computer technology in the plastic money industry

see also: International Organization for Standardization (ISO), ISO (International Organization for Standardization)

ISO-Normen

issuance brand – the leading brand under which a card is issued

cf.: issuance mark, issuing brand, issuing mark

opp.: acceptance brand, acceptance mark

Markenname und -zeichen, unter denen eine Karte ausgegeben wird

issuance mark – the leading brand under which a card is issued

cf.: issuance brand, issuing brand, issuing mark

opp.: acceptance brand, acceptance mark

Markenname und -zeichen, unter denen eine Karte ausgegeben wird

issue, to – to sell a card to a person and to transmit the card to the cardholder

eine Karte ausgeben

issuer – a bank which issues cards, receives the card-holder transactions from the members / merchants, guarantees the payment and collects the respective amounts from the cardholders

kartenausgebende Bank, Karten-emittent

cf.: card issuer, card issuing bank, cardholder bank, issuer bank, issuing bank, issuing institution, issuing member, paying bank

opp.: acquirer, acquirer bank, acquiring bank, acquiring institution, acquiring member, beneficiary bank

Autorisierungszen-
trale / Genehmigungs-
zentrale der karten-
ausgebenden Bank

issuer authorization centre – the site where the authorization actually takes place by the issuer

opp.: aquirer authorization centre

see also: authorization centre

Verarbeitung von
kartenbezogenen
Daten und Transak-
tionen, die nicht Au-
torisierungen sind

issuer back-office processing – the processing of all batch functions related to the cardholder data base and the cardholders transactions

opp.: acquirer back-office processing

see also: issuer batch processing

kartenausgebende
Bank, Karten-
emittent

issuer bank – a bank which issues cards, receives the cardholder transactions from the members / merchants, guarantees the payment and collects the respective amounts from the cardholders

cf.: card issuer, card issuing bank, cardholder bank, issuer, issuing bank, issuing institution, issuing member, paying bank

opp.: acquirer, acquirer bank, acquiring bank, acquiring institution, acquiring member, beneficiary bank

Stapelverarbeitung
von kartenbezoge-
nen Daten und
Transaktionen

issuer batch processing – the processing of all batch functions related to the cardholder data base and the cardholder transactions

opp.: acquirer batch processing

see also: issuer back-office processing

Land, in dem die
kartenausgebende
Bank domiziliert ist

issuer country – the country where a card is issued

opp.: acquirer country

Code des Landes,
in dem die karten-
ausgebende Bank
domiziliert ist

issuer country code – a code in the transaction data defining the issuer country

opp.: acquirer country code

see also: country code

issuer economics – revenue, cost and margin situation of an issuer

opp.: acquirer economics

see also: card economics

Ertrags-, Aufwands- und Gewinnsituation einer kartenausgebenden Bank

issuer host – the processing system designated by the issuer as the preferred system to provide authorizations

cf.: IHS (issuer host system), issuer host system (IHS), primary, primary processing system

opp.: acquirer host, acquirer host system (AHS), AHS (acquirer host system)

see also: alternate, alternate processing system, back-up processing system, down-option processing system, dynamic stand-in processing system

Autorisierungs- computer der kartenausgebenden Bank

issuer host system (IHS) – the processing system designated by the issuer as the preferred system to provide authorizations

cf.: (IHS) issuer host system, issuer host, primary, primary processing system

opp.: acquirer host, acquirer host system (AHS), AHS (acquirer host system)

see also: alternate, alternate processing system, back-up processing system, down-option processing system, dynamic stand-in processing system

Autorisierungs- computer der kartenausgebenden Bank

issuer identification number (IIN) – a number designating an issuer

cf.: IIN (issuer identification number)

see also: bank identification number (BIN), BIN (bank identification number)

Bankleitzahl der kartenausgebenden Bank

issuer liability – the capability of the issuer to fulfil its financial obligations

opp.: acquirer liability

see also: liability, liability shift

Fähigkeit einer kartenausgebenden Bank, ihren finanziellen Verpflichtungen nachzukommen

issuer on-line processing – the processing of the requests for authorizations received from merchants or other members

Online-Verarbeitung von Genehmigungsanfragen

Unternehmen, das
EDV-Dienstleistun-
gen im Auftrag der
kartenausgebenden
Bank erbringt

issuer processor – a processor providing IT service for an issuer

opp.: acquirer processor

see also: processor

Genehmigungszen-
trale der karten-
ausgebenden Bank

issuer site – the place where the issuer host system (IHS) is located

cf.: issuer authorization centre

Geschäft im
Zusammenhang
mit der Karten-
ausgabe, Karten-
inhabergeschäft

issuing – all activities concerning the issuance of cards, the receipt of cardholder transactions from the members / merchants, the guaranteeing of the payments and the collection of the respective amounts from the cardholders

cf.: card issuance, card issuing business, issuing business

opp.: acquiring business, merchant acquiring business

kartenausgebende
Bank, Karten-
emittent

issuing bank – a bank which issues cards, receives the cardholder transactions from the members / merchants, guarantees the payment and collects the respective amounts from the cardholders

cf.: card issuer, card issuing bank, cardholder bank, issuer, issuer bank, issuing institution, issuing member, paying bank

opp.: acquirer, acquirer bank, acquiring bank, acquiring institution, acquiring member, beneficiary bank

Markenname und
-zeichen, unter
denen eine Karte
ausgegeben wird

issuing brand – the leading brand under which a card is issued

cf.: issuance brand, issuance mark, issuing mark

opp.: acceptance brand, acceptance mark

Geschäft im
Zusammenhang
mit der Karten-
ausgabe, Karten-
inhabergeschäft

issuing business – all activities concerning the issuance of cards, the receipt of cardholder transactions from the members / merchants, the guaranteeing of the payments and the collection of the respective amounts from the cardholders

cf.: card issuance, card issuing business, issuing

opp.: acquiring business, merchant acquiring business

issuing institution – a bank which issues cards, receives the cardholder transactions from the members / merchants, guarantees the payment and collects the respective amounts from the cardholders

cf.: card issuer, card issuing bank, cardholder bank, issuer, issuer bank, issuing bank, issuing member, paying bank

opp.: : acquirer, acquirer bank, acquiring bank, acquiring institution, acquiring member, beneficiary bank

kartenausgebende Bank, Karten-emittent

issuing licence – the right granted by a licensor to a licensee to issue cards

opp.: acquiring licence

see also: licence

Lizenz für das Karteninhaber-geschäft; Lizenz, Karten auszugeben

I

issuing mark – the leading brand under which a card is issued

cf.: issuance brand, issuance mark, issuing brand

opp.: acceptance brand, acceptance mark

Markenname und -zeichen, unter denen eine Karte ausgegeben wird

issuing member – a bank which issues cards, receives the cardholder transactions from the members / merchants, guarantees the payment and collects the respective amounts from the cardholders

cf.: card issuer, card issuing bank, cardholder bank, issuer, issuer bank, issuing bank, issuing institution, paying bank

opp.: acquirer, acquirer bank, acquiring bank, acquiring institution, acquiring member, beneficiary bank

kartenausgebende Bank, Karten-emittent

issuing-before-acquiring rule – a rule that a bank has to issue cards before acquiring member establishments

Regel, dass eine Bank vor der Ab-rechnung von Ver-tragsunternehmen Karten ausgeben muß

item charge – the fee charged per transaction

cf.: transaction charge, transaction fee

Transaktionsentgelt

JCB	**JCB** – an international card system where the business is carried on by JCB International and its licensees see also.: JCB card, JCB International
JCB-Karte	**JCB card** – a card issued by JCB or a licensed bank see also: JCB, JCB International
JCB International	**JCB International** – an international card organisation which carries on both the issuing and acquiring business itself and through licensees see also: JCB, JCB card
Beitrittsentgelt	**joining fee** – a single payment by the cardholder to receive a card cf.: entrance fee
gemeinsame Haftung	**joint liability** – the combined liability of two or more parties opp.: several liability see also: liability
julianisches Datum, numerisch fortlaufendes Datum	**Julian date** – numeric day of the year starting with 001 on January 1st cf.: entrance fee
Schlüssel, der im Rahmen eines Verschlüsselungsverfahrens verwendet wird	**key** – a mathematical value which is used in an algorithm to protect data within a network cf.: encryption key
Schlüsselgebiet	**key area** – an important region for an issuer / acquirer
Schlüsselindikatoren	**key indicators** – values used to track performance of an issuer or an acquirer
Schlüsselverwaltung	**key management** – the secure generation, allocation, distribution and replacement of keys for a cryptosystem
Schlüsselvertragsunternehmen	**key merchant** – an important merchant for an issuer
Schlüssel. der dazu verwendet wird, um andere Schlüssel zu verschlüsseln	**key-encryption key** – a key used for the sole purpose of encrypting other keys

J
K

large-value payment – a payment of a very large amount between participants in the financial markets which require timely settlement

Zahlung über einen sehr hohen Betrag

laser card – a card on which information is stored using optimal recording techniques
cf.: optical memory card

optische Speicherkarte

laser engraving – the application of information on a card by laser imprint

Anbringen der Daten auf einer Karte per Laserdruck

laser-engraved photograph – a photograph of the genuine cardholder which is engraved on a card for security purposes

gelasertes Foto

laser-engraved signature – the signature of the genuine cardholder which is engraved on the card for security purposes

gelaserte Unterschrift

late charge – a fee levied for late payment
cf.: late fee, late payment fee

Entgelt bei verspäteter Zahlung

late fee – a charge levied for late payment
cf.: late charge, late payment fee

Entgelt bei verspäteter Zahlung

late payment fee – a charge levied on late payment
cf.: late charge, late fee

Entgelt bei verspäteter Zahlung

lawful cardholder – the cardholder to whom the card was legally issued
cf.: genuine cardholder, legitimate cardholder, rightful cardholder, true cardholder

rechtmäßiger Karteninhaber

leased line – the communications system where data are transmitted between two endpoints which are permanently connected
cf.: dedicated line, private line

Standleitung

legible reproduction fee – a fee for providing a microfiche of a sales slip for a retrieval request

Entgelt für die Übermittlung einer lesbaren Leistungsbelegskopie

legitimate cardholder – the cardholder to whom the card was legally issued
cf.: genuine cardholder, lawful cardholder, rightful cardholder, true cardholder

rechtmäßiger Karteninhaber

Fähigkeit einer kartenausgebenden oder einer vertragsunternehmensabrechnenden Bank, ihren finanziellen Verpflichtungen nachzukommen

liability – the ability of an acquirer or an issuer to meet its financial obligations
see also: acquirer liability, issuer liability, liability shift

Haftungsübergang, Übergang der Haftung vom Acquirer auf den Issuer oder umgekehrt

liability shift – a point from which liability passes from acquirer to issuer or vice-versa
see also: acquirer liability, issuer liability, liability

Lizenz für das Kartengeschäft; Lizenz, Karten auszugeben und Vertragsunternehmen abzurechnen

licence – the right granted by a licensor to a licensee to issue cards and to acquire merchants
see also: acquirer licence, issuer licence

Lizenzvertrag

licence agreement – contract between a bank and a payment system concerning one / more product licence / s
see also: membership agreement

Lizenzentgelt

licensing fee – a fee payable by a member of a card organization under a licence agreement

Ladung einer elektronischen Geldbörse zulasten des Kontos eines Karteninhabers auf das Pool-Konto

linked load – a load(ing) transaction whereby electronic value is transferred from the cardholder's account to an electronic purse / issuer's float account
opp.: unlinked load

Liquiditätsrisiko

liquidity risk – the risk that a debtor is unable to meet their financial obligations in a timely manner due to temporary illiquidity

Eingabedatum einer Kartennummer in die Sperrliste

listing date – the date of the entry of a card number in the stoplist
cf.: entry date

echte einsatzfähige Karte

live card – a genuinely issued card that can be used
cf.: specimen card, test card

eine elektronische Geldbörse laden

load an electronic purse, to – to transfer value from the cardholder's account to the electronic purse / issuer's float account

cf.: fund an electronic purse, to
opp.: unload an electronic purse, to

load authorization request – a request to authorize a load(ing) transaction for an electronic purse
opp.: load authorization response

Genehmigungsan-frage für eine La-detransaktion

load authorization response – a response to a load authorization request for an electronic purse
opp.: load authorization request

Genehmigung / Ab-lehnung einer La-detransaktion

load trigger value – the balance of an electronic purse below or at which a card initiated load will be triggered

Betrag, ab dem die elektronische Geld-börse selbst auf das Ladeerforder-nis hinweist

load(ing) device – a terminal (e.g. an ATM, a POS terminal or a telephone) for loading value into electronic purses
cf.: load(ing) terminal

Ladeterminal

load(ing) fee – a fee charged for loading an electronic purse

Ladeentgelt

load(ing) terminal – a device for loading value into electronic purses

Ladeterminal

load(ing) transaction – a transaction where value is transferred from the cardholder's account to an electronic purse / issuer's float
opp.: unload(ing) transaction
see also: merchant transaction, payment transaction, purchase transaction, retail transaction, sales transaction

Ladetransaktion, Ladung

load(ing) value – the amount that is loaded into an electronic purse

Ladebetrag

loaded value – the actual amount stored in an electronic purse at a given time

geladener Betrag

lobby ATM – an ATM located in a bank lobby
see also: drive-through ATM, in-bank ATM, in-branch ATM, indoor ATM, off-premises ATM, off-site ATM, outdoor ATM, through-the-wall ATM

Foyer-Geldausgabe-automat, Foyerau-tomat, Lobby-Geld-ausgabeautomat, Lobbyautomat

nur örtlich/regional einsetzbare Karte	**local card** – a card designated for local use only see also: domestic card, international card
Vertragsunter-nehmens-Genehmi-gungsgrenze	**local floor limit** – a maximum amount above which a particular transaction requires an authorization at the point of sale cf.: domestic floor limit, floor limit, merchant floor limit see also: international floor limit, intra-European floor limit
dezentrale PIN-Überprüfung	**local PIN checking** – the decentralized verification of a PIN
Transaktionsdatum	**local transaction date** – the date when a transaction takes place at the point of sale
Transaktions-zeitpunkt	**local transaction time** – the time when a transaction takes place at the point of sale
Reisestellenkarte	**lodge(d) card** – a card which is deposited at a travel agency for convenient payment of a company's travel expenses cf.: travel account card
Transaktions-protokoll	**log** – an activity file of card transactions for analysis and reporting purposes see also: logging analysis, logging data
Analyse der gespeicherten Daten	**logging analysis** – the process of analysing the logged card transactions see also: log, logging data
gespeicherte Daten	**logging data** – the data concerning card transactions contained in the log see also: log, logging analysis
Ergebnis der Analyse der gespeicherten Daten	**logging report** – the result of the logging analysis
Lorokonto	**loro account** – a bank account held by one bank for another bank opp.: nostro account
Verlust- oder Diebstahlsmeldung	**lost & stolen report** – a report of a cardholder to the issuer concerning the loss or theft of the credit card

lost card – a card which was lost by the cardholder, and found and used by a dishonest finder

verlorene Karte

low risk area – an area where fraud / counterfeit cases rarely occur
opp.: high risk area

Gebiet mit niedrigem Risiko

low risk merchant – a merchant where cards are misused and counterfeit cards are used rarely
opp.: high risk merchant

Vertragsunternehmen mit niedrigem Risiko

low risk outlet – an outlet where cards are misused and counterfeit cards are used rarely
cf.: low risk point of sale
opp.: high risk outlet, high risk point of sale

Niederlassung eines Vertragsunternehmens mit niedrigem Risiko

low risk point of sale – an outlet where cards are misused and counterfeit cards are used rarely
lcf.: ow risk outlet
opp.: high risk outlet, high risk point of sale

Niederlassung eines Vertragsunternehmens mit niedrigem Risiko

low risk postal area – an area in which the risk of interception and theft of a mailed card is low
opp.: high risk postal area

Postbezirk mit niedrigem Risiko

low traffic area – a region with a low number of transactions and/or a low volume
cf.: low volume area
opp.: high traffic area, high volume area

Gebiet mit niedrigem Umsatz

low value transaction – a transaction of a lower amount
opp.: high value transaction

kleinere Kartentransaktion

low volume area – a region with a low number of transactions and/or a low turnover
cf.: low traffic area
opp.: high traffic area, high volume area

Gebiet mit niedrigem Umsatz

low volume merchant – a merchant with a low number of transactions and/or a low turnover
opp.: high volume merchant

Vertragsunternehmen mit niedrigem Umsatz

Branche mit niedrigem Umsatz

low volume sector – a business sector with a low number of transactions and/or a low turnover

opp.: high volume sector

Prüfziffer (nach dem Luhn-Verfahren)

Luhn check digit – the digit on a card number which is calculated by using the Luhn formula and the purpose of which is to check the integrity of the preceding number

see also: Luhn formula

Prüfziffernermittlung (nach dem Luhn-Verfahren)

Luhn formula – the check digit routine for a card number from which a Luhn check digit is obtained as a result

see also: Luhn check digit

Maestro

Maestro – a licensed debit card system with the licences being granted by MasterCard International

see also: Maestro card, MasterCard International

Maestro-Karte

Maestro card – a debit card issued by a licensee of Maestro International

see also: Maestro, MasterCard International

Magnetstreifen

magnetic stripe – a stripe with a magnetic layer on the reverse side of the card, on which information concerning details of the card can be stored on magnetic tracks

see also: chip

Magnetstreifenfeld

magnetic stripe area – the area on a card on which its magnetic stripe is located

Magnetstreifenterminal, POS-Terminal mit einem Magnetstreifenleser

magnetic stripe ATM – an ATM which contains a magnetic stripe reader

see also: chip ATM, magnetic stripe terminal

Magnetstreifenkarte

magnetic stripe card – a card with a magnetic stripe, on which information concerning details of the card is encoded on tracks

see also: chip card

Magnetstreifenfälschung

magnetic stripe counterfeiting – the duplication of the data contained on the magnetic stripe of a card onto another card or the falsification of data contained on the magnetic stripe of a card

magnetic stripe reader – a device which reads information recorded on the magnetic track of a card

Magnetstreifen-leser

magnetic stripe specifications – the data outlining the details of a magnetic stripe
see also: chip specifications, POS terminal specifications

Magnetstreifen-Spezifikationen

magnetic stripe tapping – the retrieval of the data contained on the magnetic stripe of a card

Kopieren eines Magnetstreifens

magnetic stripe terminal – a POS terminal which contains a magnetic stripe reader
see also: chip terminal, magnetic stripe ATM

Magnetstreifenterminal, POS-Terminal mit einem Magnetstreifenleser

magnetic stripe transaction – a transaction whereby transaction data is captured directly from the magnetic stripe of the card
opp.: chip transaction

Magnetstreifen-Transaktion

magnetic stripe writer – a device which writes information on a magnetic stripe of a card

Magnetstreifen-codiergerät

magnetic track – a linear path on a magnetic stripe along which data is recorded

Spur auf einem Magnetstreifen

mail order – a transaction effected by mail to be paid by a credit card
cf.: mail order transaction
see also: mail order / telephone order transaction (MO / TO transaction), MO / TO transaction (mail order / telephone order transaction

Kreditkarten-transaktion aufgrund einer postalischen Bestellung

mail order fraud – the misuse of card data by ordering goods via mail order

Betrug mittels schriftlicher Bestellung

mail order transaction – a transaction effected by mail to be paid by a credit card
cf.: mail order
see also: mail order / telephone order transaction (MO / TO transaction), MO / TO transaction (mail order / telephone order transaction

Kreditkartentransaktion aufgrund einer postalischen Bestellung

M

Kreditkartentransaktion aufgrund einer postalischen oder telefonischen Bestellung

mail order / telephone order transaction (MO / TO transaction) – a transaction effected by mail or by telephone to be paid by a credit card

cf.: MO / TO transaction (mail order / telephone order transaction)

see also: mail order transaction, telephone order transaction

Kartenangebot per Brief

mail solicition – a card offered by a letter

see also: solicited offer, unsolicited offer

Massenkarte

mainstream card – a card which is issued to a considerable proportion of the population

cf.: broad card, mass card

opp.: gold card, preferred card, premier card, premium card, prestige card, privilege card, up-market card, up-scale card

größere Währungseinheit

major currency unit – the large unit of a currrency in a particular country

opp.: minor currency unit

zahlen

make payments, to – to give money in cash or cash-like substitutes

cf.: pay, to

Bargeldauszahlung am Kassenschalter einer Bank(filiale)

manual cash advance – the process whereby the cardholder obtains cash from a cashier in a bank branch

cf.: OTC cash advance (over-the-counter cash advance), over-the-counter cash advance (OTC cash advance)

von einem Karteninhaber initiierte Ladung einer elektronischen Geldbörse

manual load(ing) – a loading transaction of an electronic purse initiated by the cardholder

cf.: cardholder-initiated load(ing)

opp.: card-initiated load(ing)

beleggebundene Transaktion, manuelle Transaktion

manual transaction – a transaction carried out by using paper drafts

cf.: imprinter transaction, paper-based transaction

opp.: electronic transaction

Marketing-Management

marketing management – the management of card and merchant marketing

opp.: operations management

mass card – a card which is issued to a considerable proportion of the population

cf.: broad card, mainstream card

opp.: gold card, preferred card, premier card, premium card, prestige card, privilege card, up-market card, up-scale card

Massenkarte

mass transit application – an off-line POS solution catering to the special needs of the mass transit industry which generally has low maximum transaction amounts

see also: QPS (quick payment service), quick payment service (QPS), rapid payment service (RPS), RPS (rapid payment service)

offline POS-Lösung für Verkehrsmittel

MasterCard – a licensed card system with the licences being granted by MasterCard International

see also: MasterCard card, MasterCard Electronic card, MasterCard International

MasterCard

MasterCard card – a card issued by a licensee of MasterCard International

see also: MasterCard, MasterCard International

MasterCard-Karte

M

MasterCard Electronic card – an online-only credit card issued by a licensee of MasterCard International

see also: MasterCard, MasterCard International

MasterCard Electronic-Karte

MasterCard International – an international payment systems organization which is the licensor of MasterCard cards and Maestro cards

see also: Maestro, Maestro card, MasterCard, MasterCard card, MasterCard Electronic card

MasterCard International

MasterCard SecureCode – a standard for secure payments with MasterCard and Maestro cards in the Internet / in the virtual world

see also: Verified by Visa

sichere Zahlungsform mit MasterCard- und Maestro-Karten im Internet / in der virtuellen Welt, MasterCard SecureCode

matching signature – a signature corresponding to the specimen signature on a card

opp.: non-matching signature

übereinstimmende Unterschrift

gesättigter Karten-
markt; Kartenmarkt,
der voll entwickelt ist

mature card market – a developed card market
cf.: saturated card market
opp.: developing card market, emerging card market

Höchstbetrag je
Transaktion

maximum amount – the maximum amount a cardholder
can pay or withdraw with the respective card in one transaction

der maximal von
einem Geldaus-
gabeautomaten aus-
gegebene Betrag

maximum ATM withdrawal amount – the maximum
amount which can be dispensed by an ATM
opp.: minimum ATM withdrawal amount
see also: ATM limits

Höchstanzahl von
Transaktionen inner-
halb eines Zeitraums

maximum card uses – the maximum number of times
that the cardholder may use or attempt to use his card in a
given period

maximaler
Ladebetrag

maximum load(ing) value – the maximum amount that
can be loaded into an electronic purse in one transaction

maximal geladener
Betrag

maximum loaded value – the maximum amount that
can be loaded in total into an electronic purse

elektronischer Kauf/
Verkauf von Waren/
Dienstleistungen mit-
tels eines Mobil-
telefons

m-business – the electronic purchase/sale of goods/
services by a mobile phone
cf.: m-commerce
see also: m-payment, mobile payment

Chipkarte, Karte
mit Mikrochip

MC card (microcircuit card) – a card which contains a
microchip
cf.: chip card, IC card (integrated circuit card), integrated
circuit card (IC card), microcircuit card (MC card)
see also: controller card, magnetic stripe card, memory
card, processor card, smart card

numerischer
Branchencode

MCC (merchant category code) – a code assigned to
merchants classifying them by category of business or service
cf.: merchant category code (MCC)
see also: SIC (standard industrial classification), standard
industrial classification (SIC)

elektronischer Kauf/
Verkauf von Waren/
Dienstleistungen mit-
tels eines Mobil-
telefons

m-commerce – the electronic purchase/sale of goods/
services by a mobile phone
cf.: m-business
see also: m-payment, mobile payment

M

ME (member establishment, merchant establishment) – a legal entity with which there is an agreement to accept cards as payment for goods or services when properly presented

Kartenakzeptant, Vertrags- unternehmen

cf.: acceptor, card acceptor, member establishment (ME), merchant, merchant establishment (ME), retailer, SE (service establishment), service establishment (SE)

member – a bank participating via a credit card system as an acquirer and/or issuer

Bank, die Mitglied eines Zahlungssystems ist

member country – the country in which a member is situated

Land, in dem die Mitgliedsbank eines Zahlungssystems domiziliert ist

member country risk – the risk that a member may be prevented from settling due to force majeure (e.g. war, governmental decree)

Länderrisiko

member establishment (ME) – a legal entity with which there is an agreement to accept cards as payment for goods or services when properly presented

Kartenakzeptant, Vertrags- unternehmen

M

cf.: acceptor, card acceptor, ME (member establishment, merchant establishment), merchant, merchant establishment (ME), retailer, SE (service establishment), service establishment (SE)

member failure risk – the risk that a member may be prevented from settling due to lack of financial resources

Risiko, dass ein Mitglied eines Zahlungssystems seinen Verpflichtungen nicht nachkommt

member interface processor (MIP) – a uniform computer which is located at the member's site and linked together with all other MIPs via a worldwide communications network

Computer einer Bank, der an das weltweite Datennetz eines Zahlungssystems angeschlossen ist

cf.: MIP (member interface processor)

member operating regulations – regulations to which the issuer and the acquirer of a credit card organization must adhere to

Abwicklungsricht- linien für jede Bank innerhalb eines Zahlungssystems

cf.: member operating rules

*Abwicklungsricht-
linien für jede Bank
innerhalb eines
Zahlungssystems*

member operating rules – regulations to which the issuer and the acquirer of a credit card organization must adhere to
cf.: member operating regulations

*Risiko, dass ein Mit-
glied eines Zahlungs-
systems seinen
Verpflichtungen nicht
nachkommt*

member risk – the risk that a member of a payment system is unable to settle its obligations
cf.: settlement risk

*Dienstleistungs-
erbringer*

member service provider (MSP) – a third party that provides card and/or merchant services to a member
cf.: MSP (member service provider)

Teilnahmevertrag

membership agreement – a contract between a bank and a payment system concerning membership
see also: licence agreement

*Teilnahmebedingungen,
Mitgliedschaftsregeln*

membership rules – the rules which apply to all members

*Karte
mit Speicherchip*

memory card – a card which contains a microchip to store card information
opp.: controller card, processor card, smart card
see also: chip card, IC card (integrated circuit card), integrated circuit card (IC card), MC card (microcircuit card), microcircuit card (MC card)

Speicherchip

memory chip – a chip with a data memory and pre-programmed logic
cf.: processor chip
see also: memory card

*Kartenakzeptanz,
Vertragsunterneh-
men*

merchant – a legal entity with which there is an agreement to accept cards as payment for goods or services when properly presented
cf.: acceptor, card acceptor, ME (member establishment, merchant establishment), member establishment (ME), merchant establishment (ME), retailer, SE (service establishment), service establishment (SE)

Akzeptanz

merchant acceptance – the process of honouring a presented card by a merchant
see also: acceptance, ATM acceptance

merchant acceptance level – the density of a merchant network depending on the number of available merchants

cf.: merchant coverage

see also: acceptance level, coverage

Akzeptanzdichte

merchant accepting behaviour – the merchant accepting pattern which may be in line or deviate from the usual accepting profile

cf.: merchant accepting pattern

opp.: activity pattern, cardholder spending behaviour, cardholder spending pattern, spending pattern

Akzeptanzverhalten eines Vertrags- unternehmens

merchant accepting pattern – the merchant behaviour which may be in line or deviate from the usual accepting profile

cf.: merchant accepting behaviour

opp.: activity pattern, cardholder spending behaviour, cardholder spending pattern, spending pattern

Akzeptanzverhalten eines Vertrags- unternehmens

M

merchant account maintenance – the updates carried out so as to ensure a correct merchant database

opp.: cardholder account maintenance

Vertragsunter- nehmens-Daten- bestandspflege

merchant acquiring business – all activities concerning the collection of transactions from merchants which are submitted to the interchange system and the payment of the respective amounts to the merchants on the basis of a merchant agreement

cf.: acquiring, acquiring business, merchant business

opp.: card issuance, card issuing business, issuing, issuing business

Geschäft im Zu- sammenhang mit der Vertragsunter- nehmensabrechnung, Vertragsunter- nehmensgeschäft

merchant acquisition – the signing up of new merchants who are willing to accept the respective cards

cf.: merchant signing

Vertragsunterneh- mensgewinnung

merchant activity data – the data that reflects all transaction-related merchant information

opp.: cardholder activity data, merchant primary data

see also: activity data

Vertragsunter- nehmens- Umsatzdaten

*Vertragsunterneh-
mensvereinbarung*

merchant agreement – an agreement between an acquirer and a merchant, by which the merchant accepts the respective cards and will forward the transaction data to the acquirer

*Feststellung der
Echtheit eines Ver-
tragsunternehmens*

merchant authentication – a method to ensure the authenticity of a merchant

opp.: card authentication

*Autorisierung,
Genehmigung*

merchant authorization – an affirmative response of the issuer to the acquirer which is forwarded by the acquirer to the merchant to permit a card transaction

cf.: retail authorization, sales authorization

opp.: cash authorization

see also: authorization

*Transaktion, die bei
einem Netzwerkaus-
falls vom POS-Termi-
nal des Vertragsun-
ternehmens aufgrund
von Parametern auto-
risiert wird*

merchant authorized transaction – a transaction which, as a result of network failure between merchant and acquirer or between acquirer and issuer, is authorized by the merchant's POS terminal on the basis of parameters defined by the acquirer

see also: acquirer authorized transaction, store-and-forward transaction

*Vertragsunternehmens-
bestand, Vertrags-
unternehmensnetz*

merchant base – the entirety of the merchants of a card organization

cf.: acceptance network, merchant network

*Vertragsunter-
nehmens-Umsatz-
überwachung*

merchant behaviour monitoring – the process of regularly checking the merchants' accepting behaviour

opp.: cardholder behavoiur monitoring

*Geschäft im Zusam-
menhang mit der
Vertragsunterneh-
mensabrechnung,
Vertragsunterneh-
mensgeschäft*

merchant business – all activities concerning the collection of transactions from merchants which are submitted to the interchange system and the payments of the respective amounts to the merchants on the basis of a merchant agreement

cf.: acquiring, acquiring business, merchant acquiring business

opp.: card issuance, card issuing business, issuing, issuing business

merchant category – classification of the type of business performed by a merchant

Branchen-klassifikation

see also: MCC (merchant category code), merchant category code (MCC), SIC (standard industrial classification), standard industrial classification (SIC)

merchant category code (MCC) – a code assigned to merchants classifying them by category of business or service

numerischer Branchencode

cf.: MCC (merchant category code)

see also: merchant category, SIC (standard industrial classification), standard industrial classification (SIC)

merchant certificate – the digital assignment of a public key to a merchant which is used for electronic commerce

einem Vertrags-unternehmen zu-geordneter öffent-licher Schlüssel

opp.: card certificate

see also: certificate

merchant collusion – the cooperation / participation of a merchant in a fraud case

Kartenbetrug durch miteingeweihtes / mit-machendes Vertrags-unternehmen

cf.: merchant fraud, fraudulent merchant activity

see also: collusive merchant

M

merchant coverage – the density of a merchant network depending on the number of available merchants

Akzeptanzdichte

cf.: merchant acceptance level

see also: acceptance level, coverage

merchant database – all merchant data stored in a computer file

Vertragsunter-nehmens-Daten-bestand

opp.: cardholder database

merchant decalization – the process of attaching a decal at a merchant outlet

Auszeichnung

cf.: decalization, decalling, merchant decalling

merchant decalling – the process of attaching a decal at a merchant outlet

Auszeichnung

cf.: decalization, decalling, merchant decalization

merchant density – the penetration of merchants in a defined area

Vertragsunter-nehmensdichte

see also: ATM density, ATM penetration, merchant penetration, POS (terminal) density, POS (terminal) penetration

Vertragsunterneh-
mensverzeichnis

merchant directory – a directory containing all merchants that accept a specific card in a given area

cf.: merchant location directory

see also: ATM directory, ATM location directory, directory, travel directory

Strategie einer Bank,
sowohl für Master-
Card als auch für
Visa Vertragsunter-
nehmen abzurechnen

merchant duality – a strategy of a bank to conduct acquiring activities with both MasterCard and Visa

see also: duality

Kartenakzeptant,
Vertrags-
unternehmen

merchant establishment (ME) – a legal entity with which there is an agreement to accept cards as payment for goods or services when properly presented

cf.: acceptor, card acceptor, ME (member establishment, merchant establishment), member establishment (ME), merchant, retailer, SE (service establishment), service establishment (SE)

Vertragsunter-
nehmensdaten

merchant file – the details of a cardholder record stored in a computer

opp.: cardholder file

Vertragsunter-
nehmens-Genehmi-
gungsgrenze

merchant floor limit – the limit above which an authorization must be requested by the merchant from the acquirer

cf.: domestic floor limit, floor limit, local floor limit

see also: international floor limit, intra-European floor limit

Kartenbetrug durch
miteingeweihtes /
mitmachendes Ver-
tragsunternehmen

merchant fraud – a fraud case in which a merchant cooperates / participates

cf.: collusive fraud, fraudulent merchant activity

opp.: card fraud

see also: collusive merchant, merchant collusion

Vertragsunterneh-
mens-Umsatzdaten,
Transaktionen eines
Vertragsunternehmens

merchant history – the entirety of data reflecting all transaction-related merchant information

opp.: cardholder history

see also: merchant acitivity data, merchant history file

Umsatzdatenbestand
der Vertrags-
unternehmen

merchant history file – the file containing all transaction-related data

opp.: cardholder history file

see also: merchant activity data, merchant history

M

merchant income – an acquirer's earnings gained from the merchant business
cf.: merchant revenue

Erträge aus dem Vertragsunternehmensgeschäft

merchant instruction chart – a guideline instructing the merchants how to handle card transactions
see also: merchant operating regulations, merchant operating rules

Folder mit Vertragsunternehmens-Abwicklungsrichtlinien

merchant marketing – all measures aimed at increasing the merchant base, promoting transactions at merchants and preventing merchants from terminating their agreements
opp.: card marketing

Vertragsunternehmensmarketing

merchant network – the entirety of the merchants of a card organization
cf.: acceptance network, merchant base

Vertragsunternehmensbestand, Vertragsunternehmensnetz

merchant operating regulations – the regulations to which the merchants must adhere to
cf.: merchant operating rules
see also: merchant instruction chart

Vertragsunternehmens-Abwicklungsrichtlinien

M

merchant operating rules – the regulations to which the merchants must adhere to
cf.: merchant operating regulations
see also: merchant instruction chart

Vertragsunternehmens-Abwicklungsrichtlinien

merchant outlet – a location where goods or services can be paid for with a card
cf.: acceptance location, acceptance point, outlet

Niederlassung eines Vertragsunternehmens

merchant payment – an acquirer's payment made to a merchant on the basis of card transactions presented by the latter

Vertragsunternehmens-Bezahlung

merchant penetration – the density of merchants in a defined area
see also: ATM density, ATM penetration, merchant density, POS (terminal) density, POS (terminal) penetration

Vertragsunternehmensdichte

merchant pricing – the fixing of the discount rate and/or other charges applied in connection with merchants

Vertragsunternehmens-Preispolitik

opp.: card pricing

see also: commission, commission rate, discount, discount rate, merchant service charge (MSC), MSC (merchant service charge), percentage discount, service charge

Vertragsunternehmens-Stammdaten

merchant primary data – the data that is entered into the computer when the merchant agreement was signed and that is infrequently updated

opp.: cardholder primary cata, merchant activity

see also: primary data

Erträge aus dem Vertragsunternehmensgeschäft

merchant revenue – an acquirer's earnings gained from the merchant business

cf.: merchant income

see also: commission, commission rate, discount, discount rate, merchant service charge (MSC), MSC (merchant service charge), percentage discount, service charge

Belohnung für Karteneinzug

merchant reward – the amount paid to a merchant for picking up a blacklisted card

cf.: card retention reward, pick-up reward

Disagio, Kommission, Umsatzprovision

merchant service charge (MSC) – rate of the transaction amount to be paid by the merchant

cf.: commission, commission rate, discount, discount rate, MSC (merchant service charge), percentage discount, service charge, service fee

Vertragsunternehmensbezahlung

merchant settlement – the acquirer's payment to the merchant for card-based transactions

Vertragsunternehmensgewinnung

merchant signing – the acquisition of new merchants who are willing to accept the respective cards

cf.: merchant acquisition

Zahlungstransaktion

merchant transaction – a) a transaction which will lead to crediting the merchant and to collecting money from the cardholder or issuer, b) a transaction where the value is transferred from an electronic purse to the acceptor's electronic purse terminal

cf.: payment transaction, purchase transaction, retail transaction, sales transaction

opp.: cash advance transaction, credit transaction, load(ing) transaction, refund transaction

message switching – the technique of receiving and sending a message to and from a member, which is routed through a worldwide communication network of a card organization

Nachrichten-übermittlung

micro payment – the term used for designating payments amounting to less than approx. € 5

Kleinstbetragszahlung, Zahlung von einem Betrag etwa unter € 5

microcircuit card (MC card) – a card which contains a microchip

cf.: chip card, IC card (integrated circuit card), integrated circuit card (IC card), MC card (microcircuit card)

see also: controller card, magnetic stripe card, memory card, processor card, smart card

Chipkarte, Karte mit Mikrochip

middle-market card – a card which is positioned by the issuer between a mass card and a premium card

opp.: broad card, gold card, mainstream card, mass card, premier card, premium card, prestige card, privilege card, up-market card, up-scale card

Karte für mittlere Einkommens-schichten

M

MIF (multi-laterally [agreed] interchange fee) – a charge paid by acquirers to issuers in the case that there is no bi-laterally agreed charge for payments

cf.: default interchange fee, fall-back interchange fee, multi-laterally (agreed) interchange fee (MIF)

opp.: bilaterally (agreed) interchange fee

see also: interchange fee

Entgelt, das von der vertragsunternehmens-abrechnenden an die kartenausgebende Bank bei Fehlen einer bilateralen Verein-barung bezahlt wird

minimum ATM withdrawal amount – the minimum amount which is dispensed by an ATM

opp.: maximum ATM withdrawal amount

see also: ATM limits

der kleinste von einem Geldausgabe-automaten ausge-gebene Betrag

minimum payment – the amount which must be paid to ensure the further use of a credit card with extended credit

cf.: monthly minimum payment

Mindestzahlung

minor currency unit – the smaller unit of a currency in a particular country

opp.: major currency unit

kleinere Währungseinheit

Computer einer Bank, der an das weltweite Datennetz eines Zahlungssystems angeschlossen ist

MIP (member interface processor) – a uniform computer which is located at the member's site and linked together with all other MIPs via a worldwide communications network

cf.: member interface processor (MIP)

Kreditkartentransaktion aufgrund einer postalischen oder telefonischen Bestellung

MO / TO transaction (mail order / telephone order transaction) – a transaction effected by mail or by telephone to be paid by a credit card

cf.: mail order / telephone order transaction MO / TO transaction)

see also: mail order transaction, telephone order transaction

Zahlung per Mobiltelefon

mobile payment – the electronic payment for goods / services by a mobile phone

cf.: m-payment

see also: m-business, m-commerce

tragbares, meist kabelloses POS-Terminal

mobile POS terminal – a portable, mostly wireless POS terminal

cf.: handheld POS terminal

opp.: stationary POS terminal

see also: wireless POS terminal

Mondex, die Marke der elektronischen Geldbörse von MasterCard International

Mondex – an international electronic purse brand licensed by MasterCard International

Moneo, eine elektronische Geldbörse in Frankreich

Moneo – brand name of a French electronic purse

Geldwäsche

money laundering – the activity of integrating money coming from criminal activities into the financial system by converting cash into account-based money

Überweisungsauftrag

money order – an order to transfer money from one bank account to another

cf.: payment order

see also: bank transfer, money transfer

Geldtransfer, Überweisung

money transfer – the transfer of money from one bank account to another cf.: bank transfer

see also: money order, payment order

monthly expiry – a system by which cards expire on a monthly basis depending on the month in which they were issued

opp.: monthly issuance

see also: yearly expiry

Kartenablauf auf monatlicher Basis

monthly issuance – a system by which cards are issued on a monthly basis, with the card expiring one (or more) year(s) later at the end of the issuing month

opp.: monthly expiry

see also: yearly issuance

Kartenausgabe mit monatlichem Ab- laufdatum

monthly minimum payment – the amount which has to be paid to ensure the further use of a credit card with ex- tended credit

cf.: minimum payment

Mindestzahlung

monthly statement – the bill sent to the cardholder once a month

monatliche Karten- inhaberabrechnung

M

m-payment – the electronic payment for goods / services by a mobile phone

cf.: mobile payment

see also: m-business, m-commerce

Zahlung per Mobiltelefon

MSC (merchant service charge) – rate of the trans- action amount to be paid by the merchant

cf.: commission, commission rate, discount, discount rate, merchant service charge (MSC), percentage discount, serv- ice charge, service fee

Disagio, Kommission, Umsatzprovision

MSP (member service provider) – a third party that provides card and/or merchant services to a member

cf.: cf.: member service provider (MSP)

Dienstleistungs- erbringer

multi-application card – a card with several functions, not necessarily payment-oriented

Karte mit mehreren Funktionen

Vertragsunterneh-
mensgeschäft mit
mehreren Währungen

multi-currency acquiring – the collection of transactions from merchants in various currencies
opp.: multi-currency issuing

Karteninhaber-
geschäft mit meh-
reren Währungen

multi-currency issuing – the issuance of cards which are billed in various currencies
opp.: multi-currency acquiring

elektronische Geld-
börse mit mehreren
Währungen

multi-currency purse – an electronic purse that can be loaded with more than one currency
opp.: single-currency purse

Verarbeitung von
Transaktionen in
mehreren Währungen

multi-curreny processing – the processing of transactions in various currencies

Mehrfunktionskarte,
Mehrzweckkarte

multi-function card – a card offering more than one function

systemüberschreiten-
de Nutzungsmöglich-
keit zwischen zwei oder
mehr Kartensystemen

multi-lateral interoperability – the possibility of mutual card acceptance between two or more card systems

M

Entgelt, das von der
vertragsunternehmens-
abrechnenden an die
kartenausgebende Bank
bei Fehlen einer bila-
teralen Vereinbarung
bezahlt wird

multi-laterally (agreed) interchange fee (MIF) – a charge paid by acquirers to issuers in the case that there is no bilaterally agreed charge for payments
cf.: default interchange fee, fall-back interchange fee, MIF (multi-laterally [agreed] interchange fee)
opp.: bilaterally (agreed) interchange fee
see also: interchange fee

Markenpolitik, die
auf mehrere Marken
auf einer Karte aus-
gerichtet ist

multiple branding – the marking of a card with more than one brand
opp.: single branding, double branding

universell
einsetzbare
Zahlungskarte

multi-purpose card – a payment card which is issued by (a member of) a card organization for all purposes
cf.: three-party card, universal card
opp.: in-store card, private label card, proprietary card, single-purpose card, two-party card

gegenseitige Echt-
heitserkennung, ge-
genseitige Feststel-
lung der Echtheit

mutual authentication – a process during a transaction of an electronic purse whereby the purse terminal authenticates the purse card and the purse card authenticates the purse terminal

NDR (non-discrimination rule) – a rule under which a merchant agrees to charge the same price to a custromer regardless of the kind of payment the customer offers

cf.: non-discrimination clause, non-discrimination rule (NDR)

Gleichbehand-lungsklausel

negative checking – the checking of the negative file during an authorization request

see also: negative file

Überprüfung des Sperrdaten-bestandes

negative file – a data file containing card numbers which are not to be honoured

cf.: blacklist file, hot card file, stoplist file

see also: blacklist, hot card list, restricted card list, stoplist, warning bulletin

Sperrdatenbestand

negative interchange fee – a charge paid by the issuers to the acquirers which is applied to specific interchange transactions

opp.: interchange fee, positive interchange fee

see also: cash advance accommodation fee, cash advance interchange fee, cash advance service fee

Entgelt, das von der Bank des Karteninhabers an die bargeld-auszahlende Bank bezahlt wird

net acquirer – a member whose interchange out is higher than its interchange in

opp.: net issuer

Bank, bei der der Interchange-Vertrags-unternehmensumsatz größer ist als der Interchange-Karten-inhaberumsatz

net issuer – a member whose interchange in is higher than its interchange out

opp.: net acquirer

Bank, bei der der Interchange-Karten-inhaberumsatz größer ist als der Interchange-Vertrags-unternehmensumsatz

net settlement – a settlement system between two banks where the actual amount either to be paid or to be received is calculated

Verrechnung zwischen zwei Banken

net settlement account – the bank account which contains all the details on payments or receipts and which shows the amount either to be paid or to be received by another bank

Konto einer Bank zur Verrechnung mit einer anderen Bank

Verrechnungs-betrag

net settlement amount – the amount that is actually to be paid or to be received by a bank within the net settlement process

Verrechnungsbank

net settlement bank – a bank which holds the net settlement account

Kommunikations-system eines Zahlungssystems

network – the communication system of a card organization

Ausfall eines Geld-ausgabeautomaten-oder eines POS-Terminalsystems, Ausfall eines Zahlungssystems

network breakdown – the failure of an ATM or POS (terminal) network
cf.: network failure
see also: ATM network breakdown, POS (terminal) network breakdown

Ausfall eines Geld-ausgabeautomaten-oder eines POS-Terminalsystems, Ausfall eines Zahlungssystems

network failure – the failure of an ATM or POS (terminal) network
cf.: network breakdown
see also: ATM network breakdown, POS (terminal) network breakdown

Netzwerkbetreiber

network operator – an entity that operates a network

neu(ro)nales Netzwerksystem

neur(on)al network system – a sophisticated software system by which cardholder and merchant behaviour is monitored so as to detect fraudulent transactions
see also: expert system, parameters system

Karte, die per Post versandt wurde und beim Karteninhaber nie angelangt ist

never received card – a card which was mailed to the cardholder but which was never received
see also: intercepted card

Switching Centre

node – the computer of a card organization routing transactions between acquirers and issuers in the respective network so as to effect interchange
cf.: switch

Karte einer Nichtbank

non-bank card – a card issued by a non-bank

Wechselstube

non-bank encashment office – an authorized agent of a bank to exchange money, to encash cheques and to give cash advances
cf.: bureau de change, change bureau, exchange bureau, exchange office, foreign exchange bureau

non-cash payment – a payment effected without using cash
cf.: cashless payment
opp.: cash payment

bargeldlose Zahlung

non-contact card – a microprocessor card whereby the coupling between the electronic elements in the card and the external interface does not need pyhsical contact
cf.: contactless chip card
opp.: contact-type chip card

kontaktlose Chipkarte

non-discrimination clause – a rule under which a merchant agrees to charge the same price to a custromer regardless of the kind of payment the customer offers
cf.: NDR (non-discrimination rule), non-discrimination rule (NDR)

Gleichbehandlungsklausel

non-discrimination rule (NDR) – a rule under which a merchant agrees to charge the same price to a custromer regardless of the kind of payment the customer offers
cf.: NDR (non-discrimination rule, non-discrimination clause)

Gleichbehandlungsklausel

N

non-embossed card – a card whereby the visible card data in letters and numbers are not elevated by technical means
opp.: embossed card

gelaserte Karte

non-European interchange – (the exchange of) transaction data between Europe and overseas
opp.: intra-European interchange
see also: domestic interchange, interchange, international interchange

(Datenaustausch) grenzüberschreitende(r) Umsätze zwischen Europa und Übersee

non-European interchange fee – a charge paid by acquirers to issuers which is applied to most non-European cross-border transactions
cf.: inter-regional interchange fee
opp.: European interchange fee, intra-European interchange fee
see also: domestic interchange fee, international interchange fee, interchange fee

Entgelt, das von der vertragsunternehmensabrechnenden Bank an die kartenausgebende Bank bei grenzüberschreitenden nicht-europäischen Transaktionen bezahlt wird

Transaktion ohne Vorlage einer Karte

non-face-to-face transaction – a transaction where at the time of the transaction the card is not present
cf.: remote transaction
opp.: face-to-face transaction, walk-in transaction
see also: signature-on-file transaction

nichtgarantierter Scheck

non-guaranteed cheque – a cheque which is not guaranteed
opp.: guaranteed cheque
see also: non-guaranteed payment, non-guaranteed transaction

nichtgarantierte Zahlung

non-guaranteed payment – a transaction where the payment is not guaranteed for the payee
cf.: non-guaranteed transaction
opp.: guaranteed payment
see also: non-guaranteed cheque

nichtgarantierte Zahlung

non-guaranteed transaction – a transaction where the payment is not guaranteed for the payee
cf.: non-guaranteed payment
opp.: guaranteed payment
see also:non-guaranteed cheque

Haustransaktionen; Transaktionen, bei denen die vertrags- unternehmensabrech- nende Bank und die kartenausgebende Bank identisch sind

non-interchange – the transactions where the acquirer of a specific transaction and the issuer of the card generating that transaction are the same entity
see also: interchange, on-us transaction

nicht übereinstim- mende Unterschrift

non-matching signature – a signature not correspon- ding to the specimen signature on a card
opp.: matching signature

nicht mit einer Zahlung zusam- menhängende Funktion auf einer Zahlungskarte

non-payment application – an application connected with a payment card as an add-on
opp.: payment application

non-rechargeable card – a non-reloadable pre-paid card
cf.: disposable card, non-reloadable card
opp.: rechargeable card, reloadable card

*nicht wiederauflad-
bare Wertkarte*

non-reloadable card – a non-reloadable pre-paid card
cf.: disposable card, non-rechargeable cad
opp.: rechargeable card, reloadable card

*nicht wiederauflad-
bare Wertkarte*

non-repudiation of a transaction – the non-permissi-
bility to reject a transaction
see also: repudiation of a transaction

*Unzulässigkeit / Aus-
schluß der Nichtan-
erkennung einer Trans-
aktion, Unzulässigkeit
der Zurückweisung
einer Transaktion*

non-standard account number – a credit card number
which is not 16 digits in length or does not use the Luhn formula to calculate the check digit
cf.: non-standard card account number, non-standard card
number
opp.: standard account number, standard card account number, standard card number
see also: account number, card account number, card number

*nichtstandardisierte
Kartennummer*

N

non-standard card number – a credit card number
which is not 16 digits in length or does not use the Luhn formula to calculate the check digit
cf.: non-standard account number, non-standard card account number
opp.: standard account number, standard card account number, standard card number
see also: account number, card account number, card number

*nichtstandardisierte
Kartennummer*

non-T&E business – (card) business made in the various
retail branches
cf.: retail business
opp.: T&E business
see also: non-T&E merchant

*(Karten)Geschäft
im Einzelhandel*

non-T&E merchant – a merchant in one of the various
retail branches

*Vertragsunternehmen
im Einzelhandel*

cf.: retail merchant

opp.: T&E merchant

see also: non-T&E business

Belastung eines Kreditkarteninhabers, falls eine garantierte Hotelreservierung nicht in Anspruch genommen wird

no-show transaction – a transaction of a hotel where a cardholder is charged with a given amount in the case that he fails to arrive or if the guaranteed reservation is not cancelled in time

Nostrokonto

nostro account – a bank's account held by another bank

Karte, die beim Karteninhaber nicht angekommen ist

not-received card – a card that was not received by the cardholder

gefälschte Karte mit einer Kartennummer, die nicht ausgegeben wurde

not-yet-issued card – a counterfeit(ed) card with a card number that has not been issued yet

see also: not-yet-issued fraud

Betrug mit einer gefälschten Karte mit einer Kartennummer, die nicht ausgegeben wurde

not-yet-issued fraud – fraud committed with a counterfeit(ed) card with a card number that has not been issued yet

see also: not-yet-issued card

numerischer Code

numeric code – a code made up of numeric characters

opp.: alphanumeric code

optisches Schrifterkennungsverfahren, optisches Schriftleseverfahren

OCR (optical character recognition) – a technique of electronic reading and digital conversion of numeric or alphabetic characters from printed documents

cf.: optical character recognition (OCR), optical reading

see also: OCR-A, OCR-B

optisches Schrifterkennungsverfahren OCR-A, optisches Schriftleseverfahren OCR-A

OCR-A – a character set for optical character recognition defined in ISO 1073 part 1

see also: OCR (optical character recognition), OCR-B, optical character recognition (OCR), optical reading

optisches Schrifterkennungsverfahren OCR-B, optisches Schriftleseverfahren OCR-B

OCR-B – a character set for optical character recognition defined in ISO 1073 part 2

see also: OCR (optical character recognition), OCR-A, optical character recognition (OCR), optical reading

offline

off-line – an operating mode in which POS terminals or ATMs are not connected to a central computer for an extended or brief period

opp.: on-line

off-line ATM – an ATM which is not connected to a central computer for an extended or brief period
opp.: on-line ATM

Offline-Geld-ausgabeautomat

off-line authorization – an authorization where there is no access to the issuer's database and the authorization is made, for example, by the acquirer after checking a negative file
opp.: on-line authorization

Offline-Autori-sierung, Offline-Genehmigung

off-line capability – the inability of a terminal or an ATM to go on-line with a central host
opp.: on-line capability

Offline-Eignung

off-line PIN check – a PIN check performed off-line by the terminal
opp.: on-line PIN check

Offline-PIN-Prüfung vor Ort durch Terminal

offline PIN transaction – a transaction whereby the PIN verification is carried out by the ATM or the POS terminal
see also: clear text offline PIN transaction, enciphered offline PIN transaction

Offline-PIN-Transaktion

off-line processing – the data processing carried out in batch mode operations
cf.: batch mode processing
opp.: on-line processing

Offline-Verarbeitung

off-line rate – the percentage rate of transactions performed off-line
opp.: on-line rate

Prozentsatz an Offline-Transaktionen

off-line terminal – a POS terminal which is not connected to a central computer for an extended or brief period
opp.: on-line terminal

Offline-POS-Terminal

off-line transaction – a transaction which is made at a merchant terminal or an ATM where there is no on-line dialogue with the issuer
opp.: on-line transaction

Offline-Transaktion

off-premises ATM – an ATM outside of a bank branch
cf.: off-site ATM, outdoor ATM
opp.: in-bank ATM, in- branch ATM, indoor ATM
see also: drive-through ATM, lobby ATM, through-the-wall ATM

Geldausgabe-automat außerhalb einer Bank(filiale)

Offset-Wert

offset value – a numerical value derived from a specific algorithm that is applied against the card number and encoded on the magnetic stripe of the card
cf.: PIN offset

Geldausgabe-automat außerhalb einer Bank(filiale)

off-site ATM – an ATM outside of a bank branch
cf.: off-premises ATM, outdoor ATM
opp.: in-bank ATM, in- branch ATM, indoor ATM
see also: drive-through ATM, lobby ATM, through-the-wall ATM

Transaktion, wo die kartenausgebende Bank ungleich dervertrags-unternehmensab-rechnenden Bank ist

off-us transaction – a transaction whereby the acquirer and the issuer of the card which is used for payment are different members
opp.: on-us transaction

Kundenkarte eines Mineralölun-ternehmens

oil card – a credit card issued by a oil company which can be used only in the environment of the issuer
cf.: petrol card

Online-Autorisie-rung / Genehmi-gung durch die vertragsunterneh-mensabrechnende Bank

OLA (on-line to acquirer) – an authorization mode by which a POS transaction is forwarded on-line only up to the acquirer where it is authorized off-line, e.g. by checking a negative file
cf.: on-line to acquirer (OLA)
opp.: OLI (on-line to issuer), on-line to issuer (OLI)

Online-Autorisierung / Genehmigung durch die kartenausgebende Bank

OLI (on-line to issuer) – an authorization mode by which a POS transaction is forwarded on-line via the acquirer to the issuer where it is authorized
cf.: on-line to issuer (OLI)
opp.: OLA (on-line to acquirer), on-line to acquirer (OLA)

Autorisierung / Ge-nehmigung durch einen EDV-Dienst-leister

on-behalf authorization – an authorization given by a third party on behalf of the issuer
cf.: stand-in authorization

Erbringung von EDV-Dienstleistungen durch ein Rechenzen-trum / Softwarehaus

on-behalf processing – processing made by a third party on behalf of the issuer or the acquirer

Transaktion an Bord eines Schiffes, Zuges oder Flugzeuges

on-board transaction – a transaction which takes place on board of a ship, a train or an aeroplane

on-line – an operating mode in which terminals or ATMs are connected to a central computer
opp.: off-line

online

on-line ATM – an ATM which is connected to a central computer
opp.: off-line ATM

Online-Geldausgabeautomat

on-line authorization – an authorization where there is access to the issuer's database
opp.: off-line authorization

Online-Autorisierung, Online-Genehmigung

on-line capability – the ability of a terminal to go on-line
opp.: off-line capability

Online-Eignung

on-line PIN check – a PIN check performed on-line by the central host
opp.: off-line PIN check

Online-PIN-Prüfung durch zentralen Computer

on-line processing – the data processing carried out in real-time operations
cf.: real-time processing
opp.: off-line processing

Online-Verarbeitung

on-line rate – the percentage rate of transactions performed on-line
opp.: off-line rate

Prozentsatz an Online-Transaktionen

on-line terminal – a merchant terminal which is permanently connected to a central computer and where all authorizations are generated on-line
opp.: off-line terminal
see also: on-line / off-line terminal, semi on-line terminal

Online-POS-Terminal

on-line to acquirer (OLA) – an authorization mode by which a POS transaction is forwarded on-line only up to the acquirer where it is authorized off-line, e.g. by checking a negative file
cf.: OLA (on-line to acquirer)
opp.: OLI (on-line to issuer), on-line to issuer (OLI)

Online-Autorisierung durch die vertragsunternehmensabrechnende Bank

on-line to issuer (OLI) – an authorization mode by which a POS transaction is forwarded on-line via the acquirer to the issuer where it is authorized

Online-Autorisierung durch die kartenausgebende Bank

cf.: OLI (on-line to issuer)

opp.: OLA (on-line to acquirer), on-line to acquirer (OLA)

Online-Transaktion

on-line transaction – a transaction that is approved or declined at a merchant terminal where there is an on-line dialogue with the issuer

opp.: off-line transaction

POS-Terminal, das Autorisierungen parameterabhängig online einholt oder offline erteilt

on-line / off-line terminal – a merchant terminal which according to predefined conditions either obtains authorizations on-line or authorizes off-line

cf.: semi on-line terminal

Transaktion, wo die kartenausgebende Bank gleich der vertragsunternehmensabrechnenden Bank ist

on-us transaction – a transaction where the member is both the acquirer and the issuer of the card which is used for payment

opp.: off-us transaction

offene elektronische Geldbörse

open (electronic) purse system – an electronic purse that is generally open for cardholders and merchants

opp.: closed (electronic) purse system

see also: IEP (inter-sector electronic purse), inter-sector electronic purse (IEP)

Betrag auf einer elektronischen Geldbörse vor einer Transaktion

opening balance – the balance of an electronic purse before a transaction

opp.: closing balance

Operations-Management

operations management – the management of back-office card and merchant operations

opp.: marketing management

optisches Schrifterkennungsverfahren, optisches Schriftleseverfahren

optical character recognition (OCR) – a technique of electronic reading and digital conversion of numeric or alphabetic characters from printed documents

cf.: OCR (optical character recognition), optical reading

see also: OCR-A, OCR-B

optische Speicherkarte

optical memory card – a card on which information is stored using optical recording techniques

cf.: laser card

optical reading – a technique of electronic reading and digital conversion of numeric or alphabetic characters from printed documents

cf.: OCR (optical character recognition), optical character recognition (OCR)

see also: OCR-A, OCR-B

optisches Schrifter-kennungsverfahren, optisches Schrift-leseverfahren

original card – a card which was actually issued

cf.: genuine card

opp.: counterfeit(ed) card, duplicated card, fake(d) card, false card, forge card

see also: genuine cardholder

echte Karte, Originalkarte

OTC cash advance (over-the-counter cash advance) – a cash advance at the bank's teller

cf.: manual cash advance, over-the-counter cash advance (OTC cash advance)

Bargeldauszahlung am Kassenschalter einer Bank(filiale)

outbound data – the transaction data sent from the acquirer to the clearing system

cf.: outbound file, outbound traffic, outbound transactions, outgoing data, outgoing file, outgoing traffic, outgoing transactions

opp.: inbound data, inbound file, inbound traffic, inbound transactions, incoming data, incoming file, incoming traffic, incoming transactions

von der vertrags-unternehmensab-rechnenden Bank an das Clearing-system übermittelte Umsätze

outbound file – the transaction data sent from the acquirer to the clearing system

cf.: outbound data, outbound traffic, outbound transactions, outgoing data, outgoing file, outgoing traffic, outgoing transactions

opp.: inbound data, inbound file, inbound traffic, inbound transactions, incoming data, incoming file, incoming traffic, incoming transactions

von der vertrags-unternehmensab-rechnenden Bank an das Clearing-system übermittelte Umsätze

outbound traffic – the transaction data sent from the acquirer to the clearing system

cf.: outbound data, outbound file, outbound transactions, outgoing data, outgoing file, outgoing traffic, outgoing transactions

von der vertrags-unternehmensabrech-nenden Bank an das Clearingsystem über-mittelte Umsätze opp.: inbound data, inbound file, inbound traffic, inbound transactions, incoming data, incoming file, incoming traffic, incoming transactions

von der vertrags-unternehmensab-rechnenden Bank an das Clearing-system übermittelte Umsätze

outbound transactions – the transaction data sent from the acquirer to the clearing system

cf.: outbound data, outbound file, outbound traffic, outgoing data, outgoing file, outgoing traffic, outgoing transactions

opp.: inbound data, inbound file, inbound traffic, inbound transactions, incoming data, incoming file, incoming traffic, incoming transactions

Übertragung von Um-sätzen der vertrags-unternehmensabrech-nenden Bank an das Clearingsystem

outbound transmission – the process of transmitting the outbound data by the acquirer to the clearing system

cf.: outgoing transmission

opp.: inbound transmission, incoming transmission

POS-Terminal außer-halb der Geschäfts-räumlichkeiten des Vertragsunternehmens

outdoor POS terminal – a POS terminal situated outside of a merchant's premises

von der vertrags-unternehmensab-rechnenden Bank an das Clearing-system übermittelte Umsätze

outgoing data – the transaction data sent from the acquirer to the clearing system

cf.: outbound data, outbound file, outbound traffic, outbound transactions outgoing file, outgoing traffic, outgoing transactions

opp.: inbound data, inbound file, inbound traffic, inbound transactions,incoming data, incoming file, incoming traffic, incoming transactions

von der vertrags-unternehmensab-rechnenden Bank an das Clearing-system übermittelte Umsätze

outgoing file – the transaction data sent from the acquirer to the clearing system

cf.: outbound data, outbound file, outbound traffic,

outbound transactions, outgoing data, outgoing traffic, out-going transactions

opp.: inbound data, inbound file, inbound traffic, inbound transactions, incoming data, incoming file, incoming traffic, incoming transactions

outgoing traffic – the transaction data sent from the acquirer to the clearing system

cf.: outbound data, outbound file, outbound traffic, outbound transactions, outgoing data, outgoing file, outgoing transactions

opp.: inbound data, inbound file, inbound traffic, inbound transactions, incoming data, incoming file, incoming traffic, incoming transactions

von der vertragsunternehmensabrechnenden Bank an das Clearingsystem übermittelte Umsätze

outgoing transactions – the transaction data sent from the acquirer to the clearing system

cf.: outbound data, outbound file, outbound traffic, outbound transactions, outgoing data, outgoing file, outgoing traffic

opp.: inbound data, inbound file, inbound traffic, inbound transactions, incoming data, incoming file, incoming traffic, incoming transactions

von der vertragsunternehmensabrechnenden Bank an das Clearingsystem übermittelte Umsätze

outgoing transmission – the process of transmitting the outbound data by the acquirer to the clearing system

cf.: outbound transmission

opp.: inbound transmission, incoming transmission

Übertragung von Umsätzen der vertragsunternehmensabrechnenden Bank an das Clearingsystem

outlet – a location where goods or services can be paid for with a card

cf.: acceptance location, acceptance point, merchant outlet

Niederlassung eines Vertragsunternehmens

outstandings – sums that have not yet been paid

cf.: receivables

Außenstände, kreditierte Beträge

overdraft – the amount that is actually withdrawn in excess of the funds on a current account

see also: overdraft facility; overdraw, to

Überziehung

overdraft facility – the line granted for an overdraft

see also: overdraft; overdraw, to

Überziehungskredit, Überziehungsmöglichkeit, Überziehungsrahmen

overdraw, to – to withdraw money in excess of the available funds

see also: overdraft, overdraft facility

überziehen

Kartenkonto mit unbezahlten Rechnungen	**overdue cardholder account** – a cardholder account which is not covered in time
Überziehungsentgelt	**overlimit charge** – the fee levied on an overdraft cf.: overlimit fee
Überziehungsentgelt	**overlimit fee** – the charge levied on an overdraft cf.: overlimit charge
Bargeldauszahlung am Kassenschalter einer Bank(filiale)	**over-the-counter cash advance (OTC cash advance)** – a cash advance at the bank's teller cf.: manual cash advance, OTC cash advance (over-the-counter cash advance)
Zahlung einer Person an eine andere Person mittels Karte	**P2P payment (person-to-person payment)** – a payment effected from person to person through a card cf.: person-to-person payment (P2P payment) opp.: business-to-business payment (B2B payment), B2B payment (business-to-business payment)
Datex-Netz	**packet switching network** – a communications system where data packets are transmitted through special high speed lines
Kartennummer	**PAN (primary account number)** – a unique series of digits on the card created by the issuer to identify the issuer and the cardholder cf.: account number, card account number, card number, primary account number (PAN) see also: non-standard account number, non-standard card account number, non-standard card number, standard account number, standard card account number, standard card number
manuelle Kartennummerneingabe	**PAN key entry** – the process whereby the card number is keyed in instead of being read from magnetic stripe or chip
Länge einer Kartennummer	**PAN length** – the number of digits of a card number (for credit cards e.g. 16 digits)
Beleg	**paper draft** – a piece of paper which is used to document a card transaction cf.: paper slip

paper record – the data pertaining to a transaction transmitted on a paper

opp.: electronic record

see also: record

beleggebundener Transaktionsdatensatz

paper slip – a piece of paper which is used to document a card transaction

cf.: paper draft

Beleg

paper-based transaction – a transaction carried out by using paper drafts (e.g. sales slips, cash advance slips, cheques)

opp.: electronic transaction

see also: imprinter transaction

beleggebundene Transaktion

parameter – a factor or limit which affects the way that something can or should be done or made

Parameter

parameters system – a software system based on parameters, by which cardholder and merchant behaviour is monitored to detect fraudulent transactions

see also: expert system, neural network system

Parametersystem

parking card – a card issued for parking purposes

Parkkarte

parking garages application – an off-line POS solution catering to the special needs of parking garages with generally low maximum transaction amounts

see also: quick payment service (QPS), QPS (quick payment service), rapid payment service (RPS), RPS (rapid payment system)

offline POS-Lösung für Parkgaragen

P

parking meters application – an off-line POS solution where parking meters charges can be paid by card

see also: quick payment service (QPS), QPS (quick payment service), rapid payment service (RPS), RPS (rapid payment system)

offline POS-Lösung für Parkscheinautomaten

password – cardholder verification method in the e-commerce

Passwort

pay before product – a payment product where the purchase value is bought in advance for effecting a cashless payment at a later date

Zahlungsmittel, bei dem der Kaufkraftwert im vorhinein bezahlt wird

opp.: pay later product, pay now product

see also: electronic purse, pre-paid card, pre-payment card, stored value card, traveller's cheque

Zahlungsmittel, das zu einer nachträglichen Verrechnung führt

pay later product – a payment product which can be used for cashless payments and cash advances, with the statement being presented at a later date

opp.: pay before product, pay now product

see also: charge card, credit card, deferred debit card, delayed debit card

Zahlungsmittel, bei dem unverzüglich vom Girokonto abgebucht wird

pay now product – a payment product which can be used for cashless payments and cash advances, with the cardholder's current account being debited without delay at the earliest possible time

opp.: pay before product, pay later product

see also: current account linked card, debit card, immediate payment card

zahlen

pay, to – to give money in cash or cash-like substitutes

cf.: make payments, to

kartenausgebende Bank, Kartenemittent

paying bank – a bank which issues cards, receives the cardholder transactions from the members / merchants, guarantees the payment and collects the respective amounts from the cardholders

cf.: card issuer, card issuing bank, cardholder bank, issuer, issuer bank, issuing bank, issuing institution, issuing member

see also: acquirer, acquirer bank, acquiring bank, acquiring institution, acquiring member, beneficiary bank

Zahlung

payment – an act of paying money in cash or cash-like substitutes

Zahlungsfunktion

payment application – an application connected with a payment card to realize a payment

opp.: non-payment application

Zahlungsempfänger

payment beneficiary – the recipient of a payment

opp.: payment originator

payment card – a card which can be used for paying goods and services without extended credit

cf.: transaction card

see also: electronic purse, charge card, credit card, current account linked card, deferred debit card, delayed debit card, immediate payment card, pre-paid card, pre-payment card, stored value card

Zahlungskarte

payment gateway – an interface where an electronic transaction is converted by the acquirer into a standard card transaction

see also: MasterCard SecureCode, Verified by Visa

Server für E-Commerce-Zahlungen

payment guarantee – the guarantee given for a payment

Zahlungsgarantie

payment infrastructure – a system consisting of hardware and software which forms the basis of a payment scheme

Zahlungsinfrastruktur

payment instrument – a card, cheque or another means used to make a payment or withdraw cash

Zahlungsmittel

payment method – a method employed for effecting a payment

see also: payment option

Zahlungsform

payment option – a possibility offered to effect a payment

see also: payment method

Zahlungsmöglichkeit

payment order – an order to transfer money from one bank account to another

cf.: money order

see also: bank transfer, money transfer

Überweisungsauftrag

payment originator – the person initiating a payment for the benefit of another

opp.: payment beneficiary

Zahlungsauftraggeber

payment page – the page in a website where the payment data are entered

cf.: check-out page

Zahlungsseite bei einem Internet-Shop

P

Zahlungsrisiko	**payment risk** – the risk that the payer does not meet his / her payment obligations
Zahlungs-risikomanagement	**payment risk management** – the handling of payment risks so as to minimize losses
Zahlungssystem	**payment scheme** – a system for processing payment instruments, clearing the transactions and settling the debts among the parties involved cf.: payment system
Zahlungssystem	**payment system** – a scheme for processing payment instruments, clearing the transactions and settling the debts among the parties involved cf.: payment scheme
Unversehrtheit eines Zahlungssystems	**payment system integrity** – the ability of a system to remain uncorrupted despite attempted tampering
Zahlungs-transaktion	**payment transaction** – a) a transaction which will lead to crediting the merchant and to collecting money from the cardholder or issuer b) a transaction where the value is transferred from an electronic purse to the acceptor's electronic purse terminal cf.: merchant transaction, purchase transaction, retail transaction, sales transaction opp.: cash advance transaction, credit transaction, load(ing) transaction, refund transaction
bargeldlose Zah-lungsmöglichkeit in Telefonzellen	**payphone application** – a payment solution where payphone charges can be paid by card see also: quick payment service (QPS), QPS (quick payment service), rapid payment service (RPS), RPS (rapid payment system)
Transaktion mit PIN	**PBT (PIN-based transaction)** – a transaction verified by the use of a cardholder's PIN cf.: PIN-based transacition (PBT) opp.: SBT (signature-based transaction), signature-based transaction (SBT)

PCG (purchase completion guarantee) – a guarantee which allows that a purchase transaction can be completed by a reserve amount when the balance of an electronic purse is insufficient

cf.: purchase completion guarantee (PCG)

see also: PCG limit (purchase completion guarantee limit), purchase completion guarantee limit (PCG limit)

Zahlungsgarantie für eine elektronische Geldbörsentransaktion bei nicht ausreichender Ladung

PCG limit (purchase completion guarantee limit) – a determined amount for an electronic purse which allows a payment to be completed when the balance in an electronic purse is insufficient

cf.: purchase completion guarantee limit (PCG limit)

see also: PCG (purchase completion guarantee), purchase completion guarantee (PCG)

Überziehungsbetrag bei einer elektronischen Geldbörse

percentage discount – rate of the transaction amount to be paid by the merchant

cf.: commission, commission rate, discount, discount rate, merchant service charge (MSC), MSC (merchant service charge), service charge, service fee

Disagio, Kommission, Umsatzprovision

percentage fee – a fee based on for a percentage of the amount of the transaction

cf.: ad valorem fee

opp.: flat fee

Prozententgelt; wertabhängiges Entgelt

performance standard – a defined operational or business target which should be achieved

Zielerreichungsmaßstab

permanent stand-in processing system – a back-up issuer processing facility for authorizations when the primary processing system is not available

cf.: alternate, alternate processing system, back-up processing system, down-option processing system, dynamic stand-in processing system, stand-in processing system

see also: IHS (issuer host system), issuer host, issuer host system (IHS), primary, primary processing system

Ersatzgenehmigungssystem bei Systemausfall

permanent stand-in authorization – an authorization performed by a pre-determined alternate processing system used whenever the issuer is unable to respond

Genehmigung bei einem Systemausfall durch ein Ersatzsystem

cf.: alternate authorization, back-up authorization, down-option authorization, dynamic stand-in authorization, fall-back authorization, stand-in authorization

opp.: primary authorization

von der karten-ausgebenden Bank festgelegte Limits für das Ersatz-system

permanent stand-in limits – the authorization parameters set by the issuer for the alternate processing system in case the primary processing system is unable to respond

cf.: alternate limits, alternate parameters, back-up limits, back-up parameters, down-option limits, down-option parameters, dynamic stand-in limits, dynamic stand-in parameters, fall-back limits, fall-back parameters, permanent stand-in parameters, stand-in limits, stand-in parameters

von der karten-ausgebenden Bank festgelegte Limits für das Ersatz-system

permanent stand-in parameters – the authorization parameters set by the issuer for the alternate processing system in case the primary processing system is unable to respond

cf.: alternate limits, alternate parameters, back-up limits, back-up parameters, down-option limits, down-option parameters, dynamic stand-in limits, dynamic stand-in parameters, fall-back limits, fall-back parameters, permanent stand-in limits, stand-in limits, stand-in parameters

Genehmigungs-verfahren durch ein Ersatzsystem bei einem System-ausfall

permanent stand-in processing – the performance of authorizations by a pre-determined alternate processing system which is used whenever the issuer is unable to respond

cf.: alternate processing, back-up processing, down-option processing, dynamic stand-in processing, stand-in processing

opp.: primary processing

Transaktion, die bei einem System-ausfall von einem Ersatzgenehmi-gungssystem auto-risiert wird

permanent stand-in transaction – a transaction which is authorized by an alternate processing system

cf.: alternate transaction, back-up transaction, down-option transaction, dynamic stand-in transaction, stand-in transaction

opp.: primary transaction

see also: alternate processing system

persönlicher Code, persönliche Geheim-zahl, pesönliche Identi-fizierungsnummer

personal identification number (PIN) – a four to six digit secret number that authenticates the cardholder as the legitimate user of a card

cf.: PIN (personal identification number)

personalization – the provision of a card with personalized data

Versehen einer Karte mit personenbezogenen Daten

personalize a card, to – to provide a card with personalized data

eine Karte mit personenbezogenen Daten versehen

person-to-person payment (P2P payment) – a payment effected from person to person through a card
cf.: P2P payment (person-to-person payment)
opp.: business-to-business payment (B2B payment), B2B payment (business-to-business payment)

Zahlung einer Person an eine andere Person mittels Karte

petrol card – a credit card issued by a petrol company which can be used only in the environment of the issuer
cf.: oil card

Kundenkarte eines Mineralölunternehmens

phone card – a card which can be used for telephone purposes only
cf.: calling card, telephone card

Telefonkarte

photo card – a card which is provided with the cardholder's photograph on the card

Fotokarte, Karte mit Foto des Karteninhabers

physical card – a card which is corporeal
opp.: virtual card

physische Karte, tatsächlich körperlich vorhandene Karte

physical marketplace – a marketplace where products / services are physically available
opp.: electronic marketplace, virtual marketplace

physischer Markt

physical transmission – the dispatch of cash-like substitutes so as to forward payment data non-electronically
opp.: electronic transmission

beleggebundene Datenübermittlung

physically secure device – a device in which the PIN and data in clear text are physically protected against disclosure and modification
cf.: security module

Sicherheitsmodul

pick-up a card, to – to retrieve a misused or counterfeit card
cf.: confiscate a card, to; recover a card, to; retain a card, to

eine Karte einziehen

P

gesperrte Karte	**pick-up card** – a card that has been put on a blacklist cf.: blacklisted card, hot card
Prämie für Karten-einzug	**pick-up reward** – a bonus granted for withdrawing a card from circulation cf.: card retention reward, merchant reward
persönlicher Code, persönliche Geheim-zahl, persönliche Identifizierungs-nummer	**PIN (personal identification number)** – a four to six digit secret number that authenticates the cardholder as the legitimate user of a card cf.: personal identification number (PIN)
PIN-Zuteilung	**PIN allocation** – the assignment of a PIN
PIN-Eingabeversuch	**PIN attempt** – the attempted entry of a PIN
PIN-Überprüfung	**PIN checking** – a procedure in the authorization process-ing which enables the issuer to verify the PIN which was keyed in by the cardholder cf.: PIN validation, PIN verification
freie PIN-Wahl	**PIN choice** – the possibility of a cardholder to freely choose his/her own PIN cf.: PIN selection
PIN-Ausspähung	**PIN compromise** – the unlawful spying of the PIN of a card see also: PIN interception
verschlüsselte PIN-Daten	**PIN data** – the encrypted PIN as sent to the issuer host computer for verification
PIN-Schlüssel	**PIN encryption key** – a key used to encrypt and decrypt PINs
PIN-Eingabe	**PIN entry** – the input of the PIN
fehlerhafte PIN-Eingabe	**PIN error** – an erroneous entry of a PIN
PIN-Erstellung	**PIN generation** – the generation of PINs by the issuer for allocation to cardholders
PIN-Unversehrtheit	**PIN integrity** – a state whereby a PIN is only known to the genuine cardholder
PIN-Ausspähung	**PIN interception** – the unauthorized retrieval of a PIN see also: PIN compromise

PIN issuance – a procedure which enables the issuer to produce a PIN for the cardholder   *PIN-Ausgabe*

PIN length – the number of digits of a PIN   *PIN-Länge*

PIN mailer – a mailing containing a PIN   *PIN-Kuvert*

PIN offset – a numerical value derived from a specific algorithm that is applied against the card number and encoded on the magnetic stripe of the card
cf.: offset value   *Offset-Wert*

PIN pad – a device that enables the cardholder to enter a PIN at a terminal   *PIN-Eingabeeinheit, PIN-Eingabetastatur*

PIN production key (PPK) – a data encryption key used in the production of the PVV
cf.: PPK (PIN production key)   *PIN-Erstellungsschlüssel*

PIN selection – the possibility of a cardholder to freely choose his / her own PIN
cf.: PIN choice   *PIN-Auswahl*

PIN try counter – a security measure that is used to limit the number of (wrong) PIN attempts   *Zähler der PIN-Eingabeversuche*

PIN usage – the procedure by which a PIN is keyed in on a PIN pad for paying goods and services or for obtaining cash   *PIN-Einsatz*

P

PIN validation – a procedure in the authorization processing which enables the issuer to verify the PIN which was keyed in by the cardholder
cf.: PIN checking, PIN verification   *PIN-Überprüfung*

PIN verification – a procedure in the authorization processing which enables the issuer to validate the PIN which was keyed in by the cardholder
cf.: PIN checking, PIN validation   *PIN-Überprüfung*

PIN verification key (PVK) – a key used to verify a PIN code, with the calculation being based on a specific number and an algorithm
cf.: PVK (PIN verification key)   *PIN-Überprüfungsschlüssel*

PIN- *Überprüfungswert*	**PIN verification value (PVV)** – a value which is a function of the cardholder PIN and other card data and is used in the verification process of the cardholder's PIN; if this value is encoded on the card the PIN can be validated on the issuer's behalf cf.: PVV (PIN verification value)
Transaktion *mit PIN*	**PIN-based transaction (PBT)** – a transaction verified by the use of a cardholder's PIN cf.: PBT (PIN-based transaction) opp.: SBT (signature-based transaction), signature-based transaction (SBT)
noch nicht bei der kartenausgebenden Bank eingelangte Transaktion eines Karteninhabers	**pipeline transaction** – a transaction which was successfully performed by the cardholder and has not yet been received and settled by the issuer
Plastikkarte	**plastic card** – a card made of plastic
Plastikgeld	**plastic money** – all cashless means of payment in form of plastic cards
Plastikkartenhersteller	**plastics manufacturer** – the producer of plastic cards
Plus	**Plus** – a licensed ATM card system with the licences being granted by Plus International opp.: Cirrus see also: Plus card, Plus International
Plus-Karte	**Plus card** – an ATM card issued by a licensee of Plus which can be used at all ATMs connected to the Plus network cf.: Cirrus card see also: Plus, Plus International
Plus International	**Plus International** – an international ATM card organization which is the licensor for Plus cards and owned by Visa International cf.: Cirrus International see also: Plus, Plus card

POC (point of compromise) – the location where card data are obtained with the intention to commit fraudulent acts at a later time

cf.: point of compromise (POC)

Ort, von wo ein Kartenbetrug seinen Ausgang nahm

POI (point of interaction) – the place at which a payment transaction is (can be) originated

cf.: point of interaction (POI), point of sale (POS), point of service (POS), POS (point of sale, point of service)

Ort, wo eine Zahlungstransaktion generiert wird

point of compromise (POC) – the location where card data are obtained with the intention to commit fraudulent acts at a later time

cf.: POC (point of compromise)

Ort, von wo ein Kartenbetrug seinen Ausgang nahm

point of interaction (POI) – the place at which a payment transaction is (can be) originated

cf.: POI (point of interaction), point of sale (POS), point of service (POS), POS (point of sale, point of service)

Ort, wo eine Zahlungstransaktion generiert wird

point of sale (POS) – the place at which a payment transaction is (can be) originated

cf.: POI (point of interaction), point of interaction (POI), point of service POS), POS (point of sale, point of service)

Ort, wo eine Zahlungstransaktion generiert wird

point of service (POS) – the place at which a payment transaction is (can be) originated

cf.: POI (point of interaction), point of interaction (POI), point of sale (POS), POS (point of sale, point of service)

Ort, wo eine Zahlungstransaktion generiert wird

P

pool account – an account where the issuer of an electronic purse scheme holds the float

cf.: float account, funds pool account, purse pool account, underlying account

Float-Konto, Pool-Konto eines elektronischen Geldbörsensystems

POS (network) breakdown – the failure of a POS (terminal) network

see also: network breakdown, ATM network breakdown

Ausfall eines POS-Terminalsystems

POS (point of sale, point of service) – the place at which a payment transaction is (can be) originated

cf.: POI (point of interaction), point of interaction (POI), point of sale (POS), point of service (POS)

Ort, wo eine Zahlungstransaktion generiert wird

POS-Terminaldichte	**POS (terminal) density** – the penetration of POS terminals in a defined area cf.: POS (terminal) penetration see also: ATM density, ATM penetration, merchant density, merchant penetration, POS (terminal) penetration
POS-Terminal-Netz	**POS (terminal) network** – the entirety of the POS terminals within a payment system
POS-Terminaldichte	**POS (terminal) penetration** – the density of POS terminals in a defined area cf.: POS (terminal) density see also: ATM density, ATM penetration, merchant density, merchant penetration, POS (terminal) density
POS-Terminal-Spezifikationen	**POS (terminal) specifications** – the data outlining the details of a POS terminal see also: chip specifications, magnetic stripe specifications
POS-Karte	**POS card** – a card which can be used for payment at a POS terminal in a merchant location
Auszeichnung eines Vertragsunternehmens	**POS signage** – the decalization of a POS see also: ATM signage, signage
POS-System	**POS system** – a set-up consisting of a host computer, a network of transmission lines and POS terminals to enable cashless payments
POS-Technologie	**POS technology** – the technology applied in a POS system
Kassenterminal mit Zahlungsfunktion, POS-Terminal	**POS terminal** – an electronic device that accepts financial data at a point of sale and transmits the data to a computer centre for authorization, clearing and settlement cf.: EFTPOS terminal see also: integrated POS terminal
Bestand bestehender nicht gesperrter Kartennummern	**positive file** – a data file containing card numbers which are to be honoured
Entgelt, das von der vertragsunternehmens-abrechnenden Bank an die kartenausge-bende Bank gezahlt wird; Interchange Fee, Interbankenentgelt	**positive interchange fee** – a charge paid by acquirers to issuers which is applied to most interchange transactions cf.: interchange fee opp.: negative interchange fee

P

postal interception – the unauthorized retrieval of a card which is sent to the genuine cardholder by mail
cf.: postal theft

unrechtmäßiges Abfangen einer Karte auf dem Postweg

postal theft – the unauthorized retrieval of a card which is sent to the genuine cardholder by mail
cf.: postal interception

unrechtmäßiges Abfangen einer Karte auf dem Postweg

post-block fraud – the losses that are incurred after the fraud has been determined and the card has been put on the stoplist
cf.: post-status fraud
pre-block fraud, pre-status fraud
see also: post-block fraudulent transactions, post-status fraudulent transactions

Verluste, die nach Erkennen eines Betrugs anfallen

post-block fraudulent transactions – fraudulent transactions that are made after the fraud has been determined and the card has been put on the stoplist
cf.: post-status fraudulent transactions
opp.: pre-block fraudulent transactions, pre-status fraudulent transactions
see also: post-block fraud, post-status fraud

Transaktionen, die nach Erkennen eines Betrugs anfallen

post-status fraud – the losses that are incurred after the fraud has been determined and the card has been put on the stoplist
cf.: post-block fraud
opp.: pre-block fraud, pre-status fraud
see also: post-block fraudulent transactions, post-status fraudulent transactions

Verluste, die nach Erkennen eines Betrugs anfallen

post-status fraudulent transactions – fraudulent transactions that are made after the fraud has been determined and the card has been put on the stoplist
cf.: post-block fraudulent transactions
opp.: pre-block fraudulent transactions, pre-status fraudulent transactions
see also: post-block fraud, post-status fraud

Transaktionen, die nach Erkennen eines Betrugs anfallen

PIN-Erstellungs-schlüssel

PPK (PIN production key) – a data encryption key used in the production of the PVV
cf.: PIN production key (PPK)

vorautorisierte Karte

pre-approved card – a card that has been approved by the issuer prior to application

Vorausgenehmigung

pre-authorization – an authorization code given to the acquirer or to the respective merchant in advance

Vollzugsmeldung über eine Voraus-genehmigung

pre-authorization completion – a notification of the acquirer to inform the issuer of the final outcome of a previously approved pre-authorization

Möglichkeit, eine Zah-lungskarte bis zu einem vorautorisierten Betrag Offline-Transaktionen zu generieren

pre-authorized debit – a facility of a payment card which allows offline transactions up to the value of a pre-authorized amount

Dauerauftrag, Verrech-nungsermächtigung, Einzugsermächtigung, Zahlungsauftrag für wie-derkehrende Zahlungen

pre-authorized order – a cardholder's written permission to make one or more charges to his card account at a future date
see also: recurring payment, recurring transaction, standing order

Verluste, die vor dem Erkennen eines Betrugs an-fallen

pre-block fraud – the losses that are incurred before the fraud has been determined and the card has been put on the stoplist
cf.: pre-status fraud
opp.: post-block fraud, post-status fraud
see also: pre-block fraudulent transactions, pre-status fraudulent transactions

Transaktionen, die vor dem Erkennen eines Betrugs an-fallen

pre-block fraudulent transactions – fraudulent transactions that are made before the fraud has been determined and the card has been put on the stoplist
cf.: pre-status fraudulent transactions
opp.: post-block fraudulent transactions, post-status fraudulent transactions
see also: pre-block fraud, pret-status fraud

Karte mit hohem Ausgaberahmen

preferred card – a card which is issued (often as a gold card) to persons of a higher income bracket and which is provided with a high spending limit and additional features
cf.: gold card, premier card, premium card, prestige card, privilege card, up-market card, up-scale card
opp.: broad card, mainstream card, mass card

preferred file – a data file containing top card numbers which are given peferential treatment, particularly concerning higher spending limits

Datenbestand der Top-Karten-inhaber

prefix – a part of a credit card number which identifies the issuer

die ersten Stellen einer Kreditkartennummer

premier card – a card which is issued (often as a gold card) to persons of a higher income bracket and which is provided with a high spending limit and additional features

cf.: gold card, preferred card, premium card, prestige card, privilege card, up-market card, up-scale card

opp.: broad card, mainstream card, mass card

Karte mit hohem Ausgaberahmen

premium card – a card which is issued (often as a gold card) to persons of a higher income bracket and which is provided with a high spending limit and additional features

cf.: gold card, preferred card, premier card, prestige card, privilege card, up-market card, up-scale card

opp.: broad card, mainstream card, mass card

Karte mit hohem Ausgaberahmen

pre-paid card – a card which is purchased with a given value or where the purchase value is bought for a given card in advance to be used for obtaining goods or services at a later time

see also: electronic purse, pay before product, pre-payment card, stored value card, traveller's cheque

Wertkarte

P

pre-payment – payment effected in advance to obtain goods or services at a later date

cf.: advance payment

Vorauszahlung

pre-payment card – a card which is purchased with a given value or where the purchase value is bought for a given card in advance to be used for obtaining goods or services at a later time

see also: electronic purse, pay before product, pre-paid card, stored value card, traveller's cheque

Wertkarte

present a card, to – to offer a card for payment

see also: present a cheque, to

eine Karte vorlegen

einen Scheck vorlegen

present a cheque, to – to offer a cheque for payment
see also: present a card, to

Vorlage von Transaktionsdaten zur Bezahlung

presentment – a paper or electronic transaction data submitted from an acquirer to an issuer in order to collect the respective amounts

Vorlagefrist

presentment period – the timeframe in which a transaction should be presented to the issuer

Kreditlimit, Zahlungslimit, Verfügungsrahmen

pre-set limit – the amount of money a cardholder may obtain or spend with his / her card
cf.: credit limit, pre-set spending limit, spending limit

Kreditlimit, Zahlungslimit, Verfügungsrahmen

pre-set spending limit – the amount on money a cardholder may obtain or spend with his / her card
cf.: credit limit, pre-set limit, spending limit

Verluste, die vor dem Erkennen eines Betrugs anfallen

pre-status fraud – the losses that are incurred before the fraud has been determined and the card has been put on the stoplist
cf.: pre-block fraud
opp.: post-block fraud, post-status fraud
see also: pre-block fraudulent transactions, pre-status fraudulent transactions

Transaktionen, die vor dem Erkennen eines Betrugs anfallen

pre-status fraudulent transactions – fraudulent transactions that are made before the fraud has been determined and the card has been put on the stoplist
cf.: pre-block fraudulent transactions
opp.: post-block fraudulent transactions, post-status fraudulent transactions
see also: pre-block fraud, pret-status fraud

Karte mit hohem Ausgaberahmen

prestige card – a card which is issued (often as a gold card) to persons of a higher income bracket and which is provided with a high spending limit and additional features
cf.: gold card, preferred card, premier card, premium card, privilege card, up-market card, up-scale card
opp.: broad card, mainstream card, mass card

primary – the processing system, designated by the issuer as the preferred system to provide authorizations

cf.: IHS (issuer host system), issuer host, issuer host system (IHS), primary processing system

opp.: acquirer host, acquirer host system (AHS), AHS (acquirer host system)

see also: alternate, alternate processing system, back-up processing system, down-option processing system, dynamic stand-in processing system

Autorisierungs-computer der kartenausgebenden Bank

primary account number (PAN) – a unique series of digits on the card created by the issuer to identify the issuer and the cardholder

cf.: account number, card account number, card number, PAN (primary account number)

see also: non-standard account number, non-standard card account number, non-standard card number, standard account number, standard card account number, standard card number

Kartennummer

primary authorization – an authorization performed by the issuer through the primary processing system

opp.: alternate authorization, back-up authorization, down option authorization, dynamic stand-in authorization, permanent stand-in authorization, stand-in authorization

Genehmigung durch das Computersystem der kartenausgebenden Bank

P

primary card – a card which is issued to the primary cardholder and which is the basis for the issuance of additional / secondary cards to family or company members

opp.: additional card, secondary card

see also: extra card

Hauptkarte

primary cardholder – the cardholder who has the primary card when more than one card is issued to a family or a company member

opp.: additional cardholder, secondary cardholder

Hauptkarten-inhaber

primary data – the data which is entered into the computer when the card application is received and/or the merchant agreement is signed, and which is infrequently updated

opp.: activity data

see also: cardholder primary data, merchant primary data

Stammdaten

*Genehmigungsver-
fahren durch das
Computersystem
der kartenausge-
benden Bank*

primary processing – the performance of an authorization by the issuer through the primary processing system

opp.: alternate processing, back-up processing, down option processing, dynamic stand-in processing, permanent stand-in processing, stand-in processing

*Autorisierungs-
computer der
kartenausgebenden
Bank*

primary processing system – the processing system designated by the issuer as the preferred system to provide authorizations

cf.: IHS (issuer host system), issuer host, issuer host system (IHS), primary

opp.: acquirer host, acquirer host system (AHS), AHS (acquirer host system)

see also: alternate, alternate processing system, back-up processing system, down-option processing system, dynamic stand-in processing system, permanent stand-in processing system, stand-in processing system

*Ort des Computer-
systems der
kartenausgebenden
Bank*

primary site – the place where the primary processing system is located

opp.: alternate site

see also: primary processing system

P

*Transaktion durch
das Genehmi-
gungssystem der
kartenausgebenden
Bank*

primary transaction – a transaction which is authorized by the primary processing system

opp.: alternate transaction, back-up transaction, dynamic stand-in transaction, down option transaction, dynamic stand-in transaction, permanent stand-in transaction, stand-in transaction

see also: primary processing system

*Bank, die direkt
Mitglied eines Zah-
lungssystems ist;
Haupt-Lizenznehmer*

principal – a bank operating directly in the card business

cf.: principal licensee, principal member

opp.: affiliate, affiliate licensee, affiliate member

Haupt-Lizenz

principal licence – a licence which allows a bank to participate directly in the card activities of a payment system, e.g. to issue cards and to sign up merchants

opp.: affiliate licence, sublicence

principal licensee – a bank operating directly in the card business

cf.: principal, principal member

opp.: affiliate, affiliate licensee, affiliate member

Bank, die direkt Mitglied eines Zahlungssystems ist; Haupt-Lizenznehmer

principal member – a bank operating directly in the card business

cf.: principal, principal licensee

opp.: affiliate, affiliate licensee, affiliate member

Bank, die direkt Mitglied eines Zahlungssystems ist; Haupt-Lizenznehmer

privacy – the fact that no information which might permit the determination of transactions may be collected without the consent of the counterparties involved

Geheimhaltungspflicht, Schutz der Persönlichkeitssphäre, Sicherstellung der Vertraulichkeit

private card – a card which is issued to private persons

opp.: business card, company card, corporate card

Privatkarte

private key – this key is one of a pair, is used in asymmetric cryptographic algorithms and needs to be kept secret; the other key of the pair is the public key

opp.: public key

privater Schlüssel, geheimer Schlüssel

private label card – a plastic card issued by a merchant which can be used only in the issuer's environment

cf.: in-store card, proprietary card, two-party card

Kundenkarte

P

private line – a communications system where data are transmitted between two endpoints which are permanently connected

cf.: dedicated line, leased line

Standleitung

privilege card – a card which is issued (often as a gold card) to persons of a higher income bracket and which is provided with a high spending limit and additional features

cf.: gold card, preferred card, premier card, premium card, prestige card, up-market card, up-scale card

opp.: broad card, mainstream card, mass card

Karte mit hohem Ausgaberahmen

process, to – to perform a series of actions which are carried out in order to achieve a particular result

abwickeln, verarbeiten

processing – the provision of computer services

Erbringung von EDV-Dienstleistungen

Rechenzentrum

processing centre – a computer facility for processing all kinds of card transactions

Verfahrensablauf zwischen vertragsunternehmens-abrechnender und kartenausgebender Bank

processing cycle – the sequence of steps in the interchange process from presentment to arbitration

Verarbeitungstag

processing date – the day on which the data on the slip is captured or received via electronic means

EDV-Dienstleistungsunternehmen

processor – a computer service provider
see also: acquirer processor, issuer processor

Karte mit Prozessorchip, Prozessorkarte

processor card – a card which contains a processor microchip
cf.: controller card, smart card
opp.: memory card
see also: chip card, IC card (integrated circuit card), integrated circuit card (IC card), MC card (microcircuit card), microcircuit card (MC card)

Prozessorchip

processor chip – a freely programmable chip with memory and calculation capabilities
opp.: memory chip
see also: controller card, processor card, smart card

Karte für kommerzielle Einkäufe

procurement card – a card designated to be used for commercial purposes
cf.: business-to-business card, purchasing card

Produktlizenz

product licence – a licence given to a member granting the right to use a particular product

Produktregeln

product rules – the rules that apply to a particular product

PROM, Speicherart auf einem Chip

PROM (programmable ROM) – a chip where data is stored by using a programmable read-only memory
see also: EEPROM (electrical erasable programmable ROM), EPROM (erasable programmable ROM), RAM (random access memory), ROM (read-only memory)

Kundenkarte

proprietary card – a plastic card issued by a merchant which can be used only in the issuer's environment
cf.: in-store card, private label card, two-party card

protocol – procedures for the interchange of electronic messages between communication devices

Protokoll

Proton – brand name of the Belgian electronic purse

Proton, die elektronische Geldbörse in Belgien

proximity payment – a contactless payment with a chip (card) whereby there is a distance of up to 0.1 metres between card and reader

berührungslose Zahlung

see also: contactless purse, vicinity payment

PSAM (purse security application module) – the security module installed in an electronic purse terminal

PSAM, Sicherheitsmodul eines elektronischen Geldbörsenterminals

cf.: purse security application module (PSAM)

public key – this key is one of a pair, is used in asymmetric cryptographic algorithms and does not need to be kept secret (public key); the other key of the pair is the (secret) private key

öffentlicher Schlüssel

opp.: private key

public key cryptography – a set of cryptographic techniques in which two different keys - the private and the public key - are used for encrypting and decrypting data

asymmetrische Verschlüsselung, Verschlüsselung mit öffentlichem und privatem Schlüssel

cf.: asymmetric cryptography

opp.: symmetric cryptography

see also: cryptography, private key, public key

P

purchase completion guarantee (PCG) – a guarantee which allows that a purchase transaction can be completed by a reserve amount when the balance of an electronic purse is insufficient

Zahlungsgarantie für eine elektronische Geldbörsentransaktion bei nicht ausreichender Ladung

cf.: PCG (purchase completion guarantee)

see also: PCG limit (purchase completion guarantee limit), purchase completion guarantee limit (PCG limit)

purchase completion guarantee limit (PCG limit) – a determined amount for an electronic purse which allows a payment to be completed when the balance in an electronic purse is insufficient

Überziehungsbetrag bei einer elektronischen Geldbörse

cf.: PCG limit (purchase completion guarantee limit)

see also: PCG (purchase completion guarantee), purchase completion guarantee (PCG)

Zahlungs-transaktion

purchase transaction – a) a transaction which will lead to crediting the merchant and to collecting money from the cardholder or issuer; b) a transaction where the value is transferred from an electronic purse to the acceptor's electronic purse terminal

cf.: merchant transaction, payment transaction, retail transaction, sales transaction

opp.: cash advance transaction, credit transaction, load(ing) transaction, refund transaction

Karte für kommerzielle Einkäufe

purchasing card – a card designated to be used for commercial purposes

cf.: business-to-business card, procurement card

Löschdatum

purge date – the date after which a stoplisted card will disappear from the stoplist

der auf der elektronischen Geldbörse jeweils verfügbare Betrag

purse balance – the current available amount on an electronic purse

Float-Konto, Pool-Konto eines elektronischen Geldbörsensystems

purse pool account – an account where the issuer of an electronic purse scheme holds the float

cf.: float account, funds pool account, pool account, underlying account

PSAM, Sicherheitsmodul eines elektronischen Geldbörsenterminals

purse security application module (PSAM) – the security module installed in an electronic purse terminal

cf.: PSAM (purse security application module)

elektronisches Geldbörsenterminal

purse terminal – a terminal that accepts electronic purses for payment

elektronische Geldbörsentransaktion

purse transaction – a transaction with an electronic purse

see also: load(ing) transaction, merchant transaction, payment transaction, purchase transaction, retail transaction, sales transaction, unload(ing) transaction

Übertragung eines Betrages von einer elektronischen Geldbörse auf eine andere

purse-to-purse transfer – the switch of value from an electronic purse to another one

PIN-Überprüfungsschlüssel

PVK (PIN verification key) – a key used to verify a PIN code with the calculation being based on a specific number and an algorithm

cf.: PIN verification key (PVK)

PVV (PIN verification value) – a value which is a function of the cardholder PIN and other card data and is used in the verification process of the cardholder's PIN; if this value is encoded on the card the PIN can be validated on the issuer's behalf

cf.: PIN verification value (PVV)

PIN-Überprüfungswert

QPS (quick payment service) – an offline-POS solution catering to the special needs of merchants with generally low maximum transaction amounts

cf.: quick payment service (QPS), rapid payment service (RPS), RPS (rapid payment service)

see also: fast food application, mass transit application, parking garages application, parking meters application, payphone application, toll ways application, vending machines application

offline POS-Lösung für Vertragsunternehmen mit niedrigen Transaktionsbeträgen

quasi-cash transaction – a transaction whereby a money substitute such as tokens are purchased

Transaktion, bei der Geldsubstitute (z. B. Jetons) erworben werden

Quick – brand name of the Austrian electronic purse

Quick, die elektronische Geldbörse in Österreich

quick payment service (QPS) – an offline-POS solution catering to the special needs of merchants with generally low maximum transaction amounts

cf.: QPS (quick payment service), rapid payment service (RPS), RPS (rapid payment service)

see also: fast food application, mass transit application, parking garages application, parking meters application, payphone application, toll ways application, vending machines application

offline POS-Lösung für Vertragsunternehmen mit niedrigen Transaktionsbeträgen

P
Q
R

radio beacon – a fixed radio transmitting station at toll ways that detects the transponder tags presence when crossing the gates and provides a dedicated short-range communication link with the on-bordboard unit of the vehicles

auf einem Portal oberhalb der Fahrbahn installierte Datenübertragungsstation

RAM (random access memory) – a chip where data is stored by using random access memory

see also: EEPROM (electrical erasable programmable ROM), EPROM (erasable programmable ROM), PROM (programmable ROM), ROM (read-only memory)

RAM, Speicherart auf einem Chip

offline POS-Lösung
für Vertragsunter-
nehmen mit niedri-
gen Transaktions-
beträgen

rapid payment service (RPS) – an off-line POS solution catering to the special needs of merchants with generally low maximum transaction amounts

see also: fast food application, mass transit application, parking garages application, parking meters application, payphone application, toll ways application, vending machines application

Online-
Verarbeitung

real-time processing – the data processing carried out in on-line operations

cf.: on-line processing

off-line processing

Rabattsystem

rebate scheme – a scheme offering a discount to customers depending on certain parameters

Quittung

receipt – a piece of paper documenting a performed transaction

see also: ATM receipt, terminal receipt

Außenstände,
kreditierte Beträge

receivables – sums that have not yet been paid

cf.: outstandings

wiederaufladbare
Wertkarte

rechargeable card – a reloadable pre-paid card

cf.: reloadable card

opp.: non-rechargeable card, non-reloadable card

einvernehmliche
Lösung

reconciliation – an agreement between an acquirer and an issuer on financial totals

see also: reconciliation process

Vorgangsweise, um
zu einer einvernehm-
lichen Lösung zu
kommen

reconciliation process – a process between an acquirer and an issuer to reach agreement on financial totals

see also: reconciliation

Transaktions-
datensatz

record – information pertaining to a transaction, whereby the data may be a paper record or an electronic record

see also: electronic record, paper record

eine Karte
einziehen

recover a card, to – to retrieve a misused or counterfeit card

cf.: confiscate a card, to; pick-up a card, to; retain a card, to

R

recovered card – a card that has been retrieved
cf.: confiscated card, retained card

eingezogene Karte

recurring payment – a payment based on a cardholder's
written permission to make one or more charges to his card
account at a future date
cf.: recurring transaction
see also: pre-authorized order, standing order

*durchgeführte Zahlung
aufgrund eines Dau-
erauftrags / einer Ver-
rechnungsermächti-
gung / einer Einzugs-
ermächtigung, wie-
derkehrende Zahlung*

recurring transaction – a transaction based on a cardholder's written permission to make one or more charges to
his card account at a future date
cf.: recurring payment
see also: pre-authorized order, standing order

*durchgeführte Zahlung
aufgrund eines Dau-
erauftrags / einer Ver-
rechnungsermächti-
gung / einer Einzugs-
ermächtigung, wie-
derkehrende Zahlung*

referral – a telephone call made by the merchant to the acquirer to obtain an authorization, which follows a request
given by the automated authorization system
cf.: referral call
see also: call me transaction

*telefonische Geneh-
migungsanfrage nach
Aufforderung durch
ein elektronisches
Genehmigungssystem*

referral call – a telephone call made by the merchant to
the acquirer to obtain an authorization, which follows a request given by the automated authorization system
cf.: referral
see also: call me transaction

*telefonische Geneh-
migungsanfrage nach
Aufforderung durch
ein elektronisches
Genehmigungssystem*

refund an electronic purse, to – to reload an electronic
purse with a specific amount
cf.: reload an electronic purse, to

*eine elektronische
Geldbörse
(wieder)aufladen*

refund transaction – a transaction which reverses the
full or partial amount of a previous transaction
cf.: credit transaction
opp.: cash advance transaction, merchant transaction, payment transaction, purchase transaction, retail transaction,
sales transaction

Gutschrift

refusal of a card application – the rejection of a card
application
opp.: approval of a card application

*Kartenantrags-
ablehnung*

Ablehnung einer Autorisierungsanfrage / Genehmigungsanfrage

refusal of an authorization request – the rejection of an authorization request by the issuer to the acquirer which is forwarded by the acquirer to the merchant or cash advance location
opp.: approval of an authorization request, authorization

einen Kartenantrag ablehnen

refuse a card application, to – to reject a card application
opp.: approve a card application, to

Ablehnung einer Autorisierungsanfrage / Genehmigungsanfrage

refuse an authorization request, to – to reject an authorization request by the issuer
cf.: decline an authorization request, to; deny an authorization request, to
opp.: approve an authorization request, to; authorize, to

Rückerstattung, Rückvergütung

reimbursement – the repayment to someone as a result of wrong actions

eine Karte erneuern

reissue a card, to – to renew a card that has expired

Prägehöhe

relief height – the height of embossed characters from the surface of the card

eine elektronische Geldbörse (wieder)aufladen

reload an electronic purse, to – to refund an electronic purse with a specific amount
cf.: refund an electronic purse, to

wiederaufladbare Wertkarte

reloadable card – a reloadable pre-paid card
cf.: rechargeable card
opp.: non-rechargeable card, non-reloadable card

R

Mahnspesen

reminder charge – a fee which has to be paid by the cardholder if a reminder has to be made as a consequence of unpaid amounts

Transaktion ohne körperliche Vorlage einer Karte

remote payment – a payment which is effected when debtor and payee are not at the same place
see also: remote transaction

Zahlung, die erfolgt, ohne dass sich der Zahlungspflichtige und der Zahlungsempfänger am selben Ort befinden

remote transaction – a transaction where at the time of transcation the card is not present
cf.: non-face-to-face transaction
opp.: face-to-face transaction, walk-in transaction
see also: signature-on-file transaction

renewal process – the measures required for the renewal of the cards whose expiry is imminent

*Kartenerneuerungs-
vorgang*

renewals – the cards which are renewed prior to their expiration

Erneuerungskarten

representment – a transaction presented by an acquirer to an issuer to reverse a chargeback

Wiedervorlage

repudiation of a transaction – the denial of a transaction by the cardholder
see also: non-repudiation of a transaction

*Zurückweisung
einer Transaktion,
Nichtanerkennung
einer Transaktion*

reputational risk – a risk which could damage the image of a payment scheme and its brand(s)

Imagerisiko

response time – a time that a system needs to answer a specific request

Antwortzeit

restricted card list – a printout containing card numbers which are not be honoured
cf.: blacklist, hot card list, stoplist, warning, warning bulletin, warning notice bulletin
see also: blacklist file, hot card file, negative file, stoplist file

Sperrliste

retail authorization – an affirmative response of the issuer to the acquirer which is forwarded by the acquirer to the merchant to permit a card transaction
cf.: merchant authorization, sales authorization
opp.: cash authorization
see also: authorization

*Autorisierung,
Genehmigung*

R

retail business – (card) business made in the various retail branches
cf.: non T&E business
opp.: T&E business

*(Karten)Geschäft
im Einzelhandel*

retail card – credit card issued by a retailer which can be used only in the issuer's environment

*Kundenkarte eines
Einzelhandelsunter-
nehmens*

retail cheque – a cheque used for payment of goods or services
opp.: cash cheque
see also: cheque

*Scheck, mit dem Waren
oder Dienstleistun-
gen bezahlt werden*

Zahlungslimit bei
Handels- und
Dienstleistungs-
unternehmen

retail limit – the maximum amount that can be spent on goods / services by the cardholder in a given period
cf.: sales limit
opp.: cash advance limit
see also: domestic retail limit, international retail limit

Vertrags-
unternehmen im
Einzelhandel

retail merchant – a merchant in one of the various retail branches
cf.: non-T&E-merchant
opp.: T&E merchant

Zahlungs-
transaktion

retail transaction – a) a transaction which will lead to crediting the merchant and to collecting money from the cardholder or issuer; b) a transaction where the value is transferred from an electronic purse to the acceptor's electronic purse terminal
cf.: merchant transaction, payment transaction, purchase transaction, sales transaction
opp.: cash advance transaction, credit transaction, load(ing) transaction, refund transaction

Kartenakzeptant,
Vertrags-
unternehmen

retailer – a legal entity with which there is an agreement to accept cards as a means of payment for goods or services when properly presented
cf.: acceptor, card acceptor, ME (member establishment, merchant establishment), member establishment (ME), merchant, merchant establishment (ME), SE (service establishment), service establishment (SE)

R

eine Karte
einziehen

retain a card, to – to retrieve a misused or counterfeit card
cf.: confiscate a card, to; pick-up a card, to; recover a card, to

eingezogene Karte

retained card – a card that has been retrieved
cf.: confiscated card, recovered card

Aufbewahrungszeit

retention period – the minimum time the acquiring member must retain either original slips or microfilms

Behalterate,
Behaltequote

retention rate – the percentage of cards that are not cancelled with respect to the total number of cards

retina scanning – a biometric technique to verify the cardholder authentication
see also: biometric techniques, biometrics

Netzhautprüfung

retrieval message – a message of an issuer to an acquirer reporting the retrieval of a card

Karteneinzugs-benachrichtigung

retrieval request – the request of an issuer to an acquirer for either an original slip or a legible reproduction of the same

Beleganforderung

retrieval request fulfilment – the satisfaction of an retrieval request made by an acquirer by sending either an original slip or a legible reproduction of the same

Belegübersendung

retrieval system – a (computer-aided) procedure to process retrieval requests

(EDV-unterstützte) Arbeitsabläufe für die Erledigung von Beleganforderungen

return a cheque, to – to send back a cheque which was not honoured

einen Scheck zu-rückgehen lassen

reversal – a transaction from the acquirer to the issuer to neutralize a previously initiated transaction
cf.: reversal transaction, reversal transfer
see also: reversal credit, reversal debit

Storno, Storno-transaktion

reversal credit – a credit arising from a reversal of a previous debit
opp.: reversal debit
see also: reversal, reversal transaction, reversal transfer

Gutschrift infolge Stornos einer vorhergehenden Belastung

reversal debit – a debit arising from a reversal of a previous credit
opp.: reversal credit
see also: reversal, reversal transaction, reversal transfer

Belastung infolge Stornos einer vorhergehenden Belastung

R

reversal transaction – a transaction from the acquirer to the issuer to neutralize a previously initiated transaction
cf.: reversal, reversal transfer
see also: reversal credit, reversal debit

Storno, Storno-transaktion

reversal transfer – a transaction from the acquirer to the issuer to neutralize a previously initiated transaction
cf.: reversal, reversal transaction
see also: reversal credit, reversal debit

Storno, Storno-transaktion

Kartenrückseite

reverse side – the rear side of a card
cf.: card reverse
opp.: card face, card front, front side

Widerrufbarkeit

revocability – the ability to revoke a transaction
opp.: irrevocability

einen Scheck widerrufen

revoke a cheque, to – to cancel a cheque

Kreditrahmen, Überziehungsrahmen

revolving credit – a credit line which is given to the card-holder and which can be exploited up to the limit
see also: revolving credit card

Kreditrahmen, Überziehungs-rahmen

revolving credit card – a credit card with a credit line which is granted to the cardholder and which can be exploited up to the limit
see also: revolving credit

rechtmäßiger Karteninhaber

rightful cardholder – the cardholder to whom the card was legally issued
cf.: genuine cardholder, legitimate cardholder, rightful cardholder, true cardholder

Risikomanagement

risk management – the process to control all the risks associated with payment or cash advance transactions

rollierende Kartenausgabe

R

rolling issuance – a system by which cards are issued on a regular basis, usually in monthly intervals, with the card expiring one (or more) year(s) later at the end of the issuing month
cf.: monthly issuance
opp.: yearly issuance

ROM, Speicherart auf einem Chip

ROM (read-only memory) – a chip where data is stored by using a read-only memory
see also: EEPROM (electrical erasable programmable ROM), EPROM (erasable programmable ROM), PROM (programmable ROM), RAM (random access memory)

Leitwegesystem für Kartentransaktionen, Routing für Karten-transaktionen

routing system – the system according to which card transactions are sent from acquirers to issuers (and vice versa)

RPS (rapid payment service) – an off-line POS solution catering to the special needs of merchants with generally low maximum transaction amounts

cf.: QPS (quick payment service), quick payment service (QPS), rapid payment service (RPS)

see also: fast food application, mass transit application, parking garages application, parking meters application, payphone application, toll ways application, vending machines application

offline POS-Lösung für Vertragsunternehmen mit niedrigen Transaktionsbeträgen

RSA algorithm – a standardized asymmetric public key cryptosystem which leads to secure card authentication named after the first letters of the inventors Rivest, Shamir and Adleman

see also: DES (Data Encryption Standard) algorithm, Data Encryption Standard (DES) algorithm

Datenverschlüsselungsnorm, RSA

rule violation – the breach of a rule

Regelverstoß

sales authorization – an affirmative response of the issuer to the acquirer which is forwarded by the acquirer to the merchant to permit a card transaction

cf.: merchant authorization, retail authorization

opp.: cash authorization

see also: authorization

Autorisierung, Genehmigung

sales draft – paper used to document the payment by card

cf.: charge draft, sales receipt, sales slip, sales voucher

opp.: cash advance draft, cash advance slip, cash draft, cash slip

see also: transaction information document

Leistungsbeleg, Verkaufsbeleg, Zahlungsbeleg, Kartenzahlungsbeleg

sales limit – the maximum amount that can be spent on goods / services by the cardholder in a given period

cf.: retail limit

opp.: cash advance limit

see also: domestic sales limit, international sales limit

Zahlungslimit bei Handels- und Dienstleistungsunternehmen

sales receipt – paper used to document the payment by card

cf.: charge draft, sales draft, sales slip, sales voucher

opp.: cash advance draft, cash advance slip, cash draft, cash slip

see also: transaction information document

Leistungsbeleg, Verkaufsbeleg, Zahlungsbeleg, Kartenzahlungsbeleg

R
S

Leistungsbeleg,
Verkaufsbeleg,
Zahlungsbeleg,
Kartenzahlungs-
beleg

sales slip – paper used to document the payment by card
cf.: charge draft, sales draft, sales receipt, sales voucher
opp.: cash advance draft, cash advance slip, cash draft, cash slip
see also: transaction information document

Zahlungs-
transaktion

sales transaction – a) a transaction which will lead to crediting the merchant and to collecting money from the cardholder or issuer; b) a transaction where the value is transferred from an electronic purse to the acceptor's electronic purse terminal
cf.: merchant transaction, payment transaction, purchase transaction, retail transaction
opp.: cash advance transaction, credit transaction, load(ing) transaction, refund transaction

Leistungsbeleg,
Verkaufsbeleg,
Zahlungsbeleg,
Kartenzahlungs-
beleg

sales voucher – paper used to document the payment by card
cf.: charge draft, sales draft, sales receipt, sales slip
opp.: cash advance draft, cash advance slip, cash draft, cash slip
see also: transaction information document

Kartenmarkt, der voll
entwickelt ist; satu-
rierter Kartenmarkt

saturated card market – a developed card market
cf.: mature card market
opp.: developing card market, emerging card market,

Sparkonto

savings account – a bank account for savings purposes
cf.: deposit account

Transaktion mit
Unterschrift

SBT (signature-based transaction) – a transaction verified by the cardholder's signature
cf.: signature-based transaction (SBT)
opp.: PBT (PIN-based transaktion), PIN-based transaction (PBT)

Regeln eines
(Zahlungs)Systems

scheme governance – the bylaws, rules and regulations governing a (payment) scheme

Kartenakzeptant,
Vertrags-
unternehmen

SE (service establishment) – a legal entity with which there is an agreement to accept cards as a means of payment for goods or services when properly presented cf.: acceptor, card acceptor, ME (member establishment, merchant establishment), member establishment (ME), merchant, merchant establishment (ME), retailer, service establishment (SE)

secondary card – a card issued either to a member of the primary cardholder's family or a staff member of a company to whom a primary card has been issued
cf.: additional card
opp.: primary card
see also: extra card

Zusatzkarte

secondary cardholder – the cardholder who has the secondary card when more than one card is issued to a family or a company member
cf.: additional cardholder
opp.: primary cardholder

Zusatzkarteninhaber

Secure Electronic Transaction (SET) – a former credit card payment method in electronic commerce realized on a certificate-based security architecture
cf.: SET (Secure Electronic Transaction)

SET

Secure Socket Layer (SSL) – a standard for secure connections in the Internet / in the virtual world

Standard für sichere Datenübertragungen im Internet / in der virtuellen Welt, SSL

security alert – a notification given to the acquiring members concerning a fraud case

Betrugswarnung

security features – a variety of measures implemented in a card for security reasons

Sicherheitsmerkmale

security module – a device in which the PIN and data in clear text are physically protected against disclosure and modification
cf.: physically secure device

Sicherheitsmodul

self-selected PIN – a PIN not automatically produced by the card issuer but selected by the cardholder himself
see also: PIN choice, PIN selection

selbstgewählter persönlicher Code, selbstgewählte persönliche Geheimzahl, selbstgewählte persönliche Identifizierungsnummer

S

Selbstbedienungs-terminal

self-service terminal – a terminal operated by the card-holder

POS-Terminal, das entweder parameterabhängig Autorisierungen online einholt oder sie offline bearbeitet

semi on-line terminal – a merchant terminal which according to predefined conditions either obtains authorizations on-line or authorizes off-line
cf.: on-line / off-line terminal

(angestrebte) einheitliche Zahlungsverkehrsregion der 25 Länder der EU und von Island, Liechtenstein und Norwegen

SEPA (Single Euro[pean] Payment Area) – the area made up of the 25 member states of the EU plus Iceland, Liechtenstein and Norway
cf.: Single Euro[pean] Payment Area (SEPA)

Betreuungsbesuch

service call – a regular visit at a merchant by a representative of the acquirer

Disagio, Kommission, Umsatzprovision

service charge – rate of the transaction amount to be paid by the merchant
cf.: commission, commission rate, discount, discount rate, merchant service charge (MSC), MSC (merchant service charge), percentage discount, service fee

Service-Code

service code – a code on the magnetic stripe of a card which defines the range of services available to the card
cf.: SET (Secure Electronic Transaction)

Kartenakzeptant, Vertrags-unternehmen

service establishment (SE) – a legal entity with which there is an agreement to accept cards as a means of payment for goods or services when properly presented
cf.: acceptor, card acceptor, ME (member establishment, merchant establishment), member establishment (ME), merchant, merchant establishment (ME), retailer, SE (service establishment)

Disagio, Kommission, Umsatzprovision

service fee – rate of the transaction amount to be paid by the merchant
cf.: commission, commission rate, discount, discount rate, merchant service charge (MSC), MSC (merchant service charge), percentage discount, service charge

SET

SET (Secure Electronic Transaction) – a former credit card payment method in electronic commerce realized on a certificate-based security architecture
cf.: Secure Electronic Transaction (SET)

S

settlement – actual receipt or payment of amounts to a member resulting from the clearing

Abrechnung, Verrechnung

settlement account – a member's account at the settlement bank where as a result of the clearing the settlement takes place

Abrechnungskonto, Verrechnungskonto

settlement agent – a bank that maintains the member's settlement account
cf.: settlement bank, settlement institution

Abrechnungsbank, Verrechnungsbank

settlement amount – the amount which is payable to / receivable from the member's settlement account

Abrechnungsbetrag, Verrechnungsbetrag

settlement bank – a bank that maintains the member's settlement account
cf.: settlement agent, settlement institution

Abrechnungsbank, Verrechnungsbank

settlement currency – the currency of the member's settlement account

Abrechnungswährung, Verrechnungswährung

settlement fee – a fee which is paid to the settlement bank for settling amounts as a result of the clearing

Abrechnungsentgelt, Verrechnungsentgelt

settlement institution – a bank that maintains the member's settlement account
cf.: settlement agent, settlement bank

Abrechnungsbank, Verrechungsbank

settlement period – the number of days from the transaction date of a slip to the settlement date of the slip

Abrechnungszeitraum, Verrechnungszeitraum

settlement processing – the processing based on the clearing which results in the amounts a member has to pay or to receive
see also: settlement system

Abrechnungsverfahren, Verrechnungsverfahren

S

settlement risk – the risk that a member of a payment system is unable to settle its obligations
cf.: member risk

Risiko, dass ein Mitglied eines Zahlungssystems seinen Verpflichtungen nicht nachkommt

settlement system – a system provided for settling amounts from the clearing payable to / receivable from the member
see also: settlement processing

Abrechnungssystem, Verrechnungssystem

Einzelhaftung, getrennte Haftung

several liability – the single liability of an individual party

opp.: joint liability

Schattenkonto; Konto, das den Guthabensstand einer elektronischen Geldbörse beim Emittenten zeigt

shadow account – the account which shows the regularly updated balance of an electronic purse

see also: accountability, shadow accounting, shadow balance

Verfahren des Emittenten von elektronischen Geldbörsen zu deren Abstimmung, Schattenkontoführung

shadow accounting – the process of an issuer drawing up shadow balances of electronic purses after having received the respective transactions

see also: accountability, shadow accounting, shadow balance

Guthabensstand einer elektronischen Geldbörse bei deren Emittenten

shadow balance – the balance of an electronic purse account following the offset procedure of shadow accounting

see also: accountability, shadow account, shadow accounting

gemeinsam genutzter Geldausgabeautomat

shared ATM – an ATM which can be used by customers of different banks

see also: shared ATM network, shared ATM system

gemeinsam genutztes Geldausgabeautomatennetz

shared ATM network – an ATM system whereby the associated ATMs can be used by customers of different banks

see also: shared ATM, shared ATM system

gemeinsam genutztes Geldausgabeautomatensystem

shared ATM system – an ATM network whereby the associated ATMs can be used by customers of different banks

see also: shared ATM, shared ATM network

visuelle PIN-Ausspähung

shoulder surfing – a technique for visually spying out the PIN of a cardholder

numerische Branchenkategorisierung nach internationaler Norm

SIC (standard industrial classification) – merchant classification according to types of merchants

cf.: standard industrial classification (SIC)

see also: MCC (merchant category code), merchant category code (MCC)

sight deposit account – an account used for handling payment transactions
cf.: checking account, current account, demand deposit account, giro account

Girokonto

sign up a merchant, to – to win a new merchant who is willing to accept the respective credit cards

ein Vetragsunternehmen gewinnen

signage – the decalization of an ATM or a POS
see also: ATM signage, POS signage

Auszeichnung (eines Vertragsunternehmens oder eines Geldausgabeautomaten)

signature check – the comparison between the cardholder's signature on the card and on the sales or cash slip
cf.: signature verification

Unterschriftsprüfung

signature panel – the field provided on the card for the cardholder's signature
cf.: signature stripe

Unterschriftsfeld

signature stripe – the field provided on the card for the cardholder's signature
cf.: signature panel

Unterschriftsfeld

signature verification – the comparison between the cardholder's signature on the card and on the sales or cash slip
cf.: signature check

Unterschriftsprüfung

signature-based transaction (SBT) – a transaction verified by the cardholder's signature

Transaktion mit Unterschrift

signature-on-file transaction – a remote payment transaction which takes place by submitting card data and signature on a separate form
see also: non-face-to-face transaction, remote transaction

Zahlung, die durch separate Übermittlung von Kartendaten und Unterschrift erfolgt

single acquirer – an acquirer for either MasterCard or Visa transactions
opp.: dual acquirer

vertragsunternehmensabrechnende Bank, die entweder MasterCard- oder Visa-Transaktionen abrechnet

single branding – the marking of a card with one brand
opp.: multiple branding
see also: double branding

Markenpolitk, die auf eine Marke auf einer Karte ausgerichtet ist

S

Marketing einer kartenausgebenden Bank enweder für Master-Card- oder für Visa-Karten

single card marketing – marketing by an issuer for either MasterCard or Visa cards

opp.: dual card marketing

(angestrebte) einheitliche Zahlungsverkehrsregion der 25 Länder der EU und von Island, Liechtenstein und Norwegen

Single Euro[pean] Payment Area (SEPA) – the area made up of the 25 member states of the EU plus Iceland, Liechtenstein and Norway

cf.: SEPA (Single Euro[pean] Payment Area)

Bank, die entweder MasterCard- oder Visa-Karten ausgibt

single issuer – an issuer of either MasterCard or Visa cards

opp.: dual issuer

Zahlungstransaktion, die mit einer Nachricht komplett ist

single message transaction – a transaction that is complete with one message

opp.: dual message transaction

elektronische Geldbörse in einer Währung

single-currency purse – an electronic purse that can be loaded with one currency only

opp.: multi-currency purse

Kundenkarte

single-purpose card – a plastic card issued by a merchant which can be used only in the issuer's environment

cf.: in-store card, private label card, proprietary card, two-party card

opp.: three-party card, multi-purpose card, universal card

Strategie einer Bank, entweder im Master-Card- oder im Visa-Geschäft aktiv zu sein

singularity – a strategy according to which a bank carries on business either in the MasterCard or in the Visa sphere

Sistema 4B

Sistema 4B – Spanish payment systems organization

eine Karte kopieren, eine Karte fälschen

skim a card, to – to copy the data from one card to another

cf.: counterfeit a card, to; duplicate a card, to; fake a card, to; forge a card, to

Kartenfälschung

skimming – the process of copying the data from one card to another

Schlitz zum Einschub einer Karte

slot – an opening in a device for the purpose of inserting a card

S

smart card – a card which contains a processor microchip
cf.: controller card, processor card
opp.: memory card
see also: chip card, IC card (integrated circuit card), integrated circuit card (IC card), MC card (microcircuit card), microcircuit card (MC card)

Karte mit Prozessorchip, Prozessorkarte

solicited offer – an offer that is requested by a person
opp.: unsolicited offer

verlangtes Angebot

specimen card – a card which is used for marketing purposes and not for live transactions
opp.: live card
see also: test card

Musterkarte

spending limit – the amount of money a cardholder may obtain or spend with his / her card
cf.: credit limit, pre-set limit, pre-set spending limit

Kreditlimit, Zahlungslimit, Verfügungsrahmen

spending pattern – the cardholder behaviour which can be in line or deviate from the usual spending profile
cf.: activity pattern, cardholder spending behaviour, cardholder spending pattern

Zahlungsverhalten des Karteninhabers

spending volume – the total turnover generated by a cardholder with his / her card

Karteninhaberumsatz

SSL (Secure Socket Layer) – a standard for secure connections in the Internet / in the virtual world

Standard für sichere Datenübertragungen im Internet / in der virtuellen Welt, SSL

stand-alone POS terminal – a POS terminal that is not connected to the cashier terminal

nicht mit der Handelskasse verbundenes POS-Terminal

standard account number – an account number which is 16 digits in length and uses the Luhn formula to calculate the check digit
cf.: standard card account number, standard card number
opp.: non-standard account number, non-standard card account number, non-standard card number
see also: account number, card account number, card number

standardisierte Kartennummer

S

standardisierte
Kartennummer

standard card account number – an account number which is 16 digits in length and uses the Luhn formula to calculate the check digit

cf.: standard account number, standard card number

opp.: non-standard account number, non-standard card account number, non-standard card number

see also: account number, card account number, card number

standardisierte
Kartennummer

standard card number – an account number which is 16 digits in length and uses the Luhn formula to calculate the check digit

cf.: standard account number, standard card account number

opp.: non-standard account number, non-standard card account number, non-standard card number

see also: account number, card account number, card number

numerische
Branchenkategori-
sierung nach inter-
nationaler Norm

standard industrial classification (SIC) – merchant classification according to types of merchants

cf.: SIC (standard industrial classification)

see also: MCC (merchant category code), merchant category code (MCC)

Ersatzgenehmi-
gungssystem bei
Systemausfall

stand-in processing system – a back-up issuer processing facility for authorizations when the primary processing system is not available

cf.: alternate, alternate processing system, back-up processing system, down-option processing system, dynamic stand-in processing system, permanent stand-in processing system

see also: IHS (issuer host system), issuer host, issuer host system (IHS), primary, primary processing system

Genehmigung
bei einem System-
ausfall durch ein
Ersatzsystem

stand-in authorization – an authorization performed by a pre-determined alternate processing system used whenever the issuer is unable to respond

cf.: alternate authorization, back-up authorization, down-option authorization, dynamic stand-in authorization, permanent stand-in authorization

opp.: primary authorization

S

stand-in limits – the authorization parameters set by the issuer for the alternate processing system in case the primary processing system is unable to respond

cf.: alternate limits, alternate parameters, back-up limits, back-up parameters, down-option limits, down-option parameters, dynamic stand-in limits, dynamic stand-in parameters, fall-back limits, fall-back parameters, permanent stand-in limits, permanent stand-in parameters, stand-in parameters

von der karten-ausgebenden Bank festgelegte Limits für das Ersatz-system

stand-in parameters – the authorization parameters set by the issuer for the alternate processing system in case the primary processing system is unable to respond

cf.: alternate limits, alternate parameters, back-up limits, back-up parameters, down-option limits, down-option parameters, dynamic stand-in limits, dynamic stand-in parameters, fall-back limits, fall-back parameters, permanent stand-in limits, permanent stand-in parameters, stand-in limits

von der karten-ausgebenden Bank festgelegte Limits für das Ersatz-system

stand-in processing – the performance of authorizations by a pre-determined alternate processing system which is used whenever the issuer is unable to respond

cf.: alternate processing, back-up processing, down-option processing, dynamic stand-in processing, permanent stand-in processing

opp.: primary processing

Genehmigungs-verfahren durch ein Ersatzsystem bei einem Systemaus-fall

stand-in transaction – a transaction which is authorized by an alternate processing system

cf.: alternate transaction, back-up transaction, down-option transaction, dynamic stand-in transaction, permanent stand-in transaction

opp.: primary transaction

see also: alternate processing system

Transaktion, die bei einem System-ausfall von einem Ersatzgenehmi-gungssystem auto-risiert wird

standing order – an instruction to a bank by an account holder to pay a fixed amount of money to the benefit of another account at regular times

Dauerauftrag

Karteninhaber-abrechnung	**statement** – the bill sent to the cardholder cf.: cardholder statement, monthly statement
Entgelt je Karten-inhaberabrechnung	**statement fee** – a fee charged to the cardholder per statement
Zusammenstellung aller Transaktionen eines Karteninhabers	**statement history** – a complete compilation of all transactions of a cardholder
Erstellung der Karten-inhaberabrechnung/en	**statement processing** – the processing of all single transactions generated since the last statement for inclusion in the current statement
statisches Offline-Verfahren zur Feststellung der Kartenechtheit	**static off-line CAM** – a card authentication method whereby the terminal autheticates the chip by verifying the digital signature which is created during personalisation and is stored in the chip opp.: dynamic off-line CAM see also: dynamic on-line CAM
Klebeetikette	**sticker** – a polyethylene film covered on the reverse side with an adhesive material showing the logo of the card system cf.: decal
gestohlene Karte	**stolen card** – a card which was stolen from the genuine cardholder
Sperrliste	**stoplist** – a printout containing card numbers which are not to be honoured cf.: blacklist, hot card list, restricted card list, warning, warning bulletin, warning notice bulletin see also: blacklist file, hot card file, negative file, stoplist file
Sperrlisten-Ein-tragungsentgelt	**stoplist entry fee** – a fee to be paid to enter a card number on a stoplist cf.: entry fee, insertion fee, stoplist insertion fee see also: stoplist storage fee, storage fee
Sperrdatenbestand	**stoplist file** – a data file containing card numbers which are not to be honoured cf.: blacklist file, hot card file, negative file see also: blacklist, restricted card list, stoplist, warning bulletin

S

stoplist insertion fee – a fee to be paid to enter a card number on a stoplist

cf.: entry fee, insertion fee, stoplist entry fee

see also: stoplist storage fee, storage fee

*Sperrlisten-
Eintragungsentgelt*

stoplist storage fee – a fee to be paid to retain a card number on a stoplist

cf.: storage fee

see also: entry fee, insertion fee, stoplist entry fee, stoplist insertion fee

*Sperrlisten-
Verbleibeentgelt*

stoplist, to – to put a card number on a stoplist

cf.: blacklist, to

*eine Karte auf eine
Sperrliste/einen Sperr-
datenbestand setzen*

storage fee – a fee to be paid to retain a card number on a stoplist

cf.: stoplist storage fee

see also: entry fee, insertion fee, stoplist entry fee, stoplist insertion fee

*Sperrlisten-
Verbleibeentgelt*

store-and-forward function – a process carried out in a computer centre which receives transactions from different acquirer processing centres, sorts them and forwards them to different issuer processing centres

cf.: clearing function

Clearingfunktion

store-and-forward transaction – a transaction which, as a result of network failure between merchant and acquirer or between acquirer and issuer, is authorized by the merchant's POS terminal on the basis of parameters defined by the acquirer or by the acquirer himself

see also: acquirer authorized transaction, merchant authorized transaction

*Transaktion, die bei
einem Netzwerkaus-
falls vom POS-Termi-
nal des Vertragsun-
ternehmens aufgrund
von Parametern bzw.
von der vertragsun-
ternehmensabrech-
nenden Bank selbst
autorisiert wird*

S

stored-value card – a card which is purchased with a given value or where the purchase value is bought for a given card in advance to be used for obtaining goods or services at a later time

see also: electronic purse, pay before product, pre-paid card, pre-payment card, traveller's cheque

Wertkarte

Sub-Lizenz

sublicence – a licence which allows a bank to participate in the card activities of a payment system via a principal licensee
cf.: affiliate licensee
opp.: principal licence

Bank, die nicht direkt, sondern über eine andere Bank Mitglied eines Zahlungssystems ist

sublicensee – a bank participating in the card business via a principal licensee
cf.: affiliate, affiliate licensee, affiliate member
opp.: principal, principal licensee, principal member

Ersatzbeleg

substitute document – a legible microfilm copy or another reproduction of the original slip
cf.: facsimile document, facsimile draft, substitute draft

Ersatzbeleg

substitute draft – a legible microfilm copy or another reproduction of the original slip
cf.: facsimile document, facsimile draft, substitute document

Einreichungsbeleg, Summenbeleg

summary slip – a paper used to document the total amount of sales, cash advances or credits a merchant effected within a certain period

Aufschlag, Zusatzentgelt

supplementary charge – a fee which is levied in addition to the standard fee
cf.: ancillary charge, surcharge
see also: surcharge, to; surcharging

Aufschlag, Zusatzentgelt

surcharge – a fee which is levied in addition to the standard fee
cf.: ancillary charge, supplementary charge
see also: surcharge, to; surcharging

aufschlagen, zusätzlich verrechnen

surcharge, to – to levy a fee in addition to the standard fee
see also: ancillary charge, supplementary charge, surcharge, surcharging

das Aufschlagen, die Verrechnung eines Zusatzentgelts

surcharging – the practice of levying a fee in addition to the standard fee
see also: ancillary charge, supplementary charge, surcharge; surcharge, to

suspect card – a card that has become suspicious due to the cardholder's unusual spending behaviour
cf.: suspicious card

verdächtige Karte

suspect merchant – a merchant that has become suspicious due to his involvement in fraud cases
cf.: suspicious merchant

verdächtiges Vertragsunternehmen

suspect outlet – a merchant location that has become suspicious due to its involvement in fraud cases
cf.: suspicious outlet

verdächtige Niederlassung eines Vertragsunternehmens

suspect transaction – a transaction that is suspicious due to the unusual particulars
cf.: suspicious transaction

verdächtige Transaktion

suspicious card – a card that has become suspect due to the cardholder's unusual spending behaviour
cf.: suspect card

verdächtige Karte

suspicious merchant – a merchant that has become suspect due to his involvement in fraud cases
cf.: suspect merchant

verdächtiges Vertragsunternehmen

suspicious outlet – a merchant location that has become suspect due to its involvement in fraud cases
cf.: suspect outlet

verdächtige Niederlassung eines Vertragsunternehmens

suspicious transaction – a transaction that is suspect due to the unusual particulars
cf.: suspect transaction

verdächtige Transaktion

SWIFT (Society for World-wide Interbank Financial Telecommunication) – an international bank association to transmit funds, transfer instructions and administration messages

SWIFT

swipe through, to – to move a card through a reader in a POS terminal or an ATM

durchziehen

swipe-through reader – a device in a POS terminal or an ATM where a card is moved through a slot so that it can read the card data which is required for the transaction

Durchzugsleser

T

Switching-Center

switch – the computer of a card organization routing transactions between acquirers and issuers in the respective network so as to effect interchange
cf.: node

symmetrische Verschlüsselung, Verschlüsselung mit einem geheimen Schlüssel

symmetric cryptography – a set of cryptographic techniques in which devices share the same secret key in combination with algorithms, whereby the decrypting algorithm is the reverse function of the encrypting algorithm,
opp.: asymmetric cryptography, public key cryptography
see also: cryptography, private key, public key

Systemausfall

system breakdown – the outage of a system
cf.: system failure, system outage

Systemausfall

system failure – the breakdown of a system
cf.: system breakdown, system outage

Systemausfall

system outage – the failure of a system
cf.: system failure, system breakdown

Systemverfügbarkeit

system performance – the availability of a system

Systemrisiko

systemic risk – the risk that the failure of one member in a payment scheme and their inability to meet its their obligations will cause other members to be unable to meet their obligations when due

(Karten)Geschäft im T&E-Bereich, T&E-Geschäft, Reise- und Bewirtungsgeschäft

T&E business – (card) business carried on in the field of travel and entertainment
opp.: non-T&E-business, retail business
see also: T&E card, T&E merchant

Karte, die als Individualzahlungsmittel für weltweite Nutzung ausgegeben wird; T&E-Karte; Reise- und Bewirtungskarte

T&E card – a card which is issued to persons of a higher income bracket mainly for worldwide use in the fields of travel and entertainment
see also: T&E business, T&E merchant

Vertragsparter im T&E-Bereich, T&E-Vertragsunternehmen

T&E merchant – a merchant in the field of travel and entertainment
opp.: non-T&E-merchant, retail merchant
see also: T&E business, T&E card

S
T

T=0 – character-oriented asynchronous half duplex transmission protocol
see also: T=1

T=0-Protokoll

T=1 – block-oriented asynchronous half duplex transmission
see also: T=0

T=1-Protokoll

tamper evident signature panel – a signature stripe
which will immediately discolour if there is any attempt to
change a signature or numbers indent printed on it
cf.: tamper evident signature stripe

*veränderungssiche-
res Unterschrifts-
feld*

tamper evident signature stripe – a signature stripe
which will immediately discolour if there is any attempt to
change a signature or numbers indent printed on it
cf.: tamper evident signature panel

*veränderungssiche-
res Unterschrifts-
feld*

tamper, to – to falsify a card / the magnetic stripe of a card

verfälschen

tamper-resistant – the capacity of devices to resist
physical attacks up to a certain point

attackensicher

tamper-resistant ATM – the capacity of an ATM to resist
physical attacks

*attackensicherer
ATM*

tamper-resistant POS terminal – the capacity of a POS
terminal to resist physical attacks

*attackensicheres
POS-Terminal*

tamper-resistant vending machine – the capacity of a
vending machine to resist physical attacks

*attackensicherer
Verkaufsautomat*

tap a magnetic stripe, to – to copy a magnetic stripe

*einen Magnetstreifen
kopieren*

targeted merchant – a merchant who is attacked by
fraudsters

*attackiertes Ver-
tragsunternehmen*

telemarketing fraud – fraud committed by illegally ordering goods over the telephone with a valid card number
cf.: telephone fraud, telephone order fraud, telesales fraud

*Betrug bei telefoni-
schen Bestellungen
mit gültigen Kredit-
kartennummern*

telephone authorization – an affirmative response of
the issuer to the acquirer which is forwarded by the acquirer
to the merchant or cash advance location by telephone to
permit a card transaction

*telefonische
Genehmigung*

T

cf.: voice authorization

opp.: electronic authorization

see also: authorization

Telefonkarte

telephone card – a card which can be used for telephone purposes only

cf.: calling card, phone card

Betrug bei telefoni-
schen Bestellungen
mit gültigen Kre-
ditkartennummern

telephone fraud – fraud committed by illegally ordering goods over the telephone with a valid card number

cf.: telemarketing fraud, telephone order fraud, telesales fraud

telefonische Bestel-
lung, die mittels Kre-
ditkarte bezahlt wird

telephone order – a transaction effected by telephone to be paid by a credit card

Betrug bei telefoni-
schen Bestellungen
mit gültigen Kredit-
kartennummern

telephone order fraud – fraud committed by illegally ordering goods over the telephone with a valid card number

cf.: telemarketing fraud, telephone fraud, telesales fraud

Kreditkartentrans-
aktion aufgrund
einer telefonischen
Bestellung

telephone order transaction – a credit card transaction resulting from an order made by telephone

see also: mail order / telephone order transaction (MO / TO transaction), MO / TO transaction (mail order / telephone order transaction)

telefonische Geneh-
migungsanfrage

telephone request – a request by a merchant or cash advance location by telephone to permit a card transaction

cf.: voice request

opp.: electronic request

see also: authorization request

Betrug bei telefoni-
schen Bestellungen
mit gültigen Kre-
ditkartennummern

telesales fraud – fraud committed by illegally ordering goods over the telephone with a valid card number

cf.: telemarketing fraud, telephone fraud, telephone order fraud

Terminal, Daten-
endgerät

terminal – a technical device located at a point of interaction (POI) that allows payment and cash advance transactions

see also: ATM, POS terminal

T

terminal authorization – an affirmative response of the issuer to the acquirer which is forwarded by the acquirer to the merchant via a POS terminal to permit a card transaction
see also: ATM authorization, electronic authorization

Genehmigung durch ein POS-Terminal

terminal breakdown – the outage of a terminal

Terminalversagen, Terminalausfall

terminal certification – the commissioning of a terminal

Terminalabnahme, Terminalzulassung

terminal failure – the breakdown of a terminal

Terminalversagen, Terminalausfall

terminal life cycle – the service life of a terminal

Terminallebenszyklus

terminal outage – the failure of a terminal

Terminalversagen, Terminalausfall

terminal receipt – a piece of paper printed out by a terminal documenting a performed transaction
see also: ATM receipt, receipt

Quittung eines POS-Terminals

terminal reliability – the ability of a terminal to function with high availability

Terminal-zuverlässigkeit

terminal risk management – the process of managing the total risk inherent to the transactions performed by terminals
opp.: card risk management

Risikomanagement im Zusammenhang mit Terminals, Terminalrisikomanagement, Terminalrisikosteuerung

terminal transaction – an electronic transaction carried out through a terminal
opp.: imprinter transaction
see also: electronic transaction

elektronische Transaktion mittels eines POS-Terminals

terminated merchant file – the data file containing all terminated merchants

Datensatz gekündigter Vertragsunternehmen

termination of a card – the cancellation of a card according to the business conditions
cf.: cancellation of a card, card cancellation, card termination

Storno einer Karte, Kartenstorno

T

Testkarte	**test card** – a card which is used for test purposes only opp.: live card see also: specimen card
Karte, die von einer Bank mit speziellem Design ausgegeben und über einen Dritten vertrieben wird	**third party card** – a credit card with a special design which issued by a member and distributed through a third party institution cf.: affinity card, co-branded card
Betrug durch Dritte	**third party fraud** – fraud that is incurred on transactions initiated by someone other than the genuine cardholder see also: card fraud, fraud, merchant fraud
Datenverarbeitung durch ein externes Rechenzentrum	**third party processing** – the card processing which is carried out by a computer centre to whom the member has delegated it see also: third party processor
externes Rechenzentrum	**third party processor** – the computer centre to whom the member has delegated the card processing see also: third party processing
universell einsetzbare Karte	**three-party card** – a card which is issued by (a member of) a card organization for all purposes cf.: universal card opp.: in-store card, private label card, proprietary card, two-party card
Geldausgabeautomat an der Außenfront eines Gebäudes (gewöhnlich einer Bank)	**through-the-wall ATM** – an ATM located outside of a bank branch see also: drive-through ATM, in-bank ATM, in-branch ATM, indoor ATM, lobby ATM, off-premises ATM, off-site ATM, outdoor ATM
Zahlungsbetrag	**ticket value** – the amount on a sales slip
Zeit, nach der ein Abbruch der Kommunikation erfolgt	**time-out** – a condition where the authorization request is terminated because the primary site has not responded to it within the allowed time see also: time-out value

T

time-out value – the maximum time permitted between an authorization request and a response
see also: time-out

maximale Antwortzeit

tip function – a feature allowing the payment of tips with a card

Trinkgeldfunktion

token – a pre-paid item to be used at vending machines

Wertmünze

toll way operator – an institution that levies toll payments

Mauteinheber

toll ways application – an off-line POS solution catering to the special needs of this type of merchant with generally low maximum transaction amounts
see also: quick payment service (QPS), QPS (quick payment service), rapid payment service (RPS), RPS (rapid payment service)

offline POS-Lösung zur Mauteinhebung

traceability – the ability to trace transactions of cards / terminals

Nachvollziehbarkeit

track – one of three tracks on a magnetic stripe
see also: magnetic stripe, track 1, track 2, track 3, track data

Spur

track 1 – the first track on the magnetic stripe of a card; it is read-only and recorded at 8.3 bpmm; contents are defined in ISO 7813
see also: magnetic stripe, track, track 2, track 3, track data

erste Spur des Magnetstreifens

track 2 – the second track on the magnetic stripe of a card; it is read-only and recorded at 3 bpmm; contents are defined in ISO 7813
see also: magnetic stripe, track, track 1, track 3, track data

zweite Spur des Magnetstreifens

track 3 – the third track on the magnetic stripe of a card; it is a read-write track and recorded at 8.3 bpmm; contents are defined in ISO 7813
see also: magnetic stripe, track, track 1, track 2, track data

dritte Spur des Magnetstreifens

track data – the information which is encoded on the tracks of the card's magnetic stripe
see also: magnetic stripe, track, track 1, track 2, track 3

Spurdaten

T

Transaktion	**transaction** – a business matter which leads to a transfer of funds from one party to another see also: ATM cash advance transaction, ATM cash disbursement transaction, card transaction, cash advance transaction, credit transaction, load(ing) transaction, merchant transaction, payment transaction, purchase transaction, refund transaction, retail transaction, sales transaction, unload(ing) transaction
Transaktionsabbruch	**transaction abortion** – the termination of a transaction before its completion
Akkumulation von Transaktionen einer elektronischen Geldbörse im Bereich des Acquirers	**transaction aggregation** – the accumulation of electronic purse transactions for clearing in a set of total amounts per issuer; the details of these transactions are held and stored in the acquirer's domain and not transmitted to the issuer cf.: transaction truncation
Transaktionsbetrag	**transaction amount** – the value of one card transaction cf.: transaction value see also: card transaction
Transaktionsüberprüfung	**transaction analysis** – the examination of cardholder transactions cf.: transaction scoring
Transaktionsentgelt	**transaction charge** – a fee charged per transaction cf.: item charge, transaction fee
Kosten einer Transaktion	**transaction cost** – the incurred cost per transaction
Transaktionswährung	**transaction currency** – the currency in which the transaction was concluded
Transaktionsdatenbestand	**transaction data** – a file containing transaction records
Transaktionsdatum	**transaction date** – the date on which the cardholder effects a purchase or cash advance by card
Ablehnung einer Transaktion *Misslingen einer Transaktion*	**transaction denial** – the refusal of a transaction **transaction failure** – the inability to complete a transaction

transaction fee – a fee charged per transaction
cf.: item charge, transaction charge

Transaktionsentgelt

transaction history – the total of data reflecting all transaction-related cardholder information
cf.: cardholder history
opp.: merchant history
see also: cardholder acitivity data, cardholder history file

*Karteninhaber-
Umsatzdaten,
Transaktionen
eines Karten-
inhabers*

transaction identifier – digit defining the type of transaction

*Stelle, welche die Art
Transaktion definiert*

transaction information document – the paper used to
document a payment or a cash advance by card
cf.: transaction receipt
see also: cash advance draft, cash advance slip, cash draft,
cash slip, credit draft, credit slip, sales draft, sales receipt,
sales slip, sales voucher

*Beleg, der eine
Transaktion doku-
mentiert*

transaction print-out – a paper slip produced by the
POS terminal which records the transaction data

*von einem POS-Termi-
nal ausgedruckter Beleg*

transaction quality – the ability to complete a transaction with a high success rate

*Transaktions-
qualität*

transaction receipt – the paper used to document a payment or a cash advance transaction by card
cf.: transaction information document
see also: cash advance draft, cash advance slip, cash draft,
cash slip, credit draft, credit slip, sales draft, sales receipt,
sales slip, sales voucher

*Beleg, der eine
Transaktion doku-
mentiert*

transaction record – the data pertaining to a specific
transaction, either paper-based or electronically transmitted
see also: electronic record, paper record

*Transaktions-
datensatz*

transaction scoring – the examination of cardholder
transactions
cf.: transaction analysis

*Transaktions-
überprüfung*

transaction sequence number – the number defining
the sequence of transactions

*Transaktions-
folgenummer*

T

Transaktionspalette	**transaction set** – all transactions which a POS terminal is capable of carrying out (e.g. credit transaction, purchase transaction)
Transaktions-geschwindigkeit	**transaction speed** – the speed with which a transaction is performed
Transaktionsdauer	**transaction time** – the duration of a transaction
Akkumulation von Transaktionen einer elektronischen Geld-börse im Bereich des Acquirers	**transaction truncation** – the accumulation of electronic purse transactions for clearing in a set of total amounts per issuer; the details of these transactions are held and stored in the acquirer's domain and not transmitted to the issuer cf.: transaction aggregation
Transaktionsart	**transaction type** – the description of the transaction category (e.g. credit transaction, purchase transaction)
Transaktionsbetrag	**transaction value** – the amount of one card transaction cf.: transaction amount see also: card transaction
Überweisung	**transfer** – the movement of funds from one account to another one
Mindestangaben bei Kartentransaktionen	**transparency rules** – the minimum data required for a card transaction
in einem Fahrzeug installierte kabellose Datenübertragungs-einheit, Transponder	**transponder** – a wireless communication on-board unit attached to the windshield behind the rear-view mirror of vehicles that picks up and responds to an incoming signal cf.: transponder device, transponder tag, transponder unit
in einem Fahrzeug installierte kabellose Datenübertragungs-einheit, Transponder	**transponder device** – a wireless communication on-board unit attached to the windshield behind the rear-view mirror of vehicles that picks up and responds to an incoming signal cf.: transponder, transponder tag, transponder unit
in einem Fahrzeug installierte kabellose Datenübertragungs-einheit, Transponder	**transponder tag** – a wireless communication on-board unit attached to the windshield behind the rear-view mirror of vehicles that picks up and responds to an incoming signal cf.: transponder, transponder device, transponder unit

T

transponder unit – a wireless communication on-board unit attached to the windshield behind the rear-view mirror of vehicles that picks up and responds to an incoming signal
cf.: transponder, transponder device, transponder tag

in einem Fahrzeug installierte kabellose Datenübertragungseinheit, Transponder

travel account card – a card which is deposited at a travel agency for convenient payment of a company's travel expenses
cf.: lodge(d) card

Reisestellenkarte

travel assistance – the assistance rendered to a traveller if entitled to coverage

Reiseschutz

travel directory – a list of cash advance facilities and tourist-oriented enterprises in a given area
see also: ATM directory, directory, merchant directory, merchant location directory

Verzeichnis von touristisch orientierten Vertragsunternehmen und Bargeldbezugsmöglichkeiten

travel insurance – the insurance for a traveller if entitled to coverage

Reiseversicherung

travel voucher – a pre-paid document issued in the name of a person in order to claim the services as agreed

Reisegutschein

traveller's cheque – a cheque with a designated amount which is purchased in advance for effecting a cashless payment or obtaining a cash advance at a later date
see also: electronic purse, pay before product, pre-paid card, pre-payment card, stored value card

Reisescheck

trial period – a period in which a cardholder can test a card

Probierzeit

triple DES (3DES) – modified DES encryption by triple calling of the DES algorithm with alternating encryption and decryption
see also: Data Encryption Standard (DES), DES (Data Encryption Standard)

Triple-DES, 3DES

U

truck card – a card which is not issued to a cardholder but to a specific truck to pay for truck-related goods / services
see also: commercial road transport card (CRT card), CRT card (commercial road transport card), fleet card

Lkw-Flottenkarte, Lkw-Fuhrparkkarte

rechtmäßiger
Karteninhaber

true cardholder – the cardholder to whom the card was legally issued

cf.: genuine cardholder, legitimate cardholder, rightful cardholder, rightful cardholder

nicht mehr einen Scheck,
sondern nur dessen er-
faßte Daten weiterleiten

truncate a cheque, to – to forward only the data of a cheque but not the paper

delegierte
Genehmigung

truncated authorization – an authorization performed by the acquirer on behalf of the issuer, provided the transaction matches a list of parameter values set by the issuer

Zertifizierungs-
stelle

trust centre – an authority delivering keys so that participants in the system can be recognized as genuine ones

cf.: certification authority

Kundenkarte

two-party card – a plastic card issued by a merchant which can be used only in the issuer's environment

cf.: in-store card, private label card, proprietary cad

Zahlungsart

type of payment – the manner in which a payment is effected

elektronische Geld-
börse ohne in
einem Host geführte
Schattenkonten

unaccounted (electronic) purse – an electronic purse where loading, payment and unloading transactions are not centrally stored and therefore no shadow accounts exist on a host

opp.: accounted (electronic) purse

Selbstbedienungs-
terminal mit Kar-
tenzahlungsfunk-
tion, unbedientes
POS-Terminal

unattended POS terminal – a POS terminal that does not require any assistance by a cashier (e.g. at parking garages, toll ways, vending machines)

cf.: cardholder activated POS terminal, cardholder activated terminal (CAT), CAT (cardholder activated terminal)

T
U

nicht autorisierte / ge-
nehmigte Transaktion

unauthorized transaction – a transaction that was not approved by the issuer

opp.: authorized transaction

Bevölkerungsteil
ohne Bank-
verbindung

unbanked population – the number of persons or the percentage of a population not holding a bank account

opp.: banked population

unblock a card, to – to release a blocked card for use again
opp.: block a card, to

eine Kartenblockie-rung aufheben

uncollectible amount – an amount that cannot be collected

uneinbringlicher Betrag

under floor limit fraud – a fraud that was perpetrated because the transaction amount was less than the floor limit and therefore an authorization request was not made
cf.: below floor limit fraud
opp.: above floor limit fraud

Betrugsfall unter der Genehmigungsgrenze

under floor limit transaction – a transaction that does not require the merchant to call his authorization centre for authorization because the transaction amount is under the merchant floor limit
cf.: below floor limit transaction
opp.: above floor limit transaction

Transaktion unter der Genehmigungsgrenze

underlying account – an account where the issuer of an electronic purse scheme holds the float
cf.: float account, funds pool account, pool account, purse pool account

Float-Konto, Pool-Konto eines elektronischen Geldbörsensystems

unique card identification system – a numbering system that provides every card with a unique number in the card business

Karten-Nummerierungssystem

unique merchant identification system – a numbering system that provides every merchant with a unique number in the card business

Vertragsunternehmens-Nummerierungssystem

unique transaction – a transaction that cannot be identified as a retail sale or cash advance and for which there are specified SIC codes

Transaktion, die aus dem üblichen Rahmen fällt

universal card – a card which is issued by (a member of) a card organization for all purposes
cf.: three-party card
opp.: in-store card, private label card, proprietary card, two-party card
see also: universal credit card

universell einsetz-bare Karte

U

universell einsetz-
bare Kreditkarte

universal credit card – a credit card which is issued by (a member of) a card organization for all purposes

cf.: three-party card

opp.: in-store card, private label card, proprietary card, two-party card

see also: universal card

Ladung einer elektro-
nischen Geldbörse
zulasten eines bank-
eigenen Kontos auf
das Pool-Konto

unlinked load – a load(ing) transaction whereby electronic value is transferred from the account of a bank, which operates load(ing) terminals and initiates load(ing) transactions, to an electronic purse / issuer's float account

opp.: linked load

Entladen einer
elektronischen
Geldbörse

unload an electronic purse, to – the transfer of value from an electronic purse / issuer's float account to the cardholders' account

opp.: fund an electronic purse, to; load an electronic purse, to

Entladetransaktion

unload(ing) transaction – a transaction where the value is transferred from an electronic purse / issuer's float account to the cardholders' account

opp.: load(ing) transaction

see also: merchant transaction, payment transaction, purchase transaction, retail transaction, sales transaction

unbezahlte
Rechnung

unpaid balance – the balance of a statement that has remained unpaid

unbezahlt gebliebe-
ner Scheck

unpaid cheque – a cheque that has remained unpaid

unverlangtes
Angebot

unsolicited offer – an offer that was not requested by a person

opp.: solicited offer

Karte mit hohem
Ausgaberahmen

up-market card – a card which is issued (often as a gold card) to persons of a higher income bracket and which is provided with a high spending limit and additional features

cf.: gold card, preferred card, premier card, premium card, prestige card, privilege card, up-scale card

opp.: broad card, mainstream card, mass card

U

up-scale card – a card which is issued (often as a gold card) to persons of a higher income bracket and which is provided with a high spending limit and additional features
cf.: gold card, preferred card, premier card, premium card, prestige card, privilege card, up-market card
opp.: broad card, mainstream card, mass card

Karte mit hohem Ausgaberahmen

valid card – a card that has passed the valid date and has not yet expired

gültige Karte

valid date – the date embossed on the card before which the card must not be honoured

Gültigkeitsbeginn

validation – a process to verify the validity of a card
cf.: validity check

Gültigkeits-überprüfung

validity – the period during which the card can be honoured

Gültigkeit

validity check – a process to verify the validity of a card
validation

Gültigkeits-überprüfung

value chain – the entirety of the different stages of the transaction flow from the acquirer via the acquirer processor, the switch(es), the issuer processor to the issuer and the value created in this chain

Wertschöpfungs-kette

value checker – a device to show the balance of an electronic purse and the last transactions
see also: balance reader

Wertanzeiger

value date – the day on which the value of an amount commences to bear interest

Tag, an dem die Zinsberechnung für den betreffenden Wert beginnt oder endet

value-added benefit – additional benefit linked to a card to enhance its value
cf.: value-added service

Zusatzleistung

value-added service – additional service linked to a card to enhance its value
cf.: value-added benefit

Zusatzleistung

offline POS-Lösung für Verkaufs-automaten	**vending machines application** – an off-line POS solution catering to the special needs of this type of sales business with generally low maximum transaction amounts see also: quick payment service (QPS), QPS (quick payment service), rapid payment service (RPS), RPS (rapid payment service)
sichere Zahlungsform mit Visa-Karten im Internet/in der virtuellen Welt, Verified by Visa	**Verified by Visa** – a standard for secure payments with Visa cards in the Internet / in the virtual world see also: MasterCard SecureCode
berührungslose Zahlung	**vicinity payment** – a contactless payment with a chip (card) whereby there is a distance up to 1 metre between card and reader see also: contactless purse, proximity payment
nur als Nummer existierende „Karte"	**virtual card** – a „card" which only exists as a number opp.: physical card
elektronische Geschäfte, virtuelle Geschäfte, elektronischer Kauf von Waren/Dienstleistungen	**virtual commerce** – the purchase of goods / services on an electronic market place cf.: e-business, e-commerce, electronic commerce see also: electronic marketplace, virtual marketplace
elektronischer Markt, virtueller Markt	**virtual market place** – the electronic market where goods / services are offered electronically cf.: electronic marketplace opp.: physical marketplace see also: e-business, e-commerce, electronic commerce, virtual commerce
Visa	**Visa** – a licensed card system with the licences being granted by Visa International see also: Visa Electron card, Visa card, Visa International
Visa-Karte	**Visa card** – a card issued by a licensee of Visa International see also: Visa, Visa Electron card, Visa International

V

Visa Electron card – a debit card issued by a licensee of
Visa International
see also: Visa, Visa card, Visa International

*Visa Electron-Karte,
Debitkarte von Visa
International*

Visa International – an international payment systems
organization which is the licensor of the Visa cards
see also: Visa, Visa Electron card, Visa card

Visa International

voice authorization – an affirmative response of the issuer to the acquirer which is forwarded by the acquirer to the
merchant or cash advance location by telephone to permit a
card transaction
cf.: telephone authorization
opp.: electronic authorization
see also: authorization

*telefonische
Genehmigung*

voice recognition – a biometric technique to verify the
cardholder authentication
cf.: voice verification
see also: biometrics, biometric techniques

Stimmerkennung

voice request – a request by a merchant or cash advance
location by telephone to permit a card transaction
cf.: telephone request
opp.: electronic request
see also: authorization request

*telefonische Autori-
sierungsanfrage /
Genehmigungs-
anfrage*

voice verification – a biometric technique to verify the
cardholder authentication
cf.: voice recognition
see also: biometrics, biometric techniques

Stimmerkennung

waive, to – to grant an exception

*eine Ausnahme
bewilligen*

waiver – an exception

Ausnahmebewilligung

walk-in transaction – a payment transaction which takes
place by presenting a card at the point of sale
cf.: face-to-face transaction
opp.: non-face-to-face transaction, remote transaction
see also: signature-on-file transaction

*Zahlung, die durch
Vorlage einer Karte
am POS erfolgt*

Sperrliste	**warning** – a printed list of card numbers which are not to be honoured cf.: blacklist, hot card list, restricted card list, stoplist, warning bulletin, warning notice bulletin see also: blacklist file, hot card file, negative file, stoplist file, warning system
Sperrliste	**warning bulletin** – a printed list of card numbers which are not to be honoured cf.: blacklist, hot card list, restricted card list, stoplist, warning, warning notice bulletin see also: blacklist file, hot card file, negative file, stoplist file, warning system
Sperrliste	**warning notice bulletin** – a printed list of card numbers which are not to be honoured cf.: blacklist, hot card list, restricted card list, stoplist, warning, warning bulletin see also: blacklist file, hot card file, negative file, stoplist file, warning system
Sperrsystem	**warning system** – the procedure with which a card organization can transmit blacklisted card numbers to merchants, bank branches and ATMs see also: warning, warning bulletin, warning notice bulletin
Watermark-Technologie	**Watermark technology** – a card verification method by which security features are incorporated within the card during production and which requires special reading equipment at the POS
weißer Kartenrohling	**white plastic** – a plain plastic card embossed with illegally obtained card data
Kartenbetrug mit weißen Kartenrohlingen	**white plastic fraud** – a fraud case where genuine card data are obtained illegally (at the point of compromise) and then applied to a white piece of plastic which then is used to make imprints on sales slips which are then submitted for payment by a collusive merchant

wireless POS terminal – a wireless, mostly portable POS terminal
cf.: handheld POS terminal
opp.: stationary POS terminal
see also: mobile POS terminal

kabelloses, meist tragbares POS-Terminal

withdraw, to – to retrieve money

abheben

X.25 – the protocol for the interface between data terminal equipment and data communication equipment

X.25-Protokoll

yearly expiry – a system by which cards expire at the end of a calendar year
opp.: yearly issuance
see also: monthly expiry

Kartenablauf per Ende eines Kalenderjahres

yearly issuance – a system by which cards are issued at any time during a year with the card expiring at the end of a calender year
opp.: yearly expiry
see also: monthly issuance

Kartenausgabe mit per Ende eines Kalenderjahres ab-laufenden Karten

zero floor limit – a merchant floor limit which has been reduced to zero so that the merchant has to obtain an author-ization for every transaction

Null-Limit

W
XY
Z

Dr. Ewald Judt

Ewald Judt wurde 1950 in Wien geboren, studierte an der Wirtschaftsuniversität Wien und promovierte 1975 zum Dr. rer. soc. oec. Nach dem Studium war er in einigen Funktionen im österreichischen Sparkassensektor tätig. Von 1980 bis 1993 war er Geschäftsführer der Eurocard Austria Kreditkarten-Gesellschaft mbH. Seit der 1993 erfolgten Fusion der Eurocard Austria Kreditkarten-Gesellschaft mbH mit der GABE Geldausgabeautomaten-Servicegesellschaft mbH zur Europay Austria Zahlungsverkehrssysteme Gesellschaft mbH ist er dort als Geschäftsführer tätig.

Jeffrey Waldock

Jeffrey Waldock wurde 1960 in London geboren, übersiedelte 1968 mit seinen Eltern nach Österreich, machte 1978 in Wien sein Abitur und anschließend eine EDV-Ausbildung. Von 1980 bis 1983 war er in der IT-Branche als Programmierer tätig. 1984 wechselte er zur Europay Austria Zahlungsverkehrsgesellschaft mbH, wo er bis 1989 verschiedene Funktionen ausübte. Neben seinen beruflichen Tätigkeiten absolvierte er das Übersetzerstudium an der Universität Wien. Seit dessen Abschluss 1989 ist er als Übersetzer tätig, seit 1996 in seinem eigenen Übersetzungsbüro „Quick Translation".